Building the Human City

Building the Human City

William F. Lynch's Ignatian Spirituality for Public Life

John F. Kane

Foreword by
Kevin F. Burke, SJ

Shirley —
With wonderful
shared memories — and
great admiration (really!)
for your spiritual journey.

John 6/4/16

PICKWICK Publications · Eugene, Oregon

BUILDING THE HUMAN CITY
William F. Lynch's Ignatian Spirituality for Public Life

Pickwick Publications
An Imprint of Wipf and Stock Publishers
199 W. 8th Ave., Suite 3
Eugene, OR 97401

www.wipfandstock.com

PAPERBACK ISBN: 978-1-4982-3912-7
HARDCOVER ISBN: 978-1-4982-3914-1

Cataloguing-in-Publication data:

Kane, John Francis, 1942–

    Building the human city : William F. Lynch's Ignatian spirituality for public
life / John F. Kane; foreword by Kevin F. Burke, SJ.

    xxvi + 266 pp. ; 23 cm. Includes bibliographical references.

    ISBN 978-1-4982-3912-7 (paperback)
    ISBN 978-1-4982-3914-1 (hardback)

    1. Lynch, William F., 1908–1987. 2. Spirituality 3. Philosophy—Politics. I.
Title.

BT771.2 K36 2016

Manufactured in the U.S.A.   03/28/16

Permission for citation from *Christ and Apollo, Images of Hope, Christ and Prometheus*, and
Images of Faith has been granted by the University of Notre Dame Press. Permission for cita-
tion from *The Integrating Mind* (first published by Sheed & Ward, 1962) has been granted by
Curtis Brown, Ltd. Permission for use of Lynch photo has been granted by the Jesuits of the
United States Northeast Province.

For PDK and AMC

Two of the Many

Who Have Worked to Build a More Human City

And for PSC

Contents

Foreword

As I see it, we are always faced with programmatic alternatives:
We can decide to build a human city . . . Or we will decide to build
various absolute and walled cities, from which various pockets of
our humanity will always be excluded.

—William F. Lynch

A good book can read like a treasure map. Novels, biographies, histories often represent different kinds of maps and treasures, their narrative lines capable of launching all sorts of journeys. And when the subject matter rises to the occasion, they leave us not merely entertained but enriched. *Building the Human City* provides such a map. It leads not to buried gold, of course, but to something more subtle in value: the lineaments of a human and humane world.

———

When I was growing up in the 1960s, the typical junior high school curriculum included a class called "Civics." I always thought that name dull, the subject matter flat. In fact, I can't remember much about my Civics class except the vague impression that the teacher's own area of specialization was Arithmetic. But now, decades later, with an acquired appreciation for etymologies and a capacity for recognizing how some things come to be known precisely when they are missed, I muse on this name and relish it. An interdisciplinary course in history, politics, and culture: isn't this what Civics implies? Isn't this something from which our nation could benefit right now? Might it not be helpful if we all enrolled in an adult-education seminar in Civics and paid attention to the vital roots and branches evoked by that word: *civis, civitas,* civilization, citizenship, civility, the human city?

There is exactly one person I would elect to teach our nation this course. His name is William F. Lynch.

I first recall encountering Lynch in a college-level humanities class at St. Louis University in the 1970s. An eccentric Jesuit, Fr. John Walsh, taught it from his background in theater and dance. His course title meandered like a run-on sentence: *Images of God and Man and Woman in Contemporary Art, Literature, and Theater*. But the experience itself was pure electricity. It connected the dots between image and thought, imagination and action, freedom and culture. It was a dazzling, dizzying experience. Although I hardly averted to it at the time, the insights of Willian Lynch supplied the heart and soul, skeleton and skin of that course. Lynch gave learning a body.

A less remote memory pokes at me from the late 1990s. I am a newly christened professor on the faculty of a Jesuit graduate school of theology in Cambridge, Massachusetts, engaged in a light conversation over lunch with four other colleagues, all Jesuits. We are playing a game of intellectual tag with no real stakes but with oodles of wit and charm. The question of the day: who was the most brilliant Jesuit thinker ever to come from the United States? The list of candidates is impressive: John Courtney Murray, Gustave Weigel, Walter Ong, Henri Renard, Michael Buckley, George Klubertanz, and more I can't remember. Then William Lynch is mentioned and two amazing things happen in rapid sequence. First, the entire table falls silent. And then we all agree with one another! When do Jesuits ever agree on anything? When are we ever silent? But there it was. We were in the remembered presence of an American original, a genius incapable of being identified with only one academic discipline. It took our collective breath away. He had died a decade earlier but, on this day, we remembered and we knew him, even as we missed him.

William Lynch didn't write for "insiders." He wrote to overcome the dichotomy between insider and outsider. He didn't write for Catholics. He didn't write for academics. He wrote for everyone: artists and intellectuals; presidents and pipe-cleaners; people working on Madison Avenue and in Hollywood, and working class people; actors, singers, and poets—the creators and the popularizers of our culture's images—and journalists, teachers, critics and, above all, the consumers of all those images, a people living together and apart in an interwoven, divided culture.

We live through images, Lynch insisted, images of life, death, self, other, this world and what lies beyond, and so on. How we live and die remains forever tethered to those images. The responsibility this implies! "We can make or destroy the world with an image," he once wrote, to say nothing about our own lives and relationships, our individual works and dreams, our capacity to face and embrace our blessed finitude. Not surprisingly, images suffuse all his works and imagination serves as the unifying center of his seminar in Civics, his course in the art of living.

An expansive thinker, Lynch's imagination reflects multiple disciplinary interests: history and the classics; philosophy, theology, psychology, and spirituality; literature and literary criticism; drama, film, art, and the critical disciplines that engage them. A "public intellectual" and "critic" in the best sense of those terms, he lived religious faith in a way that cultivated respect for the secular. He loved the world in its tangible loveliness and so valued the gifts religious imagination might offer it. He insisted that the true imagination never seeks to escape the world but to engage it: "The task of the imagination is to imagine the real."

Lynch is less a prophet than a coach, less an artist than a critic. He mentors us in the arts of imagining the real, tutors us in the crafts of critical and civil discourse. Yet he shares at least one trait in common with great prophets and artists: Lynch always perceived the concrete present and felt the futures towards which that present aimed. In this as in many other respects Lynch calls to mind another eclectic and brilliant thinker, the German polymath, Walter Benjamin. In response to Karl Marx, who once wrote that "revolution is the locomotive of history," Benjamin countered with the suggestion that revolution is like "the emergency-brake" on history's runaway train of progress. We need to find an emergency break to stop the mindless disintegration of our political culture, to interrupt our un-civil "culture wars." But it needs to be a human revolution, a humanizing handbrake that pulls us back from the brink of intoxicating polarization. Lynch invites us, compels us, into a civil civic discourse. He helps us to imagine anew a humanizing human city. Although his greatest works were penned nearly a half a century ago, they appear today as fresh as a newly peeled orange. Now is the moment to rediscover William Lynch.

———

If, like other examples of good writing, *Building the Human City* functions like a treasure map, the treasure it leads to is the capacious imagination and productive way of William Lynch. Like no other cartographer to date, John Kane patiently sketches the whole trajectory of Lynch's audacious vision and charts an illuminating way through it. At the same time, however, he has produced something beautiful in its own right. John's book is both a map to a treasure and treasure in itself. Allow me briefly to elaborate.

Somewhere in the middle of his teaching career, John Kane remembered William Lynch. He began re-reading books he had first encountered years before. He presented papers at academic conferences, engaging colleagues in conversations about the questions Lynch awakened in him. He searched for things he hadn't yet encountered, visited the Lynch archive at Fordham University and immersed himself in previously unpublished or forgotten works. He spoke with people who knew the old Jesuit and could tell stories about him, whether in admiration or disdain. And Kane's own imagination caught fire. Lynch's vision became a passion. He not only read Lynch but began tracking texts and traditions that influenced him – classical plays by Aeschylus and Euripides, dialogues of Plato, the Spiritual Exercises of St. Ignatius, psychological and literary classics, especially Dostoyevsky, and the biblical text now re-imagined and interpreted through dramatical-ly-alert eyes. As he followed the old man down the ages, the threads that Lynch wove together slowly revealed their pattern. Or, as John prefers to say, he found himself retracing the many paths across the field of Lynch's thought, actually crossing that field from various directions and angles so as to represent its densely textured weave. The result is this book.

The beauty of this book *qua* treasure map: Kane gets Lynch right and he does so in a way at once lucid and profound. Lynch's own writings are so rich and demanding that readers hardly know where to begin, and fewer and fewer people do begin, and now even our best thinkers are not reading him, most having forgotten him. *Building a Human City* furnishes what is urgently needed: a guide to the whole that is faithful to the way to the whole. To put this paradoxically but, I think, accurately, Kane provides a balanced and insightful *overview* of Lynch's thought but does so *from the ground-level up*. This is not an overview from the sky, from the top of the mountain or a hot air balloon. We get the whole in and through the parts, but with-out drowning in the parts. John Kane's long swim in the ocean of William Lynch's intellectual world spares us that. For that we can be most grateful.

The value of this book *qua* treasure: Kane brings Lynch into our pres-ent situation of cultural impasse. He introduces a fresh way of approaching the conflicts we encounter, for example, on university campuses, within and among religious groups, or in national and local politics. He reintroduces this great Jesuit thinker into contemporary conversations about Ignatian spiritu-ality, *men and women for others*, the "faith that does justice," and Ignatian humanism. In particular, Kane spells out Lynch's constant intention to urge us towards a new spirit and sensibility in public life, that is, a spirituality for public discourse and action, for building the human city. And he helps us find contemporary examples of a Lynchian vision of that human city—a vision capable of confronting such massive challenges as immigration and climate change, terrorism and mass incarceration, the ethics of life and the dialogue of religions, the politics of hunger and the aesthetics of simple living. We not only need this book as a map to Lynch's writings; we need the wisdom of this book and the hope this spirituality of public life nurtures.

Building the Human City thus serves a triple function. First, it issues a clarion call to remember the importance of Civics, of cultivating civility, of rebuilding civilization. Second, it helps us remember one of our great Civics teachers, skillfully leading us into that master's mind and spirit. Third, as an invitation to a spirituality for contemporary public life that is both thoroughly religious and appropriately secular, it serves as a practical guide to life in community, life imagined outside of the box, life lived beyond the walls. Thanks to this book, we have a chance to remember Lynch and his realistic hope that, in this world riven by so much inhumanity, it is still possible to build a human city.

Kevin F. Burke, S.J.

Jesuit School of Theology
of Santa Clara University

Preface

In the time spent working on this book I have increasingly come to appreciate the meaning of that old platitude about "standing on the shoulders of giants." I have come to think of William Lynch as one of those giants. Yet it will also become clear as this text unfolds how much Lynch himself also stood on the shoulders of major giants of our tradition, most notably Aeschylus and Plato and Ignatius Loyola. Christ Himself remains the one from whom Lynch most drew inspiration for thought and imagination—"through, with, and in Him."

As its title suggests, this book has two inseparable goals: to provide a first overview of the work of Jesuit philosopher-theologian William F. Lynch, and thereby (since it was his focus and achievement) to outline an Ignatian spirituality for public life, a spirituality for the work of imagining and building the human city. We have, I believe, much need for such spirituality.

It is my hope, then, that this book will be more than an introduction to the thought of a (sadly) now forgotten major figure in American Catholic letters. For Lynch was in so many ways ahead of his times. He wrote from the 1950s through the mid-1980s, during times of much public turmoil in the U.S. Yet his fundamental concern with the passions and polarizations tearing then at the fabric of public life has, if anything, become more significant and needed today. For it has become a commonplace of political and cultural commentary that our public life is increasingly dominated by cultural and political warfare that shows no signs of ending. Lynch's concern, I hope to show, may have been aroused by the specific cultural wars of his time, but the Ignatian spirituality he proposed as a remedy for such conflict is even more needed today than it was then.

As a college student in the early 1960s I had heard one of Lynch's public lectures. I can still remember his startling opening image about how an ordinary bar of soap, through the seductive manipulations of advertising, can be transformed as if into the beatific vision! He must at that time have been working on *Images of Hope* (1965) since that bar of soap appears on the third page of its fifth chapter. Shortly thereafter I read *Christ and Apollo* which had been published in 1960. I know now that I really understood only parts of the book. Yet I clearly remember that I very much "felt" its thematic direction and also felt both liberated and affirmed, especially by its magnificent opening chapters on "The Definite" and "Time." Later I read *Images of Hope* (1965), *Christ and Prometheus* (1970), and *Images of Faith* (1973) as they appeared. Each time I had a similar experience: the realization that there was much that I did not understand in these often difficult and at times dense writings, yet the simultaneous sense of something important, affirming, and liberating.

Many years later, seemingly by accident, I ran across an article in *Thought*, the Fordham University quarterly which Lynch had edited in the 1950s, by the University of Chicago's Nathan Scott who lamented the fact that Lynch's writings were then (in 1991) so little known.[1] That essay sent me back to Lynch's books and led eventually to fuller comprehension and the growing sense that there was an important and still largely unrecognized vision and purpose underlying and unifying Lynch's writings. Yet it was finally something more than such comprehension that led me to pursue this study. It was above all the again experienced sense of the affirming and liberating power of his writings, now more clearly linked to my understanding of his fundamental purpose, and to my sense of the enduring need we have for their contribution to our work for common and public good.

Though it may be somewhat unorthodox for academic writing, let me explain that sense of affirmation and liberation and need by speaking autobiographically. Perhaps my brief reference to personal experience might evoke the reader's own experience of the struggles and tensions so characteristic of our times, and might thus prepare the ground for a more concrete understanding of Lynch's ideas.

Several years after leaving a very good period of intense and fairly traditional Catholic religious formation, I had come to a point where I fairly consciously "made a deal" with God. I would (and do) continue to believe and worship in traditional Catholic forms, but I would pretty much trust Him (it was unquestionably still "Him" back then) to take care of "His side of things." My need increasingly was not to become more spiritual, but to learn to be more human, to learn better how to love the world that God

---

1. Scott, "Religion."

Himself so loved. Thus my belief and prayer tended to focus increasingly on "Thy kingdom come" and "on earth as it is in heaven."

Soon enough, though, I began to stumble on a major obstacle. I was not tempted to change the basic terms of "the deal," but I often found much of the real world easier to hate than love. I lived during those years (and still do to some extent) under a seemingly strange, though actually quite widespread combination of influences. They came from both the Christian political left (typified by Dorothy Day's indictment of "this filthy, rotten system") and the Christian cultural right (typified by T.S. Eliot's jeremiad against "the wasteland" of modern culture). Such influences fueled an at times deliciously self-righteous and often quite angry activism: against the war and the bomb, against racism and consumerism, against reactionary forces in both church and society, and so on and so forth. Nor would I to this day reject much of the basic content of such activism. Yet I know that it often left me with an almost manic-depressive paralysis of spirit, with what I today would, under Lynch's influence, characterize as a deeply polarized and typically gnostic sensibility. Moments of love for the world or of manic activism were, I eventually realized, too often little more than romantic dreams fueled as much by anger as by hope. Meanwhile, ordinary, day-to-day activities were also too often depressed by such anger and by vague feelings of sullen resentment.[2]

I clearly needed (and still need) a better way to live within the tensions and conflicts of our times. I am still not much tempted to renegotiate the basic terms of my deal with God, though I regularly struggle for a better understanding of those terms and a more adequate image of and relationship to both God and the world. I am not tempted by the kind of wholesale retreat to supposedly traditional faith we hear so much about these days, nor by the leaping into various kinds of quasi-religious spirituality which often seem little more than its liberal or secular counterpart. Yet I usually manage a fair amount of sympathy for those, and not only the young, who need what I take to be such "quick fixes." For I still wrestle with my own analogous temptations.

Thus as I re-read Lynch, I gradually came to realize that he was fundamentally concerned with the need most of us have for a better way to live with the changes, conflicts and polarizations of our times, and for a way to live that directly related such public engagement with our more ultimate

2. Albert Borgmann's *Crossing*, 6–12, provides a telling analysis of the contemporary pervasiveness (left, right, and center) of such sullenness and resentment. Lynch himself provides an insightful analysis of the characteristic mood swings of his and my own "black Irish" heritage in his discussion of the work of Eugene O'Neill. See p. 33 below and CA, 81–88.

journey to God. This, I began to see, was the source of that sense of affirmation and liberation I first had and still have when working through his texts. He was not attempting to provide some new program or some new theology, at least not as I understand those terms. Nor did he suggest any quick resolutions to what, after all, are deep and often perennial political and cultural conflicts. Rather he was calling us to certain fundamental attitudes and habits, to what I will be calling fundamental forms of sensibility and spirituality that might enable us to live with those conflicts in less absolutized and polarizing ways, less enchanted by romantic fantasies or darkened by gnostic anger, and thus more able to work towards such resolutions as are human and possible. More able, in other words, to work for the improvement of our human city with realistic forms of hope, faith, and love, and also to experience such work as an essential dimension of our relationship with God.

Once again, then, my goal in this book is to explain the unifying sense of vision and purpose that develops in each of Lynch's books and through their cumulative achievement. In my title I describe that vision and purpose as "a spirituality for public life" since Lynch was primarily concerned with our ways of living in the world, above all with our ways of contributing to the contemporary human city with its many polarizations, tensions and conflicts. I describe this spirituality as "Ignatian" since we will soon enough see how much Lynch lived and thought out of his grounding in Ignatian spirituality. I also speak of "building the human city" since those are the basic terms of Lynch's own discussion. He also used, as I do in several chapter headings, key figures from Greek mythology to provide basic images of some of the most fundamental passions affecting life in the human city.

I believe that we today have much need for Lynch's contributions to such a spirituality for public life. Yet I am not here primarily concerned to relate his ideas to more recent scholarly literature and debate. Or, perhaps better, I have done so only in order to clarify the meaning of his ideas for contemporary readers. There are many fruitful connections which might be made between his ideas and our important contemporary discussions.[3] Just as there are significant critical questions that can be raised about his ideas. Yet the primary need, as I see it, is for an adequate introduction to Lynch himself, an overview of the ideas and purposes which he articulated. I hope to have begun here to meet that need.

This book moves, as did Lynch's own writings, through a gradual unfolding of his thought. The first chapter develops in greater detail ideas

---

3. See, for example, the use of Lynch's thought to contribute to the development of a Catholic theology of faith in Bednar, *Faith*.

about his vision and purpose. The second locates his work within the story of his life. Thereafter the sequence of chapters takes up the specific topics of his books in a compressed but somewhat chronological fashion. The final chapter focuses, as one form of recapitulation, on the belief and theology which grounded his entire effort.

In the first chapter I say some things about Lynch's writing, about its typically circling and "crisscrossing" style which continually returns to key themes, but typically from different angles or by adding important considerations, and thereby contributing to a gradual enlargement of understanding. I have attempted at least in part to imitate that style. Thus there is a significant repetition of key themes in the different chapters, as there is in Lynch's books and articles. Hopefully, though, the effect here will be as it is in Lynch's writings—a gradual enlargement and deepening of real understanding.

I have tried in this book to use inclusive language, but have left the general use of "man" and "mankind" in citations from Lynch. He wrote before there was widespread awareness of the need for inclusive forms of expression.

Acknowledgments

I need to thank many, many friends and colleagues who have taken the time to read or discuss various aspects of this study. That is especially true for colleagues at Regis College (of Regis University). It is one of the joys of a small liberal arts college that members of the faculty (and of administration and staff) are genuinely interested in the work of colleagues. For that very reason I will not mention specific names for fear of omitting someone, except to thank Joan Carnegie, the best secretary in the world.

I must, however, acknowledge by name a group of "New Yorkers" without whom this study could hardly have begun. They are folks who knew Bill Lynch and who gave generously of their time and critical interest. It was Joe Cunneen, the now-deceased founding editor of *Cross Currents*, who first responded to my request for assistance, and who then introduced me to both Bill Birmingham (the other long-time editor of *CC*) and to Bernard Gilligan, also now-deceased emeritus professor of Philosophy at Fordham. All had at one time or another been students and subsequently friends of Lynch's. Mary Louise Birmingham was also his friend and, with Bill, not only recounted wonderful stories, but remembered important facts and ideas. David Toolan, S.J., was a friend and companion of Lynch during his later years and a great supporter of my effort. An important writer himself, David died soon after finishing his award-winning work on environmental theology, *At Home in the Cosmos* (2001). It was Richard Geraghty who personally introduced me to Lynch (some years before I had any thought of the present project). Joe Lynch, though not related to Bill Lynch, is someone who knows and admires his ideas and who gave me important affirmation and support along the way. I also want to thank my great friend Bob Gilliam, librarian emeritus at SUNY Brockport, for answers to a variety of inquiries, and I hope he doesn't mind being included in my group of "New Yorkers."

I also give special thanks to three friends in the theological community. Above all Kevin Burke, SJ, former colleague at Regis and now professor of Systematic Theology at the Jesuit School of Theology in Berkeley, who read my text and made important suggestions, and has now written this book's "Foreword." Chris Pramuk of Xavier University's Dept. of Theology, a Merton scholar who also began his career at Regis and has more recently written an important book about race relations. Andrew Scrimgeour, Dean of Libraries Emeritus at Drew University (and formerly Dean of Regis University Library), provided invaluable help with publication. These are three of many who today articulate the importance for theology of "imagining the human city."

Along with much always congenial help from the many professionals at Wipf & Stock, especially my editor K.C. Hanson, I also want to acknowledge the detailed formatting assistance cheerfully given by Bonnie Jensen, another of those "best" secretaries.

Vince Kane has been the best copy editor a brother could ever want. Finally and most of all, my wife, Dr. Jean Demmler, has not only provided continual support, but in a professional life dedicated to social research she has been for me and for many a model for the kind of engagement in building a more human city that is this book's real subject.

Abbreviations

The following abbreviations are used in references to Lynch's books and to one book project. References throughout are to the edition identified first in the Bibliography, usually the first published edition unless otherwise noted.

BA *A Book of Admiration*

CA *Christ and Apollo*

CP *Christ and Prometheus*

IF *Images of Faith*

IH *Images of Hope*

II *The Image Industries*

IM *The Integrating Mind*

But there is another temptation which we must especially guard against: the simplistic reductionism which sees only good or evil; or, if you will, the righteous and sinners. The contemporary world, with its open wounds which affect so many of our brothers and sisters, demands that we confront every form of polarization which would divide it into these two camps.

—Pope Francis to the US Congress, September 24, 2015

1

Into the Valley of the Human

The May 23, 1960, issue of *Time* magazine carried a two-page feature article on William F. Lynch, SJ (1908–1987). Calling him "one of the most incisive Catholic intellectuals in the U.S,"[1] the article focused primarily on Lynch's just published *Christ and Apollo*. Its title, "Downward to the Infinite," not only sought to suggest the central theme of that book, but in effect gave one indication of the fundamental intention and direction that runs through the complex and rich body of Lynch's writings. For the title of this first chapter, I have used one of Lynch's own images, "into the valley of the human" (IH, 117), as another way to suggest that same fundamental intention and direction. Lynch himself probably gives the most explicit articulation of the basic intention of his work in a passage in his last published book, *Images of Faith*. There he wrote: "I repeat that everything I have ever written asks for the concrete movement of faith and the imagination through experience, through time, through the definite, through the human, through the actual life of Christ" (IF, 81).

It is my hope that this entire book will gradually unfold what Lynch meant by this description of "everything I have ever written." Yet even at this beginning point the reader may get a preliminary feel for the intention of Lynch's thought from his emphasis on the *concrete movement* of faith and imagination, and perhaps even more from his rhythmic repetition of the word "through": *through* experience, *through* time, *through* the definite, *through* the human, and *through* the actual life of Christ. Everything he wrote "asks for" this movement "into the valley of the human." Indeed he called for it with a constant, restrained urgency. Thus he continually called us to a way of thinking, to a pattern of habits and attitudes, to the development of the kind of sensibility and spirituality which would make such movement possible, and would thereby counter our regular tendency and

1 "Downward," 82.

1

temptation toward fundamentally opposed movements of mind and spirit and imagination, especially those which hunger for quick fixes, for leaps into the kind of absolute and final positions which inevitably cause deep polarizations and culture wars in the life of our city.

In its original context, Lynch's remark about "everything I have ever written" is intended to indicate where he stands on what "many . . . will say . . . happens to be precisely the central question of modern theology" (IF, 80): must theology and the Christian imagination increasingly turn its attention towards this world, towards the secular realities involved in building the human city?[2] Lynch's answer was clearly affirmative. His writings develop a deeply incarnational spirituality, or, perhaps better said, they are a sustained reflection of the significance of incarnation (and of the Incarnation) for the many dimensions of our involvement in worldly or public activity.

Images of Faith, as we will see more fully later, is about the two related meanings of its title: about our images of the nature of faith and about faith's images and imagining of this world. In taking up those topics, Lynch first criticized one very prevalent image of faith: that it is an essentially interior experience whereby the believer "ascends" to "transcendent" meaning. Rather, he argued, we need to see that faith "has a body." It is embodied in a complex of relations between self and world. Its primary location, so to speak, is external as much as internal, horizontal as much as vertical. For human faith (or a basic sense of trust) is first nurtured within and embodied in some form of family. Yet the family and its relations of faith and trust exist within that larger body of thought and practice which we call society and culture, but which seen more concretely is the pulsing life of the human city.[3] In one very important sense, then, our most basic image of faith should be an image of its social or horizontal life as embodied in a complex web of human relationships of trust and fidelity. And given that basic image of faith, it then makes good sense, to turn to the second meaning of Lynch's title, to take seriously the ways in which faith (whether religious or more basic human faith) imagines the world and to ask whether faith's images of this world lead us to the task of building such relationships in the human city or divert us from that task. Of course, the ascending or vertical movement of

---

2. Shortly after Vatican II, Richard McBrien had suggested that the Council represented a shift in Catholic and Christian thought so epochal that it deserved to be seen as a form of "Copernican revolution"—from a church-centered to a world-centered faith. See *Do We Need*, 14. Pope Francis seems today to be calling again for such a paradigm shift in Catholic thought and practice.

3. This understanding of the human city as a "body of faith" will be the primary subject of Chapter 6 below.

faith is also crucial, but typically comes later.[4] As grace (at least in Catholic understanding) builds on nature, so the ascending movement of faith builds upon faith's embodiment in and movement *through* this world, even as, of course, "vertical" faith in its turn clearly must contribute to the development of its "horizontal" body. Thus Lynch says, just before his remark about "everything I have ever written," that "I am intent on creating, and in a very imaginable way, a body for faith and, very specially, a political and social embodiment of faith" (IF, 80). Nor was this his intent only for his last book. It was true for everything he had ever written.

Of course, all that Lynch meant by faith having a body and contributing to the human city will only gradually become clear in the course of this book. Yet the idea is so central to all of Lynch's work that I want to emphasize it from the first. For, as I have already suggested in the "Preface," the goal of this book is to introduce (or perhaps in some cases to reintroduce) Lynch to the kind of philosophically and theologically educated audience that when he was writing knew at least some of his work. I want to introduce him by providing, for the first time, an overview of his work, and thus a clearer sense of what I have been calling its overall intention and direction. In doing so, I hope also to argue that the issues Lynch addressed—which I have suggested in this book's title by mention of public life, and the human city—are still very much with us, as is our need for the kind of sensibility, imagination, and spirituality he saw as crucial if we are adequately to address them.

Such an overview is needed because, while Lynch wrote numerous essays and a series of well-received books, the explicit focus of these writings was almost always some particular topic about contemporary public life.[5] And those topics varied quite widely. He wrote about cinema and the current state of the literary imagination. He also wrote about mental illness and hope, and about modern technical development and the growing secularity of the human city. He was everywhere concerned with what he saw as basic issues in U.S. culture and politics (in the broadest sense of that word). He

---

4. In his essay "Culture and Belief," the first of Lynch's mature writings published just as he had begun his tenure as editor of *Thought*, he argues that it is true for all of us (and not just for the child) that "vertical" faith (in God) is typically dependent on a prior, "horizontal" experience of faith, on a sense of fundamental trust nurtured by culture and society. See also IM, 97–120, where Lynch later reprinted the essay.

5. The one exception was *An Approach to the Metaphysics of Plato through the Parmenides*, Lynch's first book and his only typically academic and purely theoretical one. It will be discussed below in Chapter 3.

was, in other words, primarily a cultural critic and an essayist—what might today be referred to as a "public intellectual."[6]

Yet he brought to his essays about particular, topical issues both an uncommonly deep appropriation of foundational philosophical and theological ideas and a deeply integrated sensibility. His thinking and writing, in other words, while topical and contemporary, were thoroughly grounded in fundamental aspects of Western philosophy and Christian thought. Nor did he simply bring such fundamental thinking to bear on the particular issue at hand in a given writing. He was also always concerned to call for and lead us towards a shift or development in the foundations of our own thinking and feeling. Thus it can be said that the goal of Lynch's essays was invariably twofold: both to make a specific contribution to thought about some particular issue or concern, and simultaneously to contribute to the development of the fundamental or foundational kind of sensibility we need as we seek, in our struggles with such issues and concerns, to build a more human world. This second goal has not been adequately appreciated by many who have taken up Lynch's writings. Yet it gradually becomes clearer as one seeks to understand the unity of thought and purpose that runs through his quite diverse writings.

Of course, since the central concern of his writing was to bring the resources of Christian faith into sustained engagement with different arenas of the human and secular activities of our world—with the arts and sciences, with culture and politics, with building the human city—one could perhaps understand the whole of Lynch's work as contributing to a "theology of the world" or a "theology of secularity." For such themes were current on the theological scene when he wrote. Yet it is, I believe, more faithful to both his intent and his achievement to understand him as calling for and contributing to a *spirituality* for public life or for human activity in the secular world. For though he was extremely well grounded in both philosophy and theology, he was not much concerned with contributing to the standard questions of ecclesial theology or academic philosophy. Rather the concern which gave unity to his different writings was his desire to communicate a form of both Socratic and Ignatian therapy for cultural and political activity, a practical wisdom that might guide our "concrete movement" through time and through the definite dimensions of worldly action and experience. If there must be an academic category to help us locate Lynch's work, then he is perhaps best understood as a philosopher. Yet he was a *Christian* philosopher concerned with what Christ might bring to the spirit and sensibility

---

6. See Kane, "William F. Lynch."

that moves us as we build or fail to build the human city—a philosopher concerned, as I have said, with both spirituality and sensibility.

I should, at this point, provide some further clarification since the words "spirituality" and "sensibility" are easily and often misunderstood. It will be clear to anyone who has the least acquaintance with his writings that they do not deal with the kind of immediate pieties and practices found in much very good spiritual writing. Lynch was indeed much concerned with practices, with habits of mind, spirit, and imagination. Yet his concern operated at such a fundamental level—with such focus on the foundational ideas and fundamental spirit at work in the movement of mind and imagination—that it is best to see him as working towards the retrieval and development of a *fundamental* or *foundational* spirituality for worldly activity. Of course the best spiritual writers have always been concerned to get to the roots or foundations of mind and spirit, and to work there for an always-needed transformation. Yet relatively few in recent history have done so with the categories and concerns of a deeply schooled philosophical mind that was also thoroughly grounded in the traditions of Christian theology and Western literature and was simultaneously so focused on public life.[7]

I have also linked such spirituality with the related (though not typically connected) and equally problematic word "sensibility." Just as spirituality can too easily suggest specifically religious practices or something primarily interior or otherworldly, so sensibility might readily suggest something especially refined or aesthetic, contrasted with "sense" and the hurly-burly of the ordinary world. Yet Lynch continually fought against any sensibility, whether in religion or in the arts, which embodied a form of elitist separation from the everyday life of ordinary people. He used the word "sensibility," as well as more frequently used terms like "image" and "imagination," to indicate the concrete, sensory, bodily ways we touch and enter the actual world. To give here but one example, Lynch regularly criticized any understanding of religion that focused narrowly on "the saving of souls." At one point he remarked that "saving souls" all too typically means something like "saving . . . the top of the head" and failing to give faith any "relation to human reality, to *sensibility*, or to all the mighty energies of the imagination's bloodstream" (CA, 139).[8] Indeed that striking image of

---

7. The concern for spirituality among some liberation theologians and the somewhat broader concern to relate "mysticism and politics" are other contemporary examples of such foundational spiritual writing.

8. Emphasis added. I shall have occasion soon enough (see, for example, pp. 100–102 below) to discuss Lynch's use of the terms "image" and "imagination" and "imagining."

imagination's *bloodstream* itself perhaps best suggests what Lynch meant by "sensibility."

In this book, then, I want to show how Lynch was a Christian philosopher concerned to bring the resources of both faith and thought to the elucidation, recommendation, and even inculcation of fundamental forms of sensibility and spirituality which he saw as especially needed today in the vast and increasingly secular project of building the global human city.

Yet before leaving this first indication of the overall character and intent of his thought and writings, let me add still another clarification. Lynch did not anyplace develop some broad overview of "a fundamental spirituality for worldly activity." He was not a "systematic" thinker, at least not in the most typical sense of that word. Rather he was in all he wrote concerned to understand, and to help us understand, a number of basic ideas which he saw as crucial or foundational for our ability to respond to the challenges of our times. It has been said that most truly significant thinkers typically come to only one or a few fundamental insights. Their significance derives from the way in which, over time, they explore and elaborate those insights. That certainly was the case for Lynch. There is real unity of thought in all he wrote, yet there is also great diversity and difference. For he never ceased to explore the many different but analogous forms and manifestations of the fundamental insights that so concerned him. And he wrote in ways that challenge us to enter into that exploration so that we, too, might achieve not simply some conceptual clarity, but that deeper kind of understanding which contributes to the development of basic habits of thought, imagination, and practice—basic habits of spirit and sensibility.

Acclaim, Neglect, and Renewed Interest

Bill Lynch was almost 52 years old when he first began to receive the kind of national recognition suggested by the May 1960 article in *Time*. Before then he had been known mainly in Catholic academic and literary circles, both as editor of Fordham University's quarterly, *Thought,* and as a gifted writer whose work appeared primarily in its pages. Flannery O'Connor probably spoke for many others in 1955 when she referred to Lynch as "one of the most learned priests in this country."[9] Yet by 1960 he had quite literally burst onto the national scene with the publication, in quick succession, of three very well received and quite different books. In 1959, his *An Approach to the Metaphysics of Plato Through the Parmenides* was applauded by Plato specialists both here and abroad as a learned, if controversial, interpretation

9. O'Connor, *Habit of Being,* 119.

of Plato's *Metaphysics*. In 1959 Lynch also published *The Image Industries,* a far more popular book which called for the collaboration of artists, critics, theologians, and an informed public in a struggle to raise the quality of cinema in the U.S. It was discussed in Hollywood's trade journal, *Variety,* and received several national book awards.[10] *Christ and Apollo,* Lynch's study of "the dimensions of the literary imagination" (the book's subtitle), was published in early 1960. It received significant commentary not only in *Time,* but in *The New York Times Book Review*[11] and in a wide range of both scholarly journals and journals of opinion. In 1963 The New American Library published a paperback edition in its prestigious Mentor-Omega Series.[12]

The year 1960, then, might also stand as a symbol for the start of the most productive period in Lynch's work as a writer and lecturer. In 1962 he published *The Integrating Mind,* a collection of essays on society and culture *cf Wilbur* in the U.S. 1965 saw the publication of what has probably been Lynch's most widely read and most influential book, *Images of Hope,* a study of mental illness and hope. It then also appeared almost immediately (1966) in the Mentor-Omega Series.[13] Then in 1970 came another multiple award winner, *Christ and Prometheus.*[14] It represented Lynch's effort to develop a new understanding in religious circles of the growing secularity of the modern human project ("the secular city")—thus a new understanding of the relationship between Christ and Prometheus. In 1973 Lynch's last published book, *Images of Faith,* focused directly on growing polarizations and culture wars in the U.S., a topic that had been an increasing concern for him throughout the 1960s.[15] Each of his books wrestled with major concerns at issue in both church and society during "the tumultuous 60s," and each contributed to a gradual enlargement of Lynch's depiction of the fundamental habits and attitudes we need in living with and moving through those concerns.

Throughout these years, Lynch was much in demand as a lecturer and writer. Early in the decade he had chosen to leave a faculty position at Georgetown to devote himself more fully to writing as his primary form of public engagement. His essays and reviews appeared in numerous journals, most frequently in *Commonweal, America,* and *Cross Currents.* He spoke often on

10. The National Catholic Book Award as Most Distinguished Catholic Book for 1959, and the Thomas More Medal for Creative Catholic Publishing.

11. July 31, 1960, 4.

12. It has since been kept in print by several other publishers.

13. It has since stayed in print at the University of Notre Dame Press.

14. It received the 1971 National Catholic Book Award and the 1971 Conference on Christianity and Literature Book Award.

15. See his essay "Divided We Stand" in *The Integrating Mind,* 38–62, as well as *Christ and Prometheus* in its entirety.

the university and conference lecture circuit and also served as a visiting professor at a number of universities, most notably several times at Princeton.

It is not surprising that Lynch's voice and writings commanded significant attention during the 1960s and early 1970s, a period when many
of the most fundamental issues which still challenge us, both in church
and society, came to particularly sharp and often polarized focus. What is
perhaps surprising, and cause of dismay for those who most appreciated
Lynch's work, is how quickly a body of work once accurately described as
"seminal"[16] seems to have been forgotten. *Images of Faith* (1973), his last
book, was well, but not widely reviewed.[17] Nor does it seem to have been
widely read. Two subsequent book projects never came to publication,
though most of the second eventually appeared during the 1970s and early
1980s as essays in journals where Lynch continued to publish.[18] In retirement in the 1980s Lynch made an effort to start a new journal of cultural
criticism called *New York Images*. Three issues appeared (in 1984, 1985, and
1986), but it never caught on and was known only to a small readership.[19]

At the time of Lynch's death in January 1987, Jesuit writer and political
activist Dan Berrigan would praise him as "a luminous spirit whose work
lifted American Catholicism more than a few notches in the direction of
intellectual maturity." Yet Berrigan would also note "the remarkable public
neglect that marked his later years."[20] Several years later, University of Chicago professor Nathan Scott, then still a national leader in the field of religion and literature, published an essay in *Thought* on "the legacy of William
F. Lynch, S.J." He too spoke of Lynch's "remarkable intelligence" and praised
him for "one of the most remarkably sensitive and original explorations of
the interior life in the literature of our period." Yet Scott also complained of

16. Introducing an essay by Lynch, the editors of the British Jesuit journal *The
Month* note that "Father Lynch . . . has been described by American literary critics as
one of the seminal thinkers of our time." Lynch, "The Life," 5.

17. one appreciative review referred to Lynch as "one of the subtlest, soundest
philosophical voices in the United States today." Kenny, "Faith."

18. The first project which he took up after *Images of Faith,* probably during 1973
and 1974, was tentatively titled *A Book of Admiration*. A draft manuscript can be found
in the archives at Fordham University. Various forms of the second project, on which
Lynch seems to have begun work in the mid-1970s, can also be found in those archives.
It was most typically titled *The Drama of the Mind* and was to have been a study of the
philosophical and cultural significance of both classical and contemporary theater. See
below (p. 90 n. 1) for a record of the published parts of this second project.

19. Copies can be found at the Fordham University Library.

20. Berrigan, "Father William Lynch," 4. Berrigan further described Lynch as "rare
as radium and twice as bright. Grandly human, grand in learning, a man of scope and
sociability."

"the neglect [Lynch] has suffered in recent theological literature." One is, he lamented, "astonished to remark how much for [contemporary theologians] Lynch is as if he had never been."[21]

As noted above in this book's "Preface," my own study of Lynch's work was in part occasioned by Scott's essay. As also noted, I had heard Lynch speak when I was a college student, and had over the years read most of his books. I mention this again to explain how, when I read Scott's essay, I realized that Scott himself had given ironic testimony to his lament about how Lynch had been forgotten. For his essay clearly reveals that Scott knew little of Lynch's later books.[22] I do not say this to be mean-spirited or to score points. The work Scott knew, especially *Christ and Apollo,* he knew very well, and his essay remains one of the finest published interpretations of Lynch's thought. Yet it was the deficiency I saw in Scott's essay that sent me looking for other writings about Lynch, and to the discovery that, aside from the many fine reviews of his books there had been little further commentary or discussion. Just scattered essays and one unpublished doctoral dissertation.[23] I did find quite a few references and footnotes in books where an author, sometimes a major figure, praised Lynch's "original" or "groundbreaking" writing on a given topic, but then typically made little direct use of his ideas.[24] Perhaps the ultimate testimony to "the remarkable public neglect" that Lynch had suffered was provided by a librarian who helped my search for secondary literature on Lynch. Having found very little, he remarked in amazement: "It's as if he wrote on water."[25]

Yet there has more recently been renewed interest in Lynch's thought. Most notable is the first book on Lynch, *Faith as Imagination* by Gerald Bednar,[26] which draws on the significance of Lynch's understanding of the analogical character of imagination for the development of a contemporary theology of faith. Other recent theological appropriations of aspects of

21. Scott, "Religion," 156, 151–52.

22. In this regard Scott seems typical of those who once knew Lynch's work. For Lynch seems to have been known above all as the author of *Images of Hope* and *Christ and Apollo.* It also seems that he was known (and is still remembered) in different circles for just one or the other of these books, either as a significant early figure in the field of religion and literature, or as one of the early Catholic contributors to the study of psychology and religion.

23. Finnegan, "Lynch."

24. See, for instance, Hart, *Unfinished,* 248 n. 110. See also Fowler, "Vocation," 21, and *Stages,* 36 n. 38; 116 nn. 9, 16; 211 n. 10.

25. Personal correspondence from Robert Gilliam, Librarian Emeritus, State University of New York (Brockport).

26. Bednar, *Faith.*

Lynch's thought have been Francesca Murphy's *Christ the Form of Beauty,*[27] which makes significant use of Lynch's thought for the development of a Christian aesthetics, William Spohn's use of Lynch's discussion of imagination in *Go and Do Likewise: Jesus and Ethics,*[28] and most recently Paul Lakeland's *The Liberation of the Laity,*[29] which draws on Lynch's understanding of secularity for developing a much needed contemporary theology of the laity. Lynch has also been the subject of extensive discussion in three recent literary studies: John Neary's *Like and Unlike God: Religious Imaginations in Modern and Contemporary Fiction,*[30] Denis Donoghue's *Adam's Curse: Reflections on Religion and Literature,*[31] and the extended introduction by Glen Arbery ("The Act Called Existence") to the most recent edition of *Christ and Apollo.*[32] Even more recently, David Bentley Hart included a short chapter, "Infinite Lit: On William Lynch's *Christ and Apollo,*" in a recent collection of critical essays [33]

A Gradual Enlargement of Understanding

Yet all of these relatively recent studies either focus on only one of Lynch's books or draw on some particular aspect of his thought for the development of their own particular (and typically theological) concerns.[34] They give testimony to the enduring power of his ideas. They also suggest, however, that there is not yet much awareness of the more fundamental and unifying concern which runs through his diverse writings. That is, to repeat, his concern to articulate a basic practical wisdom that calls us to forms of spirituality and sensibility which we need to meet challenges raised by the

27. Murphy, *Christ.*

28. Spohn, *Ethics.*

29. Lakeland, *Laity.*

30. Neary, *Like.*

31. Donoghue, *Adam's Curse.*

32. Arberry, "Act."

33. Hart, "Infinite Lit." It will soon enough become clear, if it is not already, why I find Hart's clever chapter title misleading even though his discussion of Lynch is significant.

34. Neary and Donoghue and Hart, for example, like Murphy, focus almost exclusively on *Christ and Apollo* and understand it primarily in terms of the *religious* dimensions of the literary imagination. Yet Lynch's primary interest in literature, as we will see in chap. 4 below, actually moved in a different direction. While not uninterested in the religious dimensions of literature (discussed in chaps. 7 and 8 of *Christ and Apollo*), he was primarily concerned with the significance of faith (of Christ) for the contemporary development of mainstream or *secular* drama and fiction.

ideological and political polarizations of our times. Thankfully, one more recent book, *The Ignatian Tradition* by Kevin F. Burke, SJ, and Eileen Burke Sullivan, does give chapter length coverage to Lynch's contribution to Ignatian spirituality.[35]

Yet it clearly is not enough for me simply to keep repeating the claim that there is this broader unity of purpose in Lynch's writings. I must begin the work of explaining that unity, but I must do so in a way that corresponds to the way he himself worked—in gradual steps that lead in time to an enlargement of real understanding. For "we must not," Lynch says, summarizing one of the fundamental ideas he takes from Plato, "go too fast from the many to the one" (CA, 13, 146). Indeed we must not because finally we cannot. We *must not* seek to attain the unity (the bringing together, the integration) of real understanding—in this or in any case—by leaping quickly to some neat, perhaps clear and probably abstract formulation, and then repeating it endlessly, as I have thus far been repeating my own formulations about Lynch's contribution to a "foundational spirituality and sensibility." For we humans *cannot* attain the unity of real understanding in that way, by leaping over the many different elements which lead into and are constitutive of such understanding. Though the fact that we cannot usually does not deter us from such leaping, from moving quickly to merely notional or univocal understanding. That we regularly do so was just one manifestation of a series of related tendencies—a kind of sensibility—that Lynch was always working against.

We attain real understanding, Lynch would (and did repeatedly) say, only gradually, only by *moving through* the many different aspects of actual, finite experience.

> We must go *through* the finite, the limited, the definite, omitting none of it . . . [For] The finite is not itself a generality, to be encompassed in one fell swoop. Rather it contains many shapes and byways and clevernesses and powers and diversities and persons, and we must not go too fast from the many to the one. (CA, 7)

How else have we in fact, in the course of our lives, learned what little we really know about love or justice or, for that matter, about understanding? And how much further does each of us still have to go in the journey towards such knowledge, towards such real unity in mind, imagination, and spirit? How great still (how great always!) the temptation to stop and cling tightly to what we think we already possess? Or the correlative temptation to rush forward, attempting a quick, at times desperate grab for what can

35. Burke and Sullivan, *Ignatian*, 111–20.

in fact only gradually be received? And how typical also, especially in situations of difference and conflict, the tendency to see our thus-grasped truth in polar opposition to the errors of our adversaries. Finally, of course, to round out this picture of epistemic tendencies and temptations, how pervasive in our times is the alternative tendency simply to despair of the possibility of any real unity of understanding, to claim that the endless dance of the many is our only possibility, our post-modern fate?

We must, then, begin to move gradually, in limited steps, towards an understanding of the kind of spirituality and sensibility which were Lynch's basic concern. In fact the brief evocation of Lynch's ideas about understanding in the preceding paragraphs is itself a first small step—a first brief exemplification of the philosophical therapy whereby Lynch alerts us to the constant temptation to move (or settle) too quickly, and calls us instead to move in gradual steps "*through* the finite" towards real understanding, towards a real enlargement of spirit and sensibility. It is, moreover, important to note that the habits and practices of such movement towards real understanding are themselves expressions of one kind of epistemic sensibility—the incarnational sensibility Lynch called for—even as the habit of moving too quickly expresses a fundamentally different and deeply opposed sensibility.

In subsequent sections of this first chapter I will take three further steps into the substance of Lynch's thought. The first notes the difficulty of his writing as a way of illustrating his own practice of not moving too quickly from the many to the one. Then I will briefly sketch his understanding of the changing and challenging times during which we live. Finally I will note a few recent examples of the tendencies and temptations which arise during such times, tendencies Lynch continually called us to resist.

Succeeding chapters will, each in its own way, be further steps moving through different aspects of Lynch's thought and writing. Thus the structure of this book will be an effort to imitate, in its small way, both the style and substance of Lynch's own books. Like his writing, this book too will involve repetitions of various sorts. It will return again and again, hopefully in significantly different ways, from different angles of vision, to central themes which are repeated in different ways in those writings.

A Weaving and Horizontal Style

Lynch's books are at times dense and often difficult. In part the challenge readers face arises simply from the wide range of reference on which he drew: classical and contemporary, philosophical and theological and literary. In part it also results from his deliberate but disconcerting effort to bring the most fundamental philosophical and theological ideas into discussion of current topics and concerns, often assuming the reader's ability to grasp their connection. Yet the greatest source of difficulty is Lynch's avoidance of the kinds of quick and superficially clear writing that can seduce us into thinking that we have understood when in fact we have attained only some abstract or notional clarity. This may have been, on his part, a deliberate strategy. Yet I suspect it was as often simply the way his mind worked, a result of his own tendency to move *through* the many shapes and byways and diversities of the finite into real understanding.

He did deliberately avoid any fixed set of formulations or repeated technical jargon in elaborating his fundamental insights. It is, for instance, already evident that one of those insights had to do with our deep-seated human tendency to avoid complexity by leaping to comforting forms of clarity or unity; and the consequent tendency to fix on simplistic, either-or polarizations constructed from such easy clarities. These tendencies are rooted in the "same" fundamental temptation; yet "it" is not in fact one simple thing. In actual experience it takes many analogous forms as it comes to expression in different contexts. "It," then, is always both one and many. Thus "it" can be really understood only by careful attention to "its" many different-yet-related forms. Lynch, then, avoids speaking, as I have just been doing, of any "it." Rather he lets his terminology emerge from each specific context. In *Christ and Apollo*, for instance, he especially emphasizes the danger of "univocal" forms of literary understanding. He also warns of pervasive "gnostic" tendencies both in contemporary literature and in the broader culture. Later, in *Images of Hope*, he continues to express concern about such contemporary forms of Gnosticism, but his primary critical target is what he there calls "the absolutizing instinct." In *The Integrating Mind*, by contrast, he had spoken mostly about the "totalistic" or "totalizing" temptation and disease, and later, in *Christ and Prometheus*, he emphasizes the danger of contemporary forms of "prometheanism." In all these writings he is, in a sense, concerned about the same tendency. Yet he uses different terminology since in reality that "sameness" entails significant difference. It is, in language Lynch uses in *Christ and Apollo* and again in *The Integrating Mind*, not a univocal but an analogical "sameness." By adopting such flexible and differentiated terminology, Lynch challenges himself, and us, to move through these many forms of difference in coming to a more real understanding of the fundamental sameness.

Lynch was also, for similar reasons, wary of precise definitions. His typical procedure, even for utterly central terms like "image" and "imagination," was not "to define . . . in one step," but "to grow into our definitions"

(IF, 101).[36] This, too, seems to have been his way of not moving too quickly from the many to the one. I suspect it also was a deliberate attempt to break the captivating hold which simplistic clarities and images exercise on our minds and spirits, and thus a deliberate effort to lead us towards different ways of thinking and a different kind of sensibility.

Just as deliberate was the way in which Lynch characteristically developed his ideas in the course of his books. He says, for instance, in his introduction to *Christ and Apollo*, that the book is "an exploration" which "nowhere speaks its final mind at any one point and cannot (or should not) be judged with finality at any one point" (xi–xii).[37] The same could be said of most of his writing. For there is rarely a simple linear progression in the development of his argument. His writing, in other words, does not move in what could be called a "vertical" or a "mathematical" fashion—leading in clear steps up to one conceptually definite conclusion, or descending in clear deductions from one fundamental starting point. Rather it moves in a more exploratory fashion, often repeating or circling back on key ideas, but always in some different context.

I often think of his writing as a form of weaving where central threads and colors appear and reappear in the gradual creation of an integrated whole. His style has also continually reminded me of Wittgenstein's description of his own *Philosophical Investigations* as continually crisscrossing the same field, but always from different points and in somewhat different directions.[38] Thus it is possible to understand the progression of Lynch's thought, both within each essay or book, and also from one book to the next, as "horizontal." His mind was never content with an easy ascent to sweeping generalizations, but always sought further exploration by moving through "the shapes and byways and clevernesses and powers and diversities" of actual existence. Perhaps Bernard Gilligan, one of Lynch's students and later a professor of philosophy at Fordham, gave the best general description of Lynch's style in a review of *Images of Hope*.

> Memorable and operative phrases, sentences and paragraphs
> abound, as the author continually pivots about the same central
> themes, but each time to see something from another angle, in

---

36. See also IH, 90, CA, 122, and CP, 22.

37. The pagination in the widely available 1975 Notre Dame Press edition of *Christ and Apollo* is identical with the original 1960 Sheed and Ward edition *except* for the introductory pages. I am here (and subsequently) citing the Notre Dame edition.

38. Wittgenstein, *Investigations*, vii.

a different perspective, in a yet more effective way, with newer implications and ever fresh applications.[39]

Gilligan also wisely advised the reader "not to attempt to read [Lynch] at one or a few prolonged sittings. [The content] will be savored, digested and reflected on slowly and by degrees."[40]

Lynch's style, then, works to frustrate our habit of the quick read and our need for simple clarities. It challenges us not to move too quickly from the many to the one. It was the most appropriate style for one concerned to criticize narrowly "univocal" thinking, to break the hold of an "absolutizing instinct" or a "totalistic temptation" on our minds and spirits, and to lead us into quite different habits of understanding and sensibility. And it is, to repeat, a style which for similar reasons I have attempted to imitate in this book.

The Discernment of Spirits in an Era of Change

A further way to understand Lynch's concern to retrieve and articulate an alternative to such absolutizing or totalizing forms of thought and sensibility is to locate that concern, as he himself did, within the historical context suggested by terms like "modernity" and "post-modern." For Lynch, as I have already indicated with phrases about "growing secularity" and "the modern project of building the global city," was very conscious of the fact that we are living within an era of momentous change.

At one point in *Christ and Prometheus*, the book which most explicitly focuses on the civilizational significance of such change, he affirms the view of those who see our era of "modernization" as only the third truly "promethean" transition in human history. It is a "moment" with parallels in the first, prehistoric emergence of human beings some million years ago (when "Prometheus descended with fire") and the second great "emergence of man" in the ancient city-states of the Indus, Nile, and Tigris-Euphrates river valleys, and somewhat later in ancient Greece (CP, 101–2). Ours, he says, is a time of the "major new explosion of energy and frontiers in the modern secular project," a time of immense "forward and autonomous movement of human action and history through the arts and sciences, through economics and politics and the whole social reality, towards great but autonomous human goals . . ." (CP, 7).[41]

39. Gilligan, "Images."

40. Ibid.

41. Lynch takes this historical schema from C. E. Black's *The Dynamics of Modernization* (1966). A similar and widely referenced schema was proposed in Karl Jaspers' *The Origin and Goal of History* (1953).

Yet Lynch was not particularly concerned to enter into the often ar-
cane historical and cultural polemics which characterize much discussion
of "modernity" or "the post-modern." He simply borrowed widely accepted
ideas from various theories and explanations in pointing to the pervasive
contemporary experience of change and the vast enlargement of horizons
characteristic of our era.[42] And he used iconic figures, like Apollo and Prometheus and Dionysus, to provide general images for the deep passions and
explosive energies characteristic of our times.[43] For he was less interested
in some overall or systematic analysis of these times than in bringing the
light of sustained critical analysis to our often angry and polarized ways of
responding to them. He was, in other words, above all concerned with the
sharp, wrenching divides which our responses have torn into both the fabric
of society and the state of our souls. And, of course, he was most fundamentally concerned with helping us discern the forms of hope and faith, of
spirituality and sensibility, which might bring healing to such trauma. As he
said at the beginning of *Christ and Prometheus,* "I would be most thankful
if [this book] should make any contribution to healing the wounds in the
divided imagination of this country at this time and building for it some
common vision. Surely that is our terrible need" (vii).

Thus Lynch regularly referred to the transitional character of our times
because of his awareness that certain perennial or fundamental human tendencies and temptations are intensified and exacerbated during such times.
That was perhaps true in a particular way for the period of "the 60s" when he
did much of his writing. But it has been (and remains) much more broadly
true for the entire "modern" and the contemporary "post-modern" era.

New possibilities, new ways of thinking and acting, have emerged in
virtually every dimension of human life, just as old securities and traditional ways have been challenged and often destroyed. Thus the tendencies
grow on every front—in the arts, in religion, in politics, in work—either to

---

42. I suspect that Lynch would, for example, have followed with interest much recent debate about "secularization," about whether the worldwide resurgence of different
forms of religiousness has shown that the whole idea of secularization is exaggerated,
or whether the extreme character of such resurgence (often "fundamentalist," yet just as
often very private and esoteric) is itself evidence of the power of the secularizing process. In *Christ and Prometheus,* as we will see later (in Chapter 7 below), Lynch simply
takes as evident both that more and more spheres of human endeavor are developing
with their own autonomous (thus "secular") dynamism and that religion can, indeed
must, retain its own integral and integrating role in human life.

43. As we will see below, Lynch understood "promethean" and "dionysian" energies
as fundamentally good, as basic elements of God's creation. Yet in actual history they
are continually distorted, and thus always need (perhaps especially today) the critical
companionship of Christ.

grasp for the new or to pull back and cling to the "tried and true." Worse, we frequently seem to have no choice, to be simply caught in the whirlwind and compelled by the force of events. Then the temptations are greater still—to move quickly, with passion and even violence, whether forward or back, toward some clarity or certainty, some secure fortress.

What thereby results, again and again, are sharp divisions and deep polarizations. Yet the passion moving both sides in such polarization is fundamentally the same—the urgent need to move quickly from the many to the one, from a sense of diversity and (at times) of fragmentation to almost any form of clarity and unity. In the face of such temptation, we need an especially strong spirituality and a well-developed sensibility if we are to resist being simply swept up by the passion and polarization—if we are, in other words, to remain in the valley of the human in order to build a truly human city.

Here, in a remarkable passage from "The City of Man," Lynch's introduction to *Images of Hope*, is how he describes our situation:

> As I see it, we are *always* faced with programmatic alternatives: We can decide to build a human city, a city of man, in which all men have citizenship, Greek, Jew, and Gentile, the black and the white, the maimed, the halt, and the blind, the mentally well and the mentally ill. This will always require an act of the imagination which will extend the idea of the human and which will imagine nothing in man it cannot contain. The idea of the human and the idea of the city of man will have to remain eternally open and flexible, ready to adjust itself to the new, to new races, and above all, to new illnesses. *How many men are up to the building of this kind of city remains to be seen . . .* Or we will decide to build various absolute and walled cities, from which various pockets of our humanity will always be excluded. They will pose as ideal cities, and will exclude the imagination, the Negro, the sick, the different. *These totalistic, these non-human cities offer an extraordinary fascination for the souls of fearful men and we are fools if we underestimate how strong and seductive they can be . . .* Whatever form these non-human cities take they will always have to be self-enclosed, will always have their own defenses, and their own weapons. The citizens spend their time reassuring each other and hating everyone else. Actually they will never be safe and the final irony will be that they will have to make war on each other. Only the city of the human will be safe . . . Our subjects indeed are hope and hopelessness; but it will turn out that one of the great hopes of all men is that they shall be human and belong to the city of man—and one of the great sources of

> our hopelessness will come from these rigid and absolutized,
> these non-human constructions that lead to the self-enclosure
> of despair. (IH, 26–7, emphasis added)

If we are to resist the pervasive temptation to retreat, or to leap forward, out of the valley of the human and into various forms of absolute, walled, but non-human cities, we need the developed practice of what Ignatian spirituality calls "the discernment of spirits." We need both the critical ability to discover and understand the many forms of that seductive temptation which call to us from all sides (above all from within), and the equally critical ability to discern or imagine realistic ways into the human city.

For Lynch, of course, Christ is the source of and the model for such discernment. Yet the real Christ offers no magic, no quick, easy, or univocal path. Our God may well be "a mighty fortress," but our God was born in the valley of the human, subject to the finitude, the temptations, and the necessary and difficult discernments of real human life in time. Thus our discernments, too, demand hard work and much suffering as we move through the journey of time and experience. They require sticking, throughout that journey, with the finite and human, with "its many shapes and byways . . . and powers and diversities." They require the back-and-forth action and passion of the human drama, "for we must not go too fast from the many to the one."

Such discernments, then, also need the support and guidance of those whose sense of the human, whose own discernments and sensibility, we can trust. Lynch's writings are one major source of such guidance and discernment. They examine many dimensions of contemporary concern. Yet, each in its own way, they typically follow the broad pattern I have just outlined: calling attention to the character of our times; exploring fundamental habits of mind, imagination, and spirit at work in a given area of contemporary experience; and making critical discernments between those sensibilities which tempt us to leave the human path in flight towards some perhaps easy but often terrible absolutes, and those which enable us to stay in the valley of the human and grow towards fuller forms of living.

This, then, is one way of understanding the foundational spirituality Lynch calls for—as a form of discernment of spirits for a time of epochal change. In subsequent chapters I will be following the pattern of such discernment in different parts of his life and writings. Here, as a third and concluding step in the present chapter, I want simply to indicate a few instances of our present need for that discernment.

Polarizations: Sacral and Secular

It seems evident, even from the daily news, that religion is today one of the spheres of life deeply torn by conflict and polarization. Nor does it just seem that way because the idea of conflict still provides the dominant way in which secular intelligence frames its understanding and frequent rejection of religion. Rather it is increasingly the most religious people whose experience of faith is deeply troubled. For we seem to have entered a period of prolonged tension and "culture warfare" in most religious traditions.

Lynch himself did not write much about contemporary religious or ecclesial conflicts. (It might be true to say that he generally had bigger fish to fry.) Indeed, *Christ and Prometheus* is really the only book where he directly took up the contemporary struggles of what he called "the religious imagination." There he addressed the very fundamental issue of religion's challenging and changing relation to the growing secularity of the global human project and thus the religious imagination's need for a more adequate understanding of and response to such secularity.

Yet one need not go to such fundamental issues to find evidence of a totalizing and polarizing spirit at work in contemporary religious conflict. Let me turn instead to contemporary Catholicism in the U.S. I take up, as but one example, *The Unhealed Wound* by Eugene Kennedy,[44] an essay about "The Church, The Priesthood, and the Question of Sexuality" (the book's subtitle). It is one of many books about the sexual and gender issues troubling the Catholic world. Its paperback edition has a lengthy "Introduction" relating its argument to what many have called the greatest crisis in the history of the Catholic Church in the U.S. That is, of course, the continuing crisis caused by revelations about the Catholic hierarchy's secretive and terribly inadequate way of dealing with sexually abusive priests.

The book has important things to say about the history and present state of Catholicism's often very inadequate dealings with human sexuality. Yet it presents its insights within a fundamental and continually reiterated framework of simplistic, dichotomous oppositions. The book's most typical formulation of that framework is its depiction of the opposition between a rigid, but now dying hierarchical system (itself founded on a disastrous dualism of spirit and flesh) and an emerging, more wholesome form of faith which will heal the wounds inflicted by that system. As I read, I gradually realize that I am back in the same world depicted in psychologist Kennedy's earlier book, *Tomorrow's Catholics/Yesterday's Church*.[45] There the pervasive

44. Kennedy, *Unhealed.*

45. Kennedy, *Tomorrow's Catholics.*

"good guys vs. bad guys" framework was signaled immediately in the book's title. There, too, important insights and arguments quickly became little more than fodder for a fundamentally simplistic polarization.

One could, of course, excuse such dichotomized thinking as the product of one writer's angry sensibility. Or perhaps as an increasingly necessary framework for popular religious journalism. Indeed in the currently divided state of Catholicism in this country there has been a parade of such "good guys vs. bad guys" books—as much from the "right" as from the "left," and on issues as disparate as women's ordination, Pius XII's role during the Holocaust, or the significance of Vatican II.

Yet this dichotomizing pattern of thought can also be found in more serious writing. In scripture scholarship, for instance, the still very present opposition between "the Christ of Faith" and "the Jesus of history" has often been accompanied by an equally simplistic ecclesial dichotomy between (in one formulation) an oppressive "Kyriarchy" and a more original "discipleship of equals." Even Pope John Paul II in his many discussions of the contemporary world seemed especially fond of framing his thinking in terms of a fundamental polarization between "a culture of death" and "a civilization of love."

This dichotomizing habit of mind is, of course, not new. It has a long and at times honorable place in Christian tradition.[46] Nor is it limited to Christianity. At one point in *Images of Hope* (231–32) Lynch presents several lengthy lists of such fundamental oppositions—between, for instance, light and dark, love and death, yin and yang, one and many—oppositions which have informed and framed the thinking of a great number of religious and philosophical systems. Yet Lynch's point in alluding to the prevalence of such oppositions is to make his own discernment between those traditions of thought which embrace the continual challenge of integrating such contraries, and those which structure the universe and human life in terms of their implacable opposition. "Since the beginning of time," he says, "the human mind and feelings have been dealing with pairs of opposites and the possible conflict between them. In some cases it means that men are trying to put difficult things together; in other cases we sense that battle lines are being drawn" (IH, 231).[47]

---

46. Two of the five traditional ways of relating "Christ and culture" analyzed by H. Richard Niebuhr, in his classic book by that name, develop from a fundamental sense of tension and opposition: "Christ against Culture" and "Christ and Culture in Paradox."

47. As we will see below in Chapter 3, *The Integrating Mind* is an analysis of the latter pattern ("battle lines being drawn") in contemporary culture, and, as the book's title suggests, a call for the former pattern ("to put difficult things together").

In many of the recent Catholic debates to which I have been referring we can too easily sense "that battle lines are being drawn." Of course
there are many important conflicts in contemporary Catholicism, important "battles" which must be fought. The history of Christianity has always
developed, at least in part, through such struggles. Yet in too many recent
conflicts, whatever the level of popularity or sophistication, the reigning
animus or spirit is absolutized or totalizing, and the result is increasingly
bitter polarization. The prevalent sensibility is not that which struggles to
hold or bring difficult things together, but of battle lines drawn, walled cities
being built, and demand for unconditional surrender.

Of course such a totalizing sensibility is hardly limited to contemporary
religious conflict, though it is certainly found there in tragic abundance.[48]
Rather it would be far more accurate to suggest that the polarizing pattern
in religious conflict is but an echo of the even more pervasive presence of
that pattern in the larger worlds of culture and politics. I have said that virtually all of Lynch's writings worked to discern various forms of such thinking
and feeling in different aspects of society and culture in the U.S. He would
today, unfortunately, have little difficulty finding even greater evidence of an
absolutizing spirit at work in this country: in deep fears and enmities about
abortion and homosexuality and, more broadly, around issues of sexuality
and gender; in our still angry and fear-filled rhetoric about racism and in
rising tensions around immigration; in our economic wars as much as our
culture wars, our wars on drugs and our larger war on crime; in the polarizations which have increasingly paralyzed domestic politics, and in the way
our "war on terrorism" has pervaded and distorted international relations.

It is clear, to take up that last example, that there must be a response to
terrorism, just as we must continue to struggle with those other very difficult
problems about race and ethnicity, sexuality and gender, economic development and economic justice. It is also probably true that terrorism itself is, at
least in part and perhaps in large part, an expression of the kind of absolutized fears and hatreds that Lynch was so concerned to counter. Yet much
of the imagery and rhetoric that has accompanied the struggle against such
terrorism also gives expression to equally absolutized ideas and passions.

I note here but one of many examples, simply because of its startling
clarity. In articulating his response to terrorism, President George W. Bush
famously called for war against "an axis of evil" and then, at the national
memorial service for the victims of "9/11," proclaimed "our responsibility
to history" to "rid the world of evil." In response, sociologist Robert Bellah

48. See, for instance, the apt title of Jules Keppel's study of fundamentalism, *The
Revenge of God.*

observed: "It is hard to exaggerate the breathtaking quality of that assertion. What even God has not done America will do."[49] Yet such rhetoric is only one very clear example of the flood of simplistic and totalized "good vs. evil" imagery that has filled TV screens and newspapers during subsequent episodes of our continuing "war on terrorism."

It may well be true that such rhetoric will be found during any war, anywhere. Indeed one of the more terrible costs of resort to war may be an almost inescapable narrowing and absolutizing of feelings and imagination on the part of many, if not most of those involved. War itself, in other words, may be a primary instance of, and thus an appropriate metaphor for, all those forms of totalizing passion which draw fixed battle lines and seek unconditional surrender. Yet the roots and forms of such passions in this country, whether in time of actual warfare or in any of our political and cultural "wars," are at least in part quite particular.

In further commentary on such rhetoric, Bellah, the foremost (though recently deceased) analyst of the role of religion in the U.S., spoke of how our dominant religious tradition, what he called "dissenting Protestantism," has influenced not just the rhetoric, but the public policy and practice of this country.[50] Established churches, he argued, must include everyone, sinners as well as saints. But dissenting church traditions are "exclusive, not inclusive; they are churches of the saved." Thus they continually promote "a tendency towards moral splitting . . . thinking of the world as divided between the saved and the damned, the good and the evil . . ." Such "moral splitting," Bellah admits, is "a general human propensity" and "dissenting Protestantism [is] only one source of it." Yet in this country that dominant religious tradition has been a primary source of this tendency which is "now secularized and pervasive in our popular culture." It is, for instance, manifest in our "infatuation with superheroes . . . whose sole purpose is to rid the world of evil . . . [and who] are usually fighting against an evil genius bent on world power . . ."

Lynch also saw such "moral splitting" as "a general human propensity" and he, too, sought to criticize its operation in the life of this nation. And for him this analytic and critical task always served a yet more important constructive task—evoking and calling us to an alternative form of spirituality and sensibility.

In this call he has recently been seconded by a now more famous Jesuit. For Pope Francis, during his 2015 visit to the U.S., stressed that "there is another temptation which we must especially guard against: the simplistic

49. Bellah, "Can We."

50. Ibid. Subsequent citations in this paragraph are from this online source.

reductionism which sees only good or evil; or, if you will, the righteous and sinners." He then noted that "The contemporary world, with its open wounds which affect so many of our brothers and sisters, demands that we confront every form of polarization which would divide it into these two camps." Thus he urged this country to "move forward together, as one, in a renewed spirit of fraternity and solidarity, cooperating generously for the common good."[51]

Like Pope Francis, Lynch's sense of that "renewed spirit" grew from his experience, perhaps especially from his life as a Jesuit. So we now turn, as a next step in exploring the spirituality and sensibility he called for, to a brief telling of the story of Lynch's life.

51. Pope Francis, "Speech."

2

A Life in Time

When he gave a public lecture, Bill Lynch often began with a concrete image to suggest his central theme and help the listener follow its development. As noted in the "Preface" above, the practice helped me the one time I heard him lecture. I still remember that ordinary bar of soap fantasized into the beatific vision, and it still helps me keep together the central affirmations and critiques of Lynch's thought: the concrete goodness and complexity of movement through ordinary life, yet the constant temptation to many forms of absolutizing escape from such complexity.

So I will follow his practice here, in beginning this chapter about his life. My goal is not biography. Rather I simply hope that a sketch of the story of his life, with several interludes to provide details about major sources of his thinking, will provide the next step in understanding the kind of spirituality and sensibility to which he called us. For his sense of that spirituality clearly grew from the movement of his own life through time.

I take my opening image, then, from Lynch's short essay "Me and the East River." It is one of only a few autobiographical writings, published late in his life for the inaugural edition of *New York Images*.[1] Lynch loved cities, especially port cities on rivers that opened to the sea and the world beyond. Such love grew, he tells us, from the accident of birth in New York and a childhood lived several hundred yards from the East River. So the river became for him a symbol of the movement of life into an ever-wider world, and it may stand here as an image for this telling of the story of his life.

The essay begins with childhood memories, one a tragic-heroic tale of admiration for a man who tried to save one of Lynch's friends who had slipped as they played on an old pier. Despite the man's best efforts, Georgie

---

1. Lynch, "Me." Its contents suggest that the essay may have been conceived as part of his *A Book of Admiration* project, though it is not part of the archival manuscript of that project.

Webster drowned, and both the tragedy and the heroism stamped themselves on Lynch's soul. We all have such stories, he then says, perhaps less tragic and heroic. Yet "small though they seem they are the stories of our salvation and worth the telling to our children and the children's children."[2]

So he tells a few of his stories and they flow gradually into mention of other rivers—"the Mississippi and its breeding of young Tom Sawyer and Huckleberry Finn; the Liffey, which created Irish Ale . . . , the Ganges that grew from mud to sacredness . . . , the Po, which after the East River I would have chosen [as symbol] for my life and its endless muddy fleshed-out dreams . . ."[3] These rivers lead to broader reflection:

> But let me go back again to the river. For I have a clue for understanding why I am so much in love with it. It has something to do with its being a symbol, like admiration itself, a symbol of *a passage of human beings into a wider and wider world*, into the making of a port and then an ocean. But you get there *only through the rough, dirty human way of this river.* You go forward, on the way no doubt to glory be, you pause, the pause becomes a retreat or withdrawal. You fall back. Yes, *always two steps forward and one back.* The step back is back into the river, back into the dirt in it, back to yourself out of glory-be, back to your limits, to regain rest and strength for another dash into the bay, the port, the ocean.[4]

The river's push to the sea images his own passions and dreams of "glory-be"; its muddy messiness the actual passage to such hopes and so their realization as "muddy fleshed-out dreams." "These rivers," he says, "will give check to the perfect dreams of any of us humans. But will help us to dream humanly."[5] Thus the essay ends evoking the everyday world:

> What does this dirty river give? It gives us a world. Twice a day, a world of sticks, stones, bubbling mud, a trip to the sea, a trip to the city, treasure of all kinds, chemicals to be washed out with much work, old thrown-out clothes, Coca-Cola bottles, imperfect messages of lovers, Georgie Websters, worn-out food, twice a day strength from the sea, strong and steady as the tug boats. *We need such a world. Of all the things we need, we need a world.*[6]

2. Lynch, "Me," 3.

3. Ibid., 4–5.

4. Ibid., 4, emphasis added.

5. Ibid., 5.

6. Ibid., emphasis added. "Twice a day" refers, of course, to the twice daily change

So I borrow a mature reminiscence as an opening image for telling something of Lynch's life, with its "two steps forward and one back" on the way to "muddy" but realized or "fleshed-out" dreams.[7] I thereby re-emphasize his fundamental sense of sticking with the finite and not moving too quickly, but moving with human and earth-bound rhythms. It is a sensibility he had learned from many sources, not least the pattern of his own life.

East Side, West Side . . .

William F. Lynch was born in New York City on June 16, 1908, to Michael J. and Mary Maloney Lynch.[8] He was, he later remarked, "probably the only human being who was born, graduated from high school, graduated from college and ordained [a priest] on Bloomsday" (BA 107)—the Dublin day celebrated with such detailed earthiness and humanity in James Joyce's *Ulysses*.

Lynch especially loved New York, the city where he spent most of his life. But that first love grew to include others. He lived for a time in Washington, D.C., and the lecture circuit took him to many other cities. He also regularly did research in the libraries and museums of European cities like London and Florence and Athens.[9]

The clearest expression of this love for cities is found in the manuscript for *A Book of Admiration*.[10] There he speaks of the way admiration leads us away from fantasy and out of ourselves into the rich, at times ugly, but always real complexity of the world. He emphasizes his admiration for port

---

of tides and thus to the objects left by low tides on mud flat shores where Lynch undoubtedly played as a boy.

7. Initially I had thought to take my opening image from one of Lynch's earliest essays, "The Meaning of Mud." Its point is fundamentally the same as the late East River essay, so much so that I marvel at both the consistency of his thought and how early he came to his basic insights. I admire, as well, his youthful wit in writing about the *meaning* of mud and doing so for a journal named *Spirit*.

8. Details about Lynch's childhood, education, and years in Jesuit training are taken from 1) Gerald Bednar's *Faith*, 2) a 1978 Georgetown undergraduate thesis by Thomas Fleming who interviewed Lynch in 1977 and 1978, and 3) other Fordham archival material, especially the manuscript for *A Book of Admiration*, Lynch's most autobiographical writing.

9. In a handwritten note (which, from its reference to the forthcoming third issue of *New York Images*, was probably written the spring or summer before he died), he speaks of planning for "the usual part of the next three years whether in Florence or London . . . where the British Museum Library [has] become a fruitful center of work for me for many years." Fordham University Archives.

10. See BA especially pages 27–29, 46–48, 80–81, 88–89.

cities, not only New York and London and Athens, but also San Francisco ("the most beautiful city in the United States"), Genoa ("gem of the Mediterranean . . . dirty and mad enough to prevent that exhaustion which comes from living with the ideal") and Malaga (which "really opens into the world"). These cities were not just symbols for Lynch. For they actually led his life into broader and deeper, but always human worlds, and not a few times saved him from being trapped within himself:

> I have to live in a port because, for good or bad, it is open to the world and I have a passion for being in or next to an opening into the whole earth. A real port opens into the whole world, where it is impossible to escape admiring, or if I am caught in one of those mental prisons, if the poison and flatness makes half entrance, then I am already half way out. (BA 27–28)

His Irish immigrant family (three brothers and a sister) lived, as noted, on Manhattan's east side. "I got myself deliberately born," he once noted rather whimsically, "on the east side of New York and spent the first twenty years of my life in somewhat questionable surroundings" (IM, 134). He attended the neighborhood Catholic school, Our Lady of Good Counsel, and then the Jesuits' all-scholarship Regis High School.

In 1926, with help from a scholarship and money his family had saved from a legal settlement (as a child he'd been hit by a beer truck while crossing Second Avenue[11]), he went to Fordham, the Jesuits' New York City university located in the Bronx. He was the first in his family and in his entire neighborhood to attend college and he graduated in 1930 with a BA in Classics.[12] Then he worked as a reporter for *The New York Herald Tribune*, a job that may have developed from sports writing he'd done at Fordham. (One obituary mentioned his life-long interest in baseball and "his beloved Yankees."[13]) He returned to Fordham in 1931 as an instructor in Greek and English, a job he continued (even as he seems to have continued newspaper work[14]) until 1934 when, at age twenty-six, he entered the Jesuits.

By that time his life had embraced not only Manhattan's east side, but the Bronx and beyond. It already involved the early stages of a relationship between the academic and the urban, between thought and the bustling life of the city, which was to be so central to his later writing.

11. Lynch, "Me," 3.

12. Ibid.

13. "Friends."

14. "William F. Lynch." This obituary reported that he worked "for *The New York Herald Tribune* from 1930 until 1934."

Such, as he saw it, is the gift of real cities. For if "we are always faced with programmatic alternatives" between flight into various walled cities and entrance into the human city,[15] then actual cities, like rivers, call us out of our walled enclaves and continually challenge us to enlarge our sense of the human.

> [I]t is we ourselves who . . . severely delimit our image of the human and refuse admission to the look of the homeless, to the addict, to the vibrations of fear set up in us by the mentally ill, to our prisoners, or the birth of a blind foetus [sic], or the enemy, or the very poor . . . It is we, ourselves, for our own narrow purposes, who delimit the glorious and open image of the human into a narrow ideology or some fatuous terms of sweet and perfect normality. It is precisely this that our great city refused to do. Although it is often ugly on the outside, even the most superficial first look at the city will tell us that it has an endless number of stories of the human image to unfold.[16]

Jesuit Training: University and World

Lynch began his years of training as a Jesuit in rural Wernersville, Pennsylvania. He completed that training with theological studies at Weston College, then located in the country outside of Boston. He was, as noted, ordained a priest on "Bloomsday," June 16, in 1945.

Yet while the years at Wernersville may have been his first extended taste of rural life, they were not an idyllic retreat from the world. Whatever his appreciation for country life or for friends like poet and literary critic Allen Tate who was deeply committed to the agrarian ideal,[17] Lynch's own sensibility was not much changed by rural experience. He certainly never indulged in nostalgia for some romantic arcadia. In fact, perhaps because of his deep immersion in the religious and cultural traditions of the West, he was among the least nostalgic of men.

Even in the fairly cloistered atmosphere at Wernersville,[18] Lynch followed his own path deeper into the world. He was a good eight years older

15. IH, 26–27. See p. 17 above.

16. Lynch, "Introduction," 3.

17. See Huff, *Allen Tate,* for a discussion of Tate's agrarianism ("The Cause of the Land," 50–71) and evidence that Lynch was among Tate's "regular correspondents and confidants" (83).

18. For an evocative description of the cloistered character of Jesuit training in the U.S. before Vatican II see Peters, *Ours.*

than other novices who had mostly just graduated from high school, and he already had his BA in Classics. Thus he did not follow the normal course of studies. As he tells the story, "I was coming out of the chapel minding my own business . . . when the dean suddenly came up to me, told me it was too late for me to get an education, that I should drop all classes, go to my room, and read Plato instead."[19] In a different telling, Lynch adds: "I read Plato and it was my first example of doing something very well and staying with it. It was like going over the sound barrier in a plane. I was a different person after that. I began to know what I could do."[20]

And do he did.

In 1939, a year after returning to Fordham from Wernersville, he completed an MA in philosophy with a thesis on Plato's psychology directed by the then well-known Aquinas scholar Anton Pegis. He received his PhD in classics in 1943 with a thesis on *The Central Problem in Aeschylus' "Eumenides"*.[21] During these years (between 1938 and 1943) he published nine essays, mostly on drama and the arts. He also taught undergraduates and directed university productions of classic drama—of *Oedipus* for Fordham's centenary celebration in 1941 and of the *Eumenides* the following year. No ordinary "campus theater," these were Greek-language productions with newly composed choral scores and choreography. The performers were all students, but Lynch enlisted the assistance of major New York theatrical talents: "Virgil Thomson, the brilliant modern composer . . . Erick Hawkins, one of America's greatest dancers . . . Martha Graham, one of America's greatest creative geniuses . . . and Lincoln Kirstein, director of the American Ballet" (and later founder of the New York City Ballet and Lynch's life-long friend).[22]

Thus Lynch's early years of Jesuit training were not a period of religious or academic seclusion. Rather they saw his growing involvement in scholarship, teaching, and the arts. The latter, especially, brought him back to engagement with the life of the city. In addition, he had the opportunity for a year of study at Princeton before going to the Jesuit seminary in Weston,

19. "Death," 462.

20. Fleming, "Metaphysics," 2–3. I will discuss Plato's significance for Lynch's thought below (see pp. 78–89).

21. As we shall see, Aeschylus and Greek drama were major influences on Lynch's thought . Yet no copy of the dissertation has been found. I suspect its ideas are given some expression in Lynch's extended discussion of the *Oresteia* in CP, 3–6, 77–80, 83–87, 89–94 and in published essays from his *Drama of the Mind* project (see below p. 90 n. 1) such as "Foundation Stones."

22. "Bringing," 45–46. This short article is Lynch's account of the productions. He notes that "many eminent scholars and theatrical people have been kind enough to consider [them] an event of some national importance" (45).

Massachusetts. It brought him for the first time into directly personal contact with the wider intellectual life of this country.[23] Lynch tells us it was
in a seminar on Platonism led by Whitney Oates, Chairman of Princeton's
Department of Classics, that he began the years of study that would lead
to the publication (in 1959) of his *An Approach to the Metaphysics of Plato
through the Parmenides*.[24] It was also the beginning of an ongoing relationship with Princeton and with the secular and Protestant academic worlds
he met there.

Through the Actual Life of Christ

Yet if Lynch's years of training were perhaps more "worldly" than that of
other young men with whom he entered the Jesuits, the most fundamental
influence on his life during those years was nonetheless the spirit and traditions of the Society of Jesus. Though it would probably be even more accurate to say that the most fundamental influence on his life—both before as
well as during and after his years of religious formation—was a deep faith in
Christ, in "the actual life of Christ," which was then given particular shape
and focus by Ignatian spirituality.

Clearly what had led Lynch to the Jesuits was a faith and admiration
nurtured by his family and his early schooling. His understanding of Christ
undoubtedly grew from early experiences—perhaps from the Rosary, with
its rhythmic, stage by stage repetition of major events in the life of Christ,
or from the Gospel narrative repeated over the years at Sunday Mass, and
from the rhythms of the liturgy as it moved through the seasons of the year
and the unfolding drama of Christ's life. At one point in *Christ and Apollo*,
for instance, Lynch challenges the view (think of Marx or Freud) that Christianity is a form of flight from time and that secular people are the real
champions of life in this world. His response is worth citing at length:

> I think that Catholic doctrine is the very reverse of this magi-
> cal idea [of flight from time]; rather it is a divine command of
> the mind and the will to enter . . . into an historical, actual and
> *eventful* set of facts which penetrate reality to the hilt. And for
> this kind of summary there are two major pieces of evidence . . .
> The first is the liturgy of the Church which in its changing year

23. The exact date of Lynch's year at Princeton is uncertain, though it clearly came
after some time at Fordham and before seminary studies at Weston. See Fleming,
"Metaphysics," 3, as well as Lynch, "Death," 462.

24. See the book's "Preface," ix. Professor Oates wrote a laudatory "Evaluation"
printed on the back jacket cover when the book first appeared.

reviews the events in the life of Christ. The second which comes to mind is the Apostles Creed itself... It is a sort of summary of the *actions* of God... The Creed begins with God and ends with eternal life for men, but in between is time, that time through which Christ passes and that time through which doctrine implicitly commands us to pass. (CA, 58–59)

Yet while Lynch's fundamental sense of faith's call to life in the world and in time undoubtedly derived from early experiences, his ability to articulate it came later. Then, not surprisingly, he gives greatest credit to St. Ignatius.[25] For Ignatian spirituality is grounded in the conviction that God is not only present, but active throughout the world. For the world is, in Jesuit poet Gerard Manley Hopkins' dramatic phrase, "charged with the grandeur of God."[26] The consequent Jesuit ideal of "finding God in all things" has led Jesuits and their associates not only to the four corners of the globe, but into all the arts and sciences of the secular and practical world as well.[27] Their spirituality grew in part from the Renaissance recovery of classical humanism, but it was nourished far more fundamentally by the focus of Ignatius' *Spiritual Exercises* on "the actual life of Christ." For the *Exercises* lead one in simultaneous meditation *through* both the events and stages of the life of Christ and the actualities and moments of one's own life. One is led to become contemporary with the Christ of the Gospels, in the detail and movements of His life, so that the detail and movements of one's own life might be open to the presence and action of Christ. "For," to again cite Hopkins, "Christ plays in ten thousand places, / Lovely in limbs, and lovely in eyes not his / To the Father through the features of men's faces."[28]

25. In his "Introduction" to CA (xiv) Lynch speaks of St. Ignatius as "one of my own abiding 'friends' and givers." He also lists Plato and Cardinal Newman.

26. Hopkins, "God's Grandeur," *Poems*, 27.

27. A fine, brief description of Jesuit spirituality and its sources is given by Ronald Modras in "Spirituality." He stresses that its sources "allowed Jesuit spirituality to become at once worldly and humanistic, seeing God as deeply immersed in all creation and in all human endeavor" (16). It put Jesuits from the beginning "at the intersection of secular culture with faith ... It put them at a boundary that allowed them to speak in a worldly way about piety and piously about the world" (32). It also led, he notes, to intriguing facts like the following: some thirty Jesuit scientists and mathematicians have the distinction of having craters of the moon named after them; Jesuits did the foundational work for the grammars and dictionaries of ninety-five languages, including Sanskrit and Chinese; and (of note because of Lynch's interest in theater and dance) a Jesuit wrote the first serious treatise on ballet. See also Modras' subsequent book *Ignatian Humanism*.

28. Hopkins, "As kingfishers catch fire," *Poems*, 51.

Ignatius and "The New Theological Age"

Lynch's own grounding in Ignatian spirituality was most fully expressed in an essay on "St. Ignatius and 'The New Theological Age'" which he contributed to a special issue of *Thought* on the occasion of the 400th anniversary of Ignatius' death.[29] The essay not only provides an analysis of some of the fundamental spiritual tendencies in what Lynch calls our "new theological age," but is also one of the most explicit early expressions of his call for an alternative spirituality. It thus gives a very good sense of how for Lynch Ignatian spirituality contributed to the development of that alternative.

Lynch began the essay with an evocation of elements of our era which he saw as characteristic, not so much of the churches, but of the wider culture. Though penned in the mid-1950s, this discussion of "the signs of the times" remains remarkably relevant today. Both religious and secular critics, he notes, have been saying that the "purely technological, superficial and secular" aspects of national life have created a world that "satisfies and attracts only the surface of the soul of man." This has, indeed, at times forced "the masses of men . . . into a surface and automatic life."[30] Yet Lynch rejected the elitist contempt often found in critiques of "our contemporary wasteland." Rather he argued that a deeper sympathy would reveal, beneath the surface features of our times, a pervasive spiritual hunger shared both by the masses and by intellectual and cultural elites. It is a twofold hunger: both to discover a more authentic sense of self and to discover or rediscover a deeper and more real sense of the divine.

Yet serious attention also reveals, Lynch argued, a fundamental flaw in these spiritual searchings characteristic of our times. While the human search for both self and God is perennial, what is most characteristic of our times is the tragic separation and even opposition of these searches.

The search for a more authentic self, despite its often bewildering and even destructive forms, is evidence of the re-emergence of the soul which, "refusing to be ignored for long, has reappeared upon the scene and begun to invade the consciousness."[31] Yet this re-emergence is typically filled with great pain and anxiety.

> [G]ranted that the life of pure surfaces has been broken down
> and granted that men have begun to realize that there are depths

---

29. Lynch, "St. Ignatius." The pages of this essay dealing with the *Spiritual Exercises* (207–15) were reprinted, with few changes, several years later in CA, 53–61. Lynch also published two shorter comments on the *Exercises*: see IM, 81–83 and "*Spiritual*."

30. Ibid., 187–88, 194.

31. Ibid., 195.

in them infinitely greater than it has been hitherto comfortable to admit, the first greeting these depths have received has been that of pain and bewilderment . . . That is because the attempt to live comfortably on the surface of the soul has failed us and we have not yet found instruments by whose help we might penetrate its depths.[32]

Rather the "instruments" we have tried—our many spiritualities and therapies, our ecstasies and fantasies—have often left us still too much on the surface, but now even more deeply frustrated and anxious.

One common result of the pain of such searching for the self is a rebound into the search for God. Yet this second dimension of contemporary spiritual awakening is then deeply flawed from the start. For it is "too influenced by recurrent sweeps of painful history in the external world or in the self . . ." So it focuses on "*an altogether other world*, one that will bear no relationship to this one or to the reality of the new self as it has been thus far discovered."[33] It seeks a God who, "in whatever form, is a reality completely external to man, who must be leaped to, by unfounded faith, by sudden, unrooted ecstasy, or even by hysterics . . ." However deep and real the need it expresses, it is nonetheless "a kind of theology, a kind of faith, a kind of leaping, which leaves the human situation untouched and in terms of which God is only being used as an escape."[34]

Lynch points to the plays of Eugene O'Neill as examples of both aspects of this contemporary spiritual search *and* of their separation. He chooses O'Neill, "not because he is among our very best and most perspicacious writers, but because he . . . has hit off, in his rough way, so many of the fundamental, popular feelings of our day."[35] Dark plays like *The Hairy Ape*, *The Emperor Jones*, and especially *Mourning Becomes Electra* give popular dramatic expression to the pain and suffering of the search for self which comes up empty. Yet O'Neill's "theological plays," like *Days Without End* and especially *Lazarus Laughed*, are, Lynch argues, "nothing but sheer leaping" out of reality. Thus O'Neill remains (and leaves his audience) either "overwhelmed by his first taste of the pain that lurks under the skin or . . . engaged in blowing bubbles in an idle dream world."[36]

32. Ibid.

33. Ibid., 198, 197.

34. Ibid., 202.

35. Ibid., 195. Lynch reprinted this discussion of O'Neill, virtually unchanged, in his chapter on "Tragedy" in CA, 81–88.

36. Ibid., 206.

Were he writing today Lynch would have little difficulty finding similar examples of this essentially gnostic sensibility in our arts and fictions, as well as in many of our spiritualities and theologies—examples of the same fear and loathing of our times, the same recoil in desperate search for the inner spark of the soul, the same rebound into leaping towards some totally transcendent God. Nor would he have to limit his search to the cinema and music of popular culture. He could as readily find examples among artists and intellectuals of high seriousness.[37] Yet his fundamental purpose would remain the same—*not* contemptuous dismissal of such contemporary Gnosticism, but sympathetic attention to the seriousness it expresses.[38] Thus he would today issue the same "double plea":

> On the one hand it is *a plea to thoughtful Christian men and women,* and especially to the theologians and writers among them, to theologize . . . in such a way that they are aware of the tremendous new spiritual forces that are now at large among us. But it is also *a plea to the modern non-Christian thinker and writer* to note the awful inadequacy, despite its power and beauty, of the point at which we have actually arrived and the final primitiveness of these separatist movements [seeking self *or* God] which now begin to overwhelm them.[39]

Lynch issues this plea to both Christian and non-Christian in the hope that they might join in the much-needed elaboration of spiritualities and sensibilities more adequate to the needs of our times. To that end he offers "a relatively brief look at the theology of St. Ignatius in the Spiritual Exercises . . . to consider whether it might not have some shocking relevancy" for our common problem.[40]

He presents Ignatius' thought in terms of two related ideas. The first is the central idea, noted above, of "finding God in the world." Lynch's way of putting this, and his reason for believing that Ignatius' ideas are particularly relevant to the painful disjunction of our contemporary spiritual hungers, is to stress "the Ignatian plea that we direct our search for God *through* time,

---

37. See Chapter 4 below for the detail of Lynch's critique of both popular and serious drama.

38. "I must repeat," he says, at the end of his discussion of O'Neill's plays, "that, despite this very critical analysis, we must have nothing but the highest respect and sympathy for this theological impulse of the dramatist, as we must have a similar awareness of and sympathy for the crude theological impulse which begins to seize on the people of these days." "St. Ignatius," 204.

39. Ibid., 206 (emphasis added).

40. Ibid., 206–7.

reality and the self."[41] For it is not by any impossible "leaping," but by "penetration" of the finite and the actual that we come both to a deeper sense
of self and finally to God. Ignatius is, Lynch says, "incredibly, remarkably
definite in his demands on the soul that the latter be altogether concrete in
its considerations . . ."[42] He demands: 1) that the person making his *Spiritual
Exercises* focus on *specific events* in the life of Christ; 2) that by the imaginative technique known as the "composition of place" she "enter as fully
as possible into the entire concreteness of each of these moments"; and 3)
that, by an "application of the senses," she not only "see with the eyes of the
imagination," but "hear" what is being said and "smell and taste" and "feel
with the touch."[43]

Thus the basic pattern of Ignatian prayer is not one of mystical withdrawal from the world, not a brief evocation of the life of Christ as mere
occasion for a leap to eternal verities. There is, Lynch emphasizes, "not a
single 'leap' in the whole book."[44] Rather Ignatius leads the believer to God
through the fullest imaginative immersion in the details of particular scenes
from the Gospels and corresponding reflection on the concrete realities of
her own life.

Complementing this fundamental element of "Ignatius' method"
Lynch notes a second which he calls Ignatius' "devotion to the time scheme
and his great patience in marching through it, part by part."[45] For Ignatius
leads the believer "*proportionally* through the life of Christ," "step by step,
forbidding him again and again to take the way of magic impatience . . . and
commanding him to stay within the pure time process as such."[46]

Of course this emphasis on time is another way of speaking about
finitude. Lynch had introduced his discussion of Ignatius by stressing "the
Ignatian plea that we direct our search for God through time, reality and
the self," just as I introduced this book about Lynch by stressing his call
"for the concrete movement of faith and imagination through experience,
through time, through the definite, through the human, through the actual
life of Christ."[47] Thus it may already be clear that time, with its limitations
and its dramatic rhythms, its "two steps forward and one back," is for Lynch
the most fundamental aspect of finitude that we are called to stay with and

41. Ibid., 214.
42. Ibid., 208.
43. Ibid., 211, 213–14.
44. Ibid., 213.
45. Ibid., 210.
46. Ibid., 208.
47. See p. 1 above.

move through. Indeed, all of his writings can well be understood as a sustained meditation on time, just as the spirituality he called for is a continual training in the necessity of movement through the forms and complexities of time.[48]

Ignatius was for Lynch one of the primary sources for this sense of the fundamental importance of time—of not moving too quickly from the many to the one. Over the course of the classic thirty-day retreat of the *Spiritual Exercises* (which Lynch would have made at least twice, at key moments in his Jesuit training) one does not simply immerse oneself in the concreteness of specific *events* in the life of Christ, but moves gradually, step by step, *through the life of Christ*—through the narrative of the Gospels, from birth to death. In the words of Lynch's own summary, Ignatius guides the retreatant "through the *mysteries of the life of Christ* as the latter advances *through the full human scheme*. For him, then, there is no separation between our advance through Christ and our advance through man and time, even unto death . . ."[49]

"Man," Lynch says elsewhere, "is a temporal, historical being who is to be understood and defined in relation to the internal time scheme he occupies, from birth to death" (IF 109). This does not mean that we are somehow trapped in time, either left with "no exit" or rescued only by the descent of the divine and subsequent ascent to glory. Rather, God has created the inescapable necessity of time as a great human good. God, Lynch says quite dramatically at one point, "will not be beaten at His own game, and His game is time" (CA 176).[50] Nor did God simply create time, for in Christ God has fully entered and embraced the movement of human time. As Lynch says, even more dramatically, "it is the time of man which He re-explored . . . [T]he new Adam takes as his instrument . . . the whole temporal process . . . [He is] an athlete . . . running with joy . . . through the whole length and breadth of the human adventure" (CA, 176).

---

48. Lynch's most detailed and explicit discussions of time are in CA, 31–64 and IF, 109–75.

49. "St. Ignatius," 210 (second emphasis added). "Perhaps," Lynch then adds, this is "enough evidence for us to call [Ignatius] the full secularist and the full theologian in the one breath . . . " (214). See below (pp. 223–25) for a subsequent presentation of Lynch's understanding of Ignatius' *Spiritual Exercises*.

50. Elsewhere Lynch says, "Let us imagine that twice God put on our mind with which to think. The first time He did it He made the world. He made it according to all the things that have parallelism and resonance with the body and spirit of man . . ." Thus God created "The most important kind of time for man," the time that "exists within himself, existing in the form of the stages of his own life . . . " (CP, 71). The second time "God put on our mind" is, of course, in the actual life of Christ.

Lynch's understanding of Ignatian spirituality, then, was the foundation for a spirituality of concrete movement "through experience, through time, through the definite, through the human." Said a bit differently, the most fundamental element of Lynch's spirituality for engagement in the world is a sensibility which embraces the temporality of human life and empowers us to move fruitfully, without transcending leaps or hopeless retreats, through the stages and limitations, the action and suffering, the "two steps forward and one back" of life in time. This spirituality and sensibility Lynch himself had learned, under Ignatius' guidance, from his own prayerful and imaginative movement "through the actual life of Christ."

Enter into the City

After his ordination to the priesthood in 1945, Lynch was assigned for a time to a Jesuit retreat house in New York City (on Staten Island) and then in 1948 was named editor of *The Messenger of the Sacred Heart*, a popularly oriented Catholic monthly. He remained editor of *The Messenger* for slightly more than a year until it ceased publication. He had no great practical success in this first stint as an editor, yet he'd be a writer and an editor till his last days. The brief period at *The Messenger* no doubt prepared him for his next and far more important assignment as editor of *Thought*, Fordham's prestigious scholarly quarterly.

Before taking the helm at *Thought* in 1950, Lynch had another opportunity for study at Princeton. We know little of his specific activities during that period. Yet it is clear that his focus was contemporary literature and those concerns about the literary imagination which came to expression in most of the writing he did during his years at *Thought*, writing which culminated in the publication of *Christ and Apollo*.[51]

Lynch began his tenure at *Thought* with a, for that publication, rare editorial statement entitled "*Ingredere in Civitatem*."[52] That title ("Enter Into the City"), he tells us at the editorial's end, "was the great word of Cardinal Suhard." It was also, he says, the idea governing the work of his predecessor, Father Gerald Groveland Walsh, SJ.

---

51. One of Lynch's early essays for *Thought*, "Adventure in Order," probably gives an indication of his studies at Princeton. He credits the phrase used for his title to Princeton professor R. P. Blackmur and at one point refers to the "brilliant seminar on the novel at Princeton" conducted by Professor Mark Schorer (43). William Birmingham, who knew Lynch at Fordham shortly thereafter, indicated (in personal correspondence) that Blackmur had indeed played a major role in Lynch's time at Princeton.

52. Lynch, "*Ingredere*."

> The fundamental drive in [Fr. Walsh's] editorship and in his own
> personal work was to help to rediscover and rebuild the order of
> the secular and the natural within Christianity . . . [E]verything
> depends upon it. To go into a Christian corner or a catacombs
> in our crisis is absurd. To try to save merely the last scraps of
> Christianity is to make certain that we lose all . . . Nothing less
> than the reformation of the natural order and the human per-
> son in their own autonomous spheres is necessary before we can
> save Christianity and make Christians.[53]

The challenge for the Christian in our time, and for a journal like
Thought, is to reject the temptation to sectarian withdrawal from the larger
"wasteland." Instead the Christian must recognize and affirm the legitimate
autonomy of the many spheres of "the natural order and the human person"
and work with others "to rebuild the order of the secular."[54]

> Not only must nature be brought back under the sovereignty
> of God, the contingent under the absolute, but *Christians must
> return to the secular,* to all the "lost frontiers." The city of man
> may very well not be Christian; but it cannot do without Chris-
> tians. It is a life and a community under God which all men
> of good will must work to save—a community of charity for
> citizens where all men can live in a unity whether of scholarship
> or of economy or of peace. For a Christian to create a catacombs
> rather than to "*enter into the city*" would be a terrible mistake.[55]

Ingredere in Civitatem, then, was to be the guiding principle for Lynch's
six and one-half years (1950–1956) as editor of *Thought*, as it was for all his
subsequent writing. It was also his clear and firm response to those Catholic
voices at the time who worried "about the loss of the purity of truth, if we
march too unwittingly into the American scene," and who urged the Church
(as some again do today) to maintain itself in a catacomb or walled city,
separate from the mainstream of society and culture.[56]

Probably the most well-known article published in *Thought* under
Lynch's editorship is the justly famous essay "American Catholics and the
Intellectual Life" by John Tracy Ellis.[57] It may also have been the most
controversial since it exposed the deficiencies of Catholic colleges and uni-

---

53. Ibid., 5.

54. Ibid., 6. This, as we shall see, is the central theme of *Christ and Prometheus* and
of Chapter 7 below.

55. Ibid., 6–7 (emphasis added).

56. Lynch, "St Ignatius," 191.

57. Ellis, "American Catholics."

versities and challenged Catholic intellectuals to move out of their secure academic catacombs into the larger intellectual and public life of this nation. Indeed, Ellis may well have published his essay in *Thought* because Lynch was already engaged in exactly that program.

The roster of others who wrote for *Thought* during the years Lynch was its editor reads not only like pages from a *Who's Who?* of contemporary Catholics, but includes many from that larger intellectual world outside Catholicism. Among Jesuit writers were Martin D'Arcy, Jean Danielou, John LaFarge, Gustav Weigel, John Courtney Murray, Walter Ong, and Fordham sociologist Joseph Fitzpatrick. Among literary figures one finds W.H. Auden, Francis Fergusson, R.P. Blackmur, W.K. Wimsatt, as well as Marshal McLuhan and Walker Percy. Thomas Merton, Jacques Maritain, Gerhart Niemeyer and Josef Pieper all contributed essays, as did Carleton Hayes, Will Herberg, and Kierkegaard-editor Walter Lowrie. Lynch also published younger scholars like William Birmingham and Joseph Cunneen, who in 1950 had founded *Cross Currents*, a journal modeled on the French Catholic *Esprit*. In 1951 Lynch invited St. Louis University philosopher James Collins to begin an annual "Review of Philosophy" which later continued for many years in the pages of *Cross Currents*.

Of course such a list of names in itself means little. At worst it might be the kind of academic "name-dropping" Lynch would have detested. I intend it simply as a symbol for the quality and direction of his work at *Thought*. I realize that readers might not recognize all (or even many) of the names I have listed, yet hope that some of these names and the many fields of thought and concern they represent—philosophy and theology, literature and the arts, sociology and history and politics—might suggest the way Lynch pursued the goal announced in his inaugural editorial. Editing *Thought* clearly was for him a form of public and imaginative action, in collaboration with many others, in building the human city. It was the kind of project he would attempt again many years later, on a much smaller scale, with *New York Images*.

Culture and Belief

Lynch's own writing developed considerably during his years at *Thought*. He taught graduate courses in philosophy at Fordham and continued work on his study of Plato's *Parmenides*.[58] Yet he also published a series of major essays in *Thought* which pointed towards the substance of his later books.

58. William Birmingham (in personal correspondence) indicated that "the original take on *Approach* was complete by Spring 1952."

"Culture and Belief," published in September 1950, was the first of these essays. In many ways it was also the first of his mature publications. As such its title could hardly have been more apt. For it encompassed all the concerns which would come to expression in those later books.

Lynch knew, of course, that his primary audience was Catholic and Christian intellectuals. Yet his focus in "Culture and Belief" was not theology or the church. Rather he wanted to direct attention to the problem of unbelief among secular artists and writers. For them, he says, "There never was a time when the mind was more affected by the terrible remoteness of God."[59] He suggests, however, that belief in God is so difficult for contemporary intellectuals because of their lack of a prior or more fundamental trust in and engagement with society and culture. That the "vertical" depends on and grows from the "horizontal" is a fundamental principle for Lynch, one way of understanding the Catholic idea that grace builds on nature. Thus religious faith typically builds upon a more natural trust in the world, especially the human world of society and culture—what later in *Images of Faith* Lynch would imagine as "the body of faith."[60] Yet it is precisely this more natural faith that so many contemporary artists and writers lacked, albeit often because of their very legitimate and important criticisms of the contemporary "wasteland."

Lynch then repeats the thought expressed in his inaugural editorial that Christians are partly responsible for this situation of alienation because of their own deliberate distancing from modern society. He also repeats the challenge of that editorial: that the Christian must "enter the city" to build the kind of society and culture which nurtures basic human trust and faith, especially the more secular or "horizontal" forms of faith.[61] His concern is that Christians understand the broader plight of secular society which comes to expression in the alienation of its elites. He wants Christians to bring the resources of their faith, their fundamental sensibility and spirituality, not primarily to an effort at religious conversion (though that perhaps might follow), but to the difficult, long-term task of building a human world within the vast and often terrifying horizons opened by the secular developments of our times.

In his subsequent essays for *Thought*, starting with "Adventure in Order" in March, 1951, and running through six major essays later incorporated into *Christ and Apollo*,[62] Lynch focused almost exclusively on the role of

---

59. Lynch, "Culture," 443.

60. See IF, 53–74. See also Chapter 6 below.

61. Lynch, "Culture," 451. See also 441 and 462.

62. These were: "Confusion in Our Theater," "Theology and the Imagination,"

secular literature and the dramatic arts in the development of such a human "body of faith." These essays are, at least in terms of Lynch's published writings, the first developed expressions of his concern with the central role of imagination in human life. His critical targets throughout these essays were the many forms of contemporary literature and literary theory which, rather than contributing to the development of adequately human cultural images, were themselves expressions of diseased or alienated forms of imagination and sensibility. Thus they not only reinforced the artist's own alienation, but spread it through the culture, either in the form of a pseudo-realism narrowly focused on humanity's lost-ness in the world or as sophisticated aesthetic fantasies designed to transcend the muddy actualities of history and society. We have seen (just above) how Lynch found both tendencies at work in the writings of O'Neill.

When it was published in 1960, *Christ and Apollo*, along with *The Image Industries* which had come out the previous year, provided a detailed critical phenomenology of such alienating tendencies in contemporary literature, drama and cinema. Yet in both books Lynch was more fundamentally concerned to bring a healing corrective to the contemporary dramatic imagination and thereby enable it to again take up its central culture-building tasks. As we have seen, Lynch found resources for such healing in the spirituality of Ignatius Loyola. Yet it was another teacher who most enabled him to understand the civic and therapeutic importance of the dramatic imagination.

Aeschylus: Builder of Athens

In *Christ and Apollo* Lynch tells us that "Aeschylus was possibly the first to teach us that . . . insight into the human condition comes only through a descent into that deeper temporality that is the very moving life of the soul . . ." (53). He means, of course, that centuries before Christ it was Aeschylus, as founder of Greek theater, who first "taught us" (in the West) the utter centrality of dramatic movement through time and the definite for knowing and making (and saving) the human.[63] For Lynch himself, Aeschylus along with Plato—he wrote his dissertation about the former and a major book

---

"Theology and the Imagination II," "Theology and the Imagination III, "St. Ignatius," and "The Imagination and the Finite."

63. Of course some narratives of Hebrew Scripture antedate Greek theater, and it is the argument of Eric Auerbach's *Mimesis*, which Lynch knew well, that they are the earliest source of the dramatic imagination of Western culture. Lynch probably meant that the Bible did not in fact "teach us" until, well after Aeschylus, it became part of mainstream Western culture through the spread of Christianity.

about the latter—are second only to the Gospels and the *Spiritual Exercises* as a fundamental source for his thought.

Yet for modern ears such claims risk sounding too aesthetic or academic, as if Aeschylus (with Plato and the Bible) was a great founder of Western "humanities" in our typically specialized sense of that term, but had little to do with the larger and harder economic and political realities that really determine the fate of the human city. Lynch himself was everywhere concerned to work against such restriction of literature (as well as theology and faith) to some refined and separated sphere. Yet what is more important here is the simple fact that for the Greeks, and especially for Aeschylus, drama played no such separated role. It had grown from earlier forms of public religious ritual and was enacted in the civic space of the amphitheater. It was a decidedly public form of theater which led its audience into ever-wider and publicly shared dimensions of sensibility and thought.[64]

In Athens, theater was, perhaps most clearly in the case of Aeschylus, a dramatic *and* theological *and* public wrestling with the most fundamental concerns facing the city. It was, Lynch stresses, both cognitive and ontological—both a major way of knowing what was most real and consequently a way of entering and also of building or enlarging reality, especially the personal and social dimensions of human reality.[65] Drama, then, was crucial in the actual building of Athens by the way it shaped and enlarged the fundamental images and rhythms, and thus the sensibility *and* the spirituality that grounded the body of its culture.

Of course, Fifth Century (B.C.E) Athens was, as we have seen, itself part of one of the great periods of revolutionary transformation in human consciousness. It was, to use Lynch's explanation, part of the second of three historic transitions during which human competence and consciousness has experienced developments of "promethean" proportions.[66] For Athens, along with other major city-states, had at that time played a crucial role in the gradual emergence of civilization from earlier tribal forms of life.

---

64. Lynch later published a wonderful article making just this point. See "Architecture and Theater." See also "Toward A Theater of Public Action," IM, 121–30, where Lynch criticizes the increasingly private character of contemporary theater. When I seek to identify contemporary parallels to such "public theater," I think of events like "Woodstock," papal "World Youth Day" festivities, the nationally-broadcast funeral rites for President Kennedy and more recent memorial services for the victims of "9/11."

65. Lynch's insistence that dramatic literature is or should be both "cognitive and ontological" (having every bit as much to do with reality as science) was the central theme of his *Drama of the Mind* project. See, Lynch, "Drama of Mind," which probably gives the best overview in print of the larger project.

66. See pp. 15–16 above and CP, 101–2.

Yet that emergence was not simply a consequence of economic or political forces, though the *polis* certainly was the center of those dynamics of human transformation. Rather the fundamental human emergence of that period was as much, if not far more fundamentally, a consequence of developments in consciousness and culture. For it involved a transformation of the fundamental images (of the human, the divine, and the world) in terms of which people understood what was real and significant, and by which they oriented the action and activity of their lives.

That transformation, to which Athens so greatly contributed, arose from the "same" shock of events, the disorientations and anxieties, the pain and polarizations, which we today experience, and which the various versions of the Prometheus myth suggest must have been experienced during the long first "moment" of primal human emergence. The people of Athens, then, also experienced the deep alienations, the sense of loss and separation from traditional forms of life, the hunger for a deeper sense of self and of the divine, and so the corresponding temptations to those leaping, magical and hysterical solutions which Lynch continually criticized.

Nor was it simply Pericles, and perhaps also Plato, who enabled Athens (and the rest of us ever since) to move through such alienations and temptations towards more human forms of life. It was also, perhaps even more fundamentally, the dramatists.

> For it was the makers of tragedy who helped largely to forge the new man of fifth century Athens, a new man who could bear the weight of reality and history.[67]

> The imagination of this great city-state of Athens [was] trained, by the theater, to move with the movements of both self and world, and to bear with both.[68]

> And we have every . . . reason to believe that the Athenians of the fifth century B.C, from the initiating moment of Aeschylus, were as capable of entering and absorbing the complexity and shock of the outer world and the reverberations of the inner human world as any other distinguished social group in history. Perhaps the dramatists were their greatest help.[69]

In *The Persians*, for instance, the earliest play we have from Aeschylus, performed just eight years after the remarkable Athenian victory over

67. Lynch, "Dramatic Making," 162.
68. Lynch, "Foundation Stones," 343–44.
69. Lynch, "Imagination of Drama,"9.

Persia's armies, Aeschylus does not indulge Athenian pride.[70] Rather his play, the only extant Greek tragedy that uses the actual events of history, is presented from the viewpoint of the defeated Persians. Aeschylus thereby challenges his people to break old patterns of tribal consciousness and enlarge their image of the human by imagining the pain of the other, the defeat and failure of the enemy. It is the gradual unfolding of this challenge in the theater itself, through the rhythms of the play's action, music and dance, that enables the people to actually begin to experience this civilizing enlargement of their sympathies and understanding.

Aeschylus does something similar, though on a much larger scale, in his last work, the *Prometheus Bound*.[71] He remembers and re-enacts, through the sacred story of Zeus and Prometheus, the very real theological struggle that would have characterized the first emergence of human freedom and skill from the restraining and sacralized forces of nature. "Something like this," Lynch comments, "is what actually must have happened, had to happen, between the secular and the sacred, man and God . . . " (CP, 62). In dramatically re-presenting that primal struggle, Aeschylus the theologian enables his people to understand their own pain and confusion at the loss of an earlier form of sacrality, the guilt and anxiety accompanying their new freedom and power, and the hunger for a new image of the relationship of "secular and sacred, man and God." It would again have been by actually entering into the theatrical but public and quasi-liturgical rhythms of the performance that those people might have begun to experience, at the deeper levels of their sensibility, an actual transformation of their images and habits of faith and spirituality.

Yet it is above all in "the great trilogy of the *Oresteia* (still perhaps the greatest theatrical achievement of man)"[72] that the full extent of Aeschylus' achievement as a builder of the human city is revealed. The trilogy enacts the full terror of the ancient practice of justice as revenge, with its endless and hopeless cycle of retribution governed by the Furies.[73] Orestes murders his mother as revenge for her murder of the just returned Agamemnon, and these murders are but the latest twists in a long and terrible cycle. Yet for Aeschylus the deeper action of the drama is imagined in the suffering, the

70. See "Dramatic Making" for Lynch's commentary on *The Persians*.

71. Lynch's commentary on Aeschylus' *Prometheus* is found throughout *Christ and Prometheus*. See, for example, CP, 3–4, 10, and 56–63. See also Chapter 7 below.

72. Lynch, "Imagination of Drama," 5. Elsewhere Lynch says the *Oresteia* "is among the very greatest achievements of the human mind" ("Drama of Mind," 18).

73. Discussions of the *Oresteia* recur throughout Lynch's later writings. Most significant is the detailed analysis in *Christ and Prometheus* (see especially CP, 4–6 and 77–95).

guilt and the sense of hopeless entrapment experienced because humanity has not yet come to a better form of justice. That suffering is reflected in the deep division within the Athenian community (at the trial of Orestes) between those who cling to the sacred obligations of the old pattern and those seeking some more adequate form of justice. It finally is Athena's vote that breaks not just the trial's deadlock, but the deeper deadlock caused by the still immensely powerful idea of justice as revenge. She votes for a more human form of justice, for law and courts and human judgment, with all their limitations. She thereby founds the city and the civilization which bears her name, a founding celebrated by the triumphal procession in the trilogy's final scene.

Thus the theologian-dramatist had again turned to sacred story as a way to imagine and understand the still very real struggles his people were experiencing in the emergence of civilization—struggles for the transformation of their images of sacrality and justice, of the divine and the human. And, again, it was the public, quasi-liturgical experience of the dramatic performance itself which contributed to that transformation.

Lynch says that it was "the genius of Aeschylus . . . to direct our thoughts to the constant dramatic process by which human civilization moves through pain toward higher moments of achievement and some verge of innocence" (CP, 3). He tells us, moreover, that in the *Agamemnon* (the first play of the trilogy) Aeschylus himself gave a fundamental description of this process:

> [E]very such story begins with a plunge into *action* . . . ; the action meets reality . . . and passes through a *suffering* history; through suffering the action reaches a new *insight*, or point of reconciliation. These words summarize all: *drama* [action], *pathos* [suffering], *mathos* [insight]. (CP, 24, emphasis added)

Later, in a passage that avoids any possible suggestion of something formulaic or mechanical, Lynch describes this process as "the fundamental Aeschylean rhythm of action and suffering, of back and forth, forward movement and check, thrust and guilt, reality and illusion . . . " (CP, 101).

What Lynch learned from Aeschylus, then, came together in his mind and spirit with what he had learned from Ignatius and from the East River. He learned again of the need to build the human city and of the utterly central role of the dramatic imagination in that task. He learned, to reiterate words cited at the beginning of this discussion of Aeschylus, the need for "descent into that deeper temporality that is the moving life of the soul" *and* the moving life of civilization. He came to understand even more fully the great human need for a "dramatic" spirituality that demanded the difficult exercise of a realistic imagination for moving, in human time and stages, into and through the actualities of the city and the world. "For the dramatic leads us by motion and stages of exploration deeper and deeper into reality and being, into men and the world."[74] He learned again the need for a spirituality that refused magic formulas, hysterical programs, and any attempts to leap beyond the asceticism of actuality and time. He learned again the need for a sensibility that trusted the real enough to stay with its actual lines and movements, even amidst fear and guilt and suffering, and to come thereby—gradually and in human stages—to the discovery or making of more adequate forms of the human city.

Of course this fundamental Aeschylean and Ignatian spirituality cannot really be learned abstractly or just notionally. It must be learned *through* the experience of action and suffering, through real movement into the city and the world which takes time and stays with complexity and difficulty. Had we a more adequate "theater of public action" like the Athenians, we too might be helped to have such experience by imaginative participation in dramatic action. Indeed we are fortunate to the extent that any of our arts—our drama and cinema and stories, our poetry and music—tutor our sensibilities in the rhythms of such spirituality. We are fortunate, too, if our religious liturgies, festivities and pieties so tutor us. Finally, though, we shall only really come to such spirituality and sensibility through the "fundamental Aeschylean rhythm" of the time and stages of our own lives and the life of our city—through the "two steps forward, one step back" pattern which Lynch had seen imaged by the tidal flows of the East River.

One Step Back

By 1956 Bill Lynch had already learned much of that "Aeschylean rhythm" from "steps back" on different occasions in his life.[75] In that year, however, he experienced a major setback, "a harrowing experience of severe mental breakdown."[76] The "illness forced him to step down" from his position at

---

74. "Imagination of Drama," 3.

75. In his "East River" essay he tells of being hospitalized for three months after the beer truck had "crushed my pelvis" ("Me," 3). *A Book of Admiration* also speaks of the painful experience, "when I was a boy," of being driven back into a "void" (60). It is not clear whether this is a reference to the same hospitalization or to some other time of setback.

76. "An Image of Hope." This unsigned obituary was presumably written by David Toolan, SJ, then an editor at *Commonweal* and also superior in the Jesuit community where Lynch had been living.

Thought and led to eventual reassignment at Georgetown University.[77] He was hospitalized for a time at Seton Institute in Baltimore and seems to have been suffering from a severe form of depression. A friend who later helped edit *Images of Hope*, the book which in many ways grew from this experience, suggests that the "catatonic patient" described at one point in that book was in fact Lynch himself.[78] Leslie Farber, the then famous psychoanalyst who became Lynch's friend, wrote at the end of his "Foreword" to *Images of Hope* that Lynch was "a man of hope [who] could not so cherish its presence had he not known the anguish of its loss" (11).[79]

We don't really know what led to the breakdown. Fellow Jesuit David Toolan, who lived with Lynch during his retirement years in the 1980s, later wrote:

> In his writings, Lynch's critique of the absolutizing, either/or imagination is generally focused on the secular world beyond the church. Yet it was impossible to know the man, as I did, without realizing that he was also wrestling with his own demons of perfectionism, the fierce moralism of Irish-American ghetto Catholicism, and a Jesuit spirituality deeply infected by American Pelagianism . . . I am fairly confident that it was the moralist perfectionism and absolutizing of his own Catholicism that led Bill Lynch, in the late 1950s, to a major psychological breakdown.[80]

There is, moreover, some evidence in *Images of Hope* to support Toolan's suggestion. While that book, as Toolan notes, is primarily concerned with absolutizing "spiritualities" that pervade the larger culture (remember that glorified bar of soap!), Lynch occasionally does speak about the way Christians, particularly those responsible for the training of priests and nuns, can distort authentic asceticism into moral rigorism and absolutism.[81]

Whatever the cause, Lynch had experienced a serious, but short-term episode of mental illness. Yet such is our own continuing fear of mental illness that we risk exaggerating its significance. Lynch, like the rest of

77. Fleming, 4. While the exact time of Lynch's breakdown is not clear, the Spring 1956 issue of *Thought* lists someone else as "acting editor." Thus it is likely that his hospitalization occurred fairly early in 1956.

78. William Birmingham (personal communication); see IH, 97.

79. At the beginning of *A Book of Admiration* Lynch chides R. D. Laing and others who found in madness "a cure-all . . . against all the established evils of the world . . ." He then adds: "I hope I love the mad as much as they, but many of us have been too close to it to lionize it or think of it in terms of ecstasy and escape" (3).

80. Toolan, "Some Biographical Reflections," 133.

81. See IH, 100, 102–3.

us, continued to struggle with setbacks and suffering later in his life.[82] He himself, moreover, seems later to have regarded his breakdown as "a mixed blessing" since it freed him to complete the writing he'd long wanted to get to.[83] It was, then, in the words of his East River meditation, "a step back . . . to your limits, to regain rest and strength for another dash into the bay, the port, the ocean." It was simply another, albeit a major moment in the "Aeschylean rhythm" of his own life.

Two Steps Forward

The five years (1957–62) Lynch next spent at Georgetown teaching English and directing the honors program were among the most productive in his life in terms of publication and national recognition. As already noted, he quickly brought out his first three books to critical acclaim. In 1960 he also edited, with fellow Jesuit Walter Burghardt, a book of readings called *The Idea of Catholicism: An Introduction to the Thought and Worship of the Church*.[84] It was a collection of essays by major modern theologians (from John Henry Newman and Karl Adam to Yves Congar and Bernard Haring) on different aspects of Catholic life and thought. Lynch himself contributed an introductory essay on "The Catholic Idea." He also continued the effort begun in *The Image Industries* to develop a more critical audience for contemporary cinema—especially in the universities.[85] And during these years he wrote most of the essays collected in *The Integrating Mind* (1962).

Yet despite, or perhaps because of, the productivity of these years, at some point Lynch decided to leave academe to take up a life of full-time writing. In 1963 he was assigned as "writer in residence" to St. Peter's College in Jersey City. He later said that he "regretted leaving Georgetown, but that was just the ordinary regret of leaving a good thing." He had left, he added, because of the sense "that I should go back to my [New York]

82. *A Book of Admiration*, for instance, speaks of the severe arthritic pain he lived with as a result of his childhood beer-truck accident. It "can be a prison . . . It makes you ache and think of self [and] tries to drive you out of the world" (32). He eventually had to have both hips replaced. And his former student, Fordham Professor Bernard Gilligan, noted (in personal correspondence) that Lynch later also suffered occasional bouts of depression.

83. Fleming, "Metaphysics," 4.

84. Burghardt, *Idea*.

85. See Lynch, "Film Festivals." The editors of *America* evidently found Lynch's call for cinema education sufficiently important that they invited television personality, producer, and critic Steve Allen to write a brief (and affirming) response in the same issue.

province and pay a debt to it."[86] A practical factor that may also have played a role in his decision was opportunity to work full-time on his study of mental illness and hope. In the "Preface" to *Images of Hope* Lynch tells us that he "was enabled to live and write for the best part of a year in residence among the actualities of the mentally ill in St. Elizabeth's [Hospital in Washington, D. C.]" (IH, 15). He gives no indication of exactly when he spent that "year in residence," but it was most likely during 1962 and 1963, after leaving Georgetown and before actually taking up residence at St. Peter's. It also seems clear, from the unusual gap in publications between 1962 and 1965, that he spent those years working on *Images of Hope* which was published in 1965.

Imagining the Human City

I cannot help but think that Lynch may also have left Georgetown because of growing dissatisfaction with the separation of university life (not just or even primarily at Georgetown) from the larger life of the city—a separation which made manifest the more pervasive separation of intellectual elites from the lives of ordinary people. That dissatisfaction—and his consequent desire to bring the arts and the university into the life of the city—comes to expression frequently in his writings.[87] For the alienation of artists and intellectuals, their often self-imposed exile to enclaves of thought or beauty, or to walled cities of criticism, contempt, and revolutionary posturing, and their consequent neglect of the more difficult vocation to build a body of faith for the human city, was a constant concern for Lynch.

In any event, the move from Georgetown represented a fairly decisive shift in Lynch's life from the university to the city. He lived for the next fifteen years at St. Peter's in Jersey City, with frequent trips for lectures and research to other parts of this country and to Europe. The shift in location reflected the development of his own response to the fundamental imperative expressed in his first editorial at *Thought*: that Christians must become more engaged in building the life of the human city. Here (again) is how he put the matter in *Images of Hope*, which he was writing at this time:

86. Fleming, "Metaphysics," 5. Georgetown University was then part of the Maryland Province of the Jesuits.

87. See, as examples, his early comments about education in his report on the Greek drama productions at Fordham ("Bringing," 45–46) as well as fundamentally similar comments in one of the last things he wrote ("Final Image," 28–30). On the dangerous separation of intellectuals from ordinary folk, see his extended comment in IM, 45–55 and his especially sharp comments in IF, 107–8. See as well pp. 67–70 below.

> We can decide to build a human city . . . This will always require
> an act of the imagination which will extend the idea of the hu-
> man . . . How many . . . are up to the building of this kind of city
> remains to be seen . . . (IH, 26)[88]

This theme of working towards an inclusive city, and thus building a "body" of hope for the mentally ill and for all of us, is central to scripts Lynch wrote for an award-winning, four-part television series on "Images of Hope" which ran during May 1965 on NBC-TV's *Catholic Hour*.[89] The same theme came even more strongly to the fore in Lynch's next two books. *Christ and Prometheus* (1970), as we have seen, was his contribution to the theological debate which followed the 1965 publication of Harvey Cox's *The Secular City*. While working on *Christ and Prometheus*, Lynch joined Dean Stanley Romaine Hopper of Drew University Divinity School in a proposal to Philip Scharper, editor at Sheed and Ward, for an ecumenical book series they would jointly edit on Christian involvement in "The City of Man." That particular project was never realized, but Lynch's last book, *Images of Faith* (1973), took up the terrible social and political divisions of the late 1960s and early 1970s and became his most sustained call for building that social and cultural body of basic civic trust which we still very much need today.

Of course Lynch never completely severed his ties with academe. He lectured widely at colleges and universities during the 1960s. He was honored by Carleton College with a visiting professorship during 1965–66 and by Muhlenberg College in 1969–70. As previously noted, he served a number of times as an adjunct visiting professor at Princeton Divinity School and he continued similar occasional teaching at the Jesuit's Woodstock Theological Seminary (something begun during his years at Georgetown). Later, in 1976–77, probably as part of his ongoing research for *The Drama of the Mind* project, he also taught for a program called "College Year in Athens."

Yet these were all brief, occasional returns to the university. His primary focus remained that "act of imagination which will extend the idea of the human," an act especially needed because of the seemingly revolutionary and deeply polarized times in which we live. In his books he worked to provide enlarged images of both secularity and faith which he hoped might contribute to healing the social and cultural polarizations characteristic of our times. Yet he also continually called others, especially intellectuals and

---

88. See above (p. 17) for the complete citation.

89. Three of the four scripts can be found in the Fordham Archives. The series received one of the first annual media awards granted by the American Foundation of Religion and Psychiatry.

artists, to resist the temptation of retreat to "various absolute and walled cities" and to contribute instead to the much-needed building of the human city. As he put the issue in an essay written during the late 1960s:

> It is our business as writers or thinkers or artists or poets to form images of the major points of life and death to help the world cope with them. For this is the central way we cope with the points and movement of life and death, by forming images of them . . . [A]ll hell breaks loose, and every manner of fantasy, when a culture does not adequately imagine . . .
>
> The first part of the hypothesis which I am proposing is that we deal with the whole of human life or death through the imagination or through violence. The second part of my hypothesis is that really, way deep down, violence is only an imitation, a cheap imitation, of the imagination . . . I hypothesize further that if we have entered upon a many sided period of serious revolution, then the real quarrel for control will occur between the men of imagination and those we now call the revolutionaries, the men of violence . . . The revolutionaries, whether on the right or the left, will attack and destroy . . . [T]he men of imagination will imagine; they will build and compose; where they destroy they will replace. They will not fall back on simple thrusts of the will but on acts of imagination . . .[90]

The constancy of Lynch's effort on behalf of such acts of imagination is perhaps nowhere better symbolized than in the journal he attempted to found during his final years. In 1978, at age seventy, Lynch had retired to New York's West Side Jesuit Community (several floors in a modest apartment building which still serve as a residence for Jesuits involved in various ministries in the New York area). His health was not good. Yet "the years that followed were, in his estimate, the happiest in his life."[91] And his "retirement" was anything but a retreat from his larger project. He not only continued research and writing, albeit in reduced fashion, but he almost single-handedly founded *New York Images* and edited its three issues.

His idea for *New York Images* was to bring together people from various disciplines and walks of life—poets and playwrights, artists and critics, sociologists and politicians and philosophers—who would comment in short, readable pieces on the current state of our images and would contribute by

---

90. Lynch, "Death," 459–60. Lynch then adds: "This in fact should be a great goal of the universities (and seminaries), to turn out men who know what is the matter and who are intent on acts of the imagination which will try to do something about it" (460).

91. Berrigan, 4.

word and by sketch or photograph to building those many images of the
human which constitute the spiritual and cultural life of the city. It was for
Lynch a return to the editorial role he'd played so well at *Thought*. It was also
a further investment in the great task of the imagination. For it took real
imagination, not just to have the idea for such a journal, but to bring it off,
to see the idea embodied and realized, even if only in several issues.

Given both the economics and sensationalist sensibilities of contemporary publishing, it is not surprising that *New York Images* did not catch
on. Yet it nonetheless remains a marvelous symbol, not only for Lynch's
consistent dedication to the life of the imagination and its role in building the human city, but even more for his understanding of the nature and
importance of these two great human things.

An Image of Death

Death, of course, is one of those very human things the imagination must
struggle with, hopefully to find and make realistic images of it. For our living as well as our dying can be terribly distorted and tormented by unreal,
fantastic images of death, whether they be terrifying or saccharin. "Part of
the vocation of the imagination should be to create true images of birth,
life and death," Lynch had said in *Images of Hope*.[92] "But," he immediately
added, "in our culture, there is nothing we are imagining, or can imagine,
less successfully than death . . ." For the image "of death as passivity and
helplessness may be the great American fear." We have "only demeaning and
corrupt images of the passive . . . The American is not equipped, therefore,
with an imagination, with a set of images, which would tell him that it is
all right to lie down in good time and die, dependently leaving it to God to
raise him up again."

Our culture of often manic activism, with its frequent recourse to the
will and to violence, and its corresponding mood swings between fantastic
utopianism and apocalyptic pessimism, is in good part caused by this lack
of adequate images of passivity and of death. Thus in *Images of Hope* Lynch
worked to develop a positive understanding of human passivity, especially
by exploring the relationship of real hope to mutuality and help and depen-
dency. Yet the theme of accepting life's passivities, especially the ultimate
passivity of death, is not limited to *Images of Hope*. It is, rather, one of those
central strands woven through many of his writings. It is central to the argument in *Christ and Apollo* that modern theater has misunderstood tragedy
by conceiving it as a promethean rebellion *against* death. It is the theme

92. The running citation which follows in this paragraph is from IH, 245–46.

of Lynch's important essay "Death as Nothingness." Finally, the concluding
sections of *Images of Faith* provide Lynch's most profound meditation on the
inevitable human passage through finitude and passivity unto death.

Perhaps because such reflection was central to his thinking and had
become embodied in his sensibility, when the time came for Lynch himself
"to lie down in good time and die," he was able to move into this final passage with real grace and no little comic drama. Here is the story as told by
David Toolan:

> One of the great gifts that Bill Lynch left me was that he let me
> take part in his dying. In late 1986, I had just become superior
> of our local Jesuit community when Bill fell very ill and spent
> about two months in Manhattan's Lennox Hill hospital. I would
> visit him every day, and step by step he took me with him in
> the process of dying. His body was failing him, but his active
> imagination, a theme that was utterly central to his thought, was
> alive and well . . . In *Images of Hope*, he speaks about the heal-
> ing power of being able to imagine a future, especially regarding
> dying and becoming finally dependent on a power not our own.
> During the last month of his life, to the great frustration of the
> doctors who wanted some straight answers from him about his
> symptoms, he moved into a twilight zone. It was as if he were ex-
> perimenting in passing over into another region—not so much
> vertically "up there" as ahead, in the unknown future. It was
> sheer play, and I found it wonderful to enter into these spaces
> with him . . . For instance, one day, as I entered his hospital
> room, he called out, "Give me your pants!" "What's happening?"
> I asked. "I'm taking a trip on a train," he answered, "and I need
> clothes." I said, "Why don't you check out whether you really
> need them." So he retired back into that twilight zone for a bit
> and then returned with a big grin. "I don't need clothes!" he said.
> "I can come as I am!" Then another problem: "I need money;
> give me some money," he said. So I asked, "Why don't you check
> that out too?" And again he checked it out and came back, again
> with a surprised smile: "The trip is free; there's no charge!" . . . It
> was extraordinary to explore this territory with him. He could
> describe where he was. On train trips, on other voyages. And
> he was always asking you to join him, come with him. He'd say:
> "COME! COME!" His own literal-minded nurse would rebuke
> him: "Father Lynch, you're not going anywhere; you're going
> to get well." She insisted on feeding him fantasy. But he would
> have none of it. "COME!" The African-American nurse for the
> patient next to him understood, was on his wave-length. "Father

Lynch," she'd cheerily say, "I'll come, I'm ready when you are." In January of 1987, he was ready, faithful to the time of the end—or the next beginning.[93]

His had been a life tutored by Aeschylean and Ignatian spiritualities and shaped by the realistic rhythms of river and city. He had struggled to stick with the real lines and stages of human action and suffering, yet always also to make that "act of the imagination which will extend the idea of the human" and to come thereby to real "muddy fleshed-out dreams." Thus he was indeed ready "to leave it to God to raise him up again."

93. Toolan, "Some Biographical Reflections," 134–135.

3

The Integrating Spirit

Just a few years after his first three books, Lynch published *The Integrating Mind* (1962), a collection of essays with the expansive subtitle "An Exploration into Western Thought." Most of the material seems to have been written for articles and lectures given after the appearance of *The Image Industries* (1959) and *Christ and Apollo* (1960), but Lynch also included his earliest major essay from *Thought*, "Culture and Belief" (1950), as well as an appendix of "chosen passages" summarizing the key ideas of his *An Approach to the Metaphysics of Plato Through the Parmenides* (1959).[1] The book received many good reviews, though it does not seem to have reached the wide readership achieved by *Christ and Apollo* and *The Image Industries*—perhaps because its general theme was quite philosophical and its particular essays quite wide-ranging.

Yet the book represents an important mid-point in Lynch's writing, and not simply because it was the fourth of his seven published books. As the appendix indicates, he clearly saw this collection as a way to bring together topical essays about U.S. politics and culture within the framework of fundamental philosophical ideas developed in his study of Plato. For those who then knew him primarily either as a literary and cinema critic or as a Plato specialist, the range of topics included gave (and still gives) a more accurate picture of the breadth of his interests as well as a sense of things to come. Indeed, in one way or another virtually all of the key ideas developed

1. IM, 17. Lynch provided no clear indication of the provenance of the different essays. He simply thanks "the editors of *Thought, Cross Currents,* and *The Critic,* the directors of the Fund for the Republic, and the President and Trustees of the College of New Rochelle, for permission to use here material which first appeared in their pages or was developed at their request" (vii). We know, as noted, that "Culture and Belief" first appeared in *Thought* (Fall 1950). "The Problem of Freedom" was published in *Cross Currents* (Spring 1960) and "Theology and Human Sensibility" in *The Critic* (April/ May, 1960). The book's opening chapter, "The Totalistic Temptation," clearly seems to have been written as its introduction.

in his subsequent books and book projects are suggested in these essays. Thus it would be accurate to say that, of all his books and essays, *The Integrating Mind* gives the clearest overall sense of the scope and direction of his work. It not only touched on most of his major topical interests, but, in its opening chapter ("The Totalistic Temptation") and in the introduction to its appendix, it clearly links those interests to his more fundamental concern for what he there calls an "integrating" mind and spirituality—"an epistemology, a way of thinking, and a corresponding set of helps for the human passions that will match the structure of reality itself" (6).[2] And it just as clearly links the need for this spirituality to pressing concerns we, both then and now, face in our struggle to build a truly human city.[3]

A brief look at the central themes of *The Integrating Mind* will, then, provide a helpful next step in our gradual unfolding of Lynch's understanding of a spirituality and sensibility for public life. It will also provide a way of suggesting the significance of Plato for Lynch—though as a result some of the sections below may involve just a bit of philosophical "heavy lifting." For despite widespread popular misinterpretations about Plato's supposed dualism and other-worldliness, his thought was central to the development of Lynch's spirituality for worldly action. As Lynch puts it at the beginning of *The Integrating Mind*, the "substantial part of fifteen years" that he spent wrestling with the *Parmenides* left "an indelible mark on me" (9). So much so that Plato must stand with Ignatius and Aeschylus as one of the basic sources on which he drew in articulating the fundamental habits of mind, spirit, and sensibility which he felt were so much needed today.

---

2. Throughout this chapter, references to *The Integrating Mind* are given simply with page numbers.

3. There is also another sense in which *The Integrating Mind* represents a "midpoint" in Lynch's writing, or perhaps one might even say something of a "turning point." The book embodies a summation of the philosophical ideas (on contrariety, for instance, and on analogy) which Lynch took from his work on Plato. That is explicitly indicated in the appendix on "The Problem of Contrariety in Plato's *Parmenides*" (147–181), and such ideas were also foundational for *Christ and Apollo*. Yet with his next book and all subsequent writing, Lynch's language shifts from such explicitly philosophical categories to a far greater emphasis on "image" and "imagination." As he tells us at the start of that next book, *Images of Hope* (13), his work on the theme of mental illness and hope gradually led him to a far broader appreciation of the role of imagination in human life. It is also quite possible that he began to realize that many of the philosophical ideas which were so clear to him were far more difficult to communicate to a broader audience and made his writings less accessible than he desired. Yet it is important to stress that his concerns and ideas remained *fundamentally* the same even as his dominant discourse shifted somewhat from philosophical categories to greater emphasis on the imagination.

Totalizing vs. Integrating

In its "Preface" Lynch gives a preliminary summary of the general argument developed in *The Integrating Mind*:

> [T]his is a book written in defense of a way of thinking and a philosophy of life that may be called both-and versus either-or. Put negatively, it is an attack on all unnecessary alternatives and unnecessary conflicts, especially in our national society. Put more philosophically, it is a defense of contrariety, that is, of the constantly recurring fact that many contraries, instead of constituting alternatives, are mutually creative of each other and cannot live without each other. (v)

Shortly thereafter he adds the following:

> This book is in substance a plea that we keep things together that belong together . . . It is first and foremost a many-phase analysis of the disease of the clear or pure idea, in the many forms of that disease that reign among us in our contemporary national culture. (3)

Typically, then, Lynch had taken up his pen to write in response to concern about "our contemporary national culture." He was particularly concerned with those deep polarizations which threatened a much-needed shared sense of national identity and purpose—what later, in *Images of Faith*, he will call our shared "body of faith." As we will soon enough see, he gives many examples of such polarizations in the book's different essays. Perhaps at this point it will suffice simply to recall the many social, political and cultural conflicts which had accompanied the progressive deepening of the Cold War through the 1950s—"McCarthyism" was but one early example—and to add that Lynch, writing in the late 50s and early 1960s, was remarkably prescient about even deeper polarizations which would arise during "the 60s" and continue still in our "culture wars."

"Divided We Stand," the book's third essay, traces the roots of such polarization to "the disease of the clear or pure idea" which the book's opening essay had spoken of as "The Totalistic Temptation." It is the temptation to see most issues and concerns in "either-or" terms, and thereby to embrace simplistic and "total" solutions which regard all opposed or alternative positions as enemies. As remedy for this disease, and condition for the maintenance or recovery of such foundational trust and unity as is necessary for the life of a nation, Lynch called for "a way of thinking and a philosophy of life that may be called both-and versus either-or." Such an integrating way of thinking and living is, he says, "one of the great and pre-eminent tasks of the civilized mind of the West" (v). It is a central aspect of our philosophical and spiritual heritage, something Lynch himself had more fully come to understand through his study of Plato. The principle Lynch took from Plato that has already been used several times—about "not moving too quickly from the many to the one"—is, as we shall see, simply one way of suggesting that more mediating or integrative sensibility which Lynch called us to recover.

For our part, we can readily begin to understand Lynch's concern about our national culture by thinking of the polarizations we continue to experience in conflicts about gender and abortion or family life and homosexuality, in clashes over taxation and gun control or individual rights and the role of government, in arguments about immigration and globalization and the environment, or in our nation's response to terrorism and its political and military relations with the rest of the world. Such issues, Lynch would say, are of immense importance and work towards their resolution will inevitably and necessarily involve argument, opposition, and conflict.[4] At times, too, such issues may involve real "either-or" choices, where exclusive moral commitments must be made and real evils fought. Yet more typically our debates and divisions do not involve (or do not simply involve) such clear and exclusive choices. Rather multiple goods and ideas are involved, typically in tension with one another. Said differently and more philosophically, fundamental "contraries" which structure human experience are involved and are, by definition, inescapably in tension with each other. Yet we, too easily seduced by "the totalistic temptation," allow such tensions to be transformed into polarizations or absolute oppositions because of our hunger for a pure and perfectly clear idea or position—or at least because of our need for perfectly clear enemies.

There are, for instance, both individual rights and common responsibilities, both the need of many freedoms and the need for law and security and governance, both the goods of the nation and the growing requirements of international community. Yet the temptation, when faced with the tensions and conflicts that emerge from such "contrary" goods, is to reduce them to moralized terms of either-or, where cause becomes crusade, our side totally right, the other totally evil. "Who does not," Lynch asks, "long at times with all his heart for the perfectly clear idea or situation?" (3). The appeal of such magnificently pure ideas and parties is immense. "These totalistic, these non-human cities," we have already heard Lynch say, "offer an

---

4. He was never held captive by any illusory image of utopian harmony. For such an image, whether from the left or the right, would itself simply be an instance of totalizing thought, a result of the hunger for some pure idea or cause which creates another "walled city" of retreat from reality.

extraordinary fascination for the souls of fearful men and we are fools if we underestimate how strong and seductive they can be" (IH, 26).[5] Thus the constant temptation, in both personal and civic life, fed by our longing "for the perfectly clear idea or situation," is to find clear-cut "either-or" polarizations everywhere. That is the response of the totalizing mind and spirit to the experience of difference and conflict. It deals with tension by absolutizing one pole of the tension and demonizing the other. We become either the party of progress or the defenders of tradition. We are either for family values or for freedom and toleration. Those who stand with us are "good Americans" and "children of the light." Those against us are not just the opposition but the enemy. Polarity escalates into polarization. We build "walled cities" of purity, simple clarity, and supposedly perfect unity—whether in an actual place (a gated-suburb, a rural enclave, or an office tower) or, more typically, in some place of the spirit, some party or program or church that is held captive by the urgency of a magnificent cause and typically also by the passionate brilliance of charismatic leaders.

There are, moreover, periods in the lives of individuals and of nations when the appeal of such clarity and purity is intensified. "We are," Lynch thought (in the late 50s and early 60s), "at such a stage of human history right now, when the demons are unusually strong and, on the surface, magnificent" (10). Nor did he just think that when he wrote those words. For his concern with our deep polarizations continued to grow and became, as we shall see, central to both *Christ and Prometheus* (1970) and *Images of Faith* (1973).

Yet the situation we face is not only part of a particular period of change and crisis, however prolonged. It is, as already suggested, a fundamental and thus perennial situation shaped by "the ineluctable and palpable presence of a contrariety in the sensible and human world . . . " (147). Said differently: it is a result of the fundamental reality that human finitude and temporality are structured, at every turn, by the presence of inescapable contraries or polar oppositions. There are, to use but a few of Lynch's examples, the basic "interior" contraries of mind and body, and thus of thought and feeling, sense and sensibility, aspiration and limitation. Then there are many analogous forms of the "external" tension between self and world: the contraries, for instance, of subject and object, activity and receptivity, individual and community, freedom and restraint. There are also temporal contraries such as past and future, continuity and change. Philosophical analysis, moreover, reveals still more fundamental contraries such as ideal and real, similarity and difference, one and many, motion and rest,

5. See p. 17 above.

and, perhaps most fundamentally, being and non-being. Such contraries, moreover, are not simply the vague abstractions they may at first seem, for they are multiply present and complexly interwoven in the actuality of our lives—in individual experience and in the life of our city. A fundamental structure of contraries, Lynch says, "takes many analogical forms" in our actual lives, "but it is always there" (15).[6] It is, to repeat, a structure of finite existence in the world and in time.

Yet the real challenge for life, as for thought, is not simply to note and enumerate the many contraries or polarities which structure human existence, but to come ever again to a lived awareness and an active sensitivity to what Lynch identifies as the fundamental reality of such "contrariety": to "the constantly recurring fact that *many contraries, instead of constituting alternatives for choice, are mutually creative of each other and cannot live without each other*" (v, emphasis added). It has been, he argues, the "passion" and the "vocation" of the mind of the West, and the great achievement of thinkers as diverse as Plato and Aquinas, Hegel and Coleridge, to help us understand this reality of "contrariety," this necessary and fruitful interpenetration of the contraries which structure our existence.[7]

Nor (again) is this just a matter of abstract theorizing, for what at first seems an apparently technical problem for philosophy in fact "spreads out . . . into a multitude of actual and concrete problems . . . " (7). "Thus the metaphysical question of contrariety or the lack of it, apparently so harmless, comes out of hiding and emerges into the forefront of our lives" (12). Those thinkers who have contributed most to our understanding of contrariety have, in other words, not simply been solving some erudite puzzle. Rather they were concerned with understanding and developing ways of thinking and patterns of practice which corresponded to the structures of contrariety which we everywhere experience, ways of thinking and patterns of practice which make possible the lived or achieved interpenetration of contraries in our individual lives and in the life of the human city.

Let me add two further notes to this introductory statement of the general problem or set of problems taken up in *The Integrating Mind*. In the first place, I want to emphasize that Lynch's understanding of integration

6. Since he is not primarily concerned to present a systematic analysis of contraries and the idea of contrariety, Lynch's examples are scattered throughout *The Integrating Mind*. Its appendix, excerpted from his book on the *Parmenides*, presents an outline of Plato's analysis of contrariety. Aside from that, Lynch's own most developed and far more accessible discussion of contraries is found in the chapter "Reality is Not Conflictual" (IH, 229–42). There he indicates how analysis of basic contraries and of their interpenetration has been central to many systems of thought, both Eastern and Western, ancient and modern.

7. See vi, 7–9, 147–48.

should not be confused with some notions of synthesis. Finite reality always remains, for him (and for Plato), unalterably complex; the poles of every contrary are and remain really different. Yet the hostility and violence that characterize the totalistic approach towards polarities is gone. As Lynch says about Plato's achievement in the *Parmenides*, "his powerful mind wove all the great contraries together, *so that they were there, but inseparably there, creating each other, depending on each other*" (8, emphasis added). Integration is not the kind of combination that reduces things to simple or univocal unities. Rather it is the interpenetration of realities that remain polar and as such (as at once distinct and yet really interpenetrating) are "mutually creative." It is a dynamic and temporal process, an inclusive process which enlarges both individual experience and the life of the city. It is not reductive and destructive as all totalizing sensibilities inevitably are.

Secondly, then, it is also important to emphasize that Lynch's ideas about the interpenetration and mutual creativity of contraries are in no way meant to suggest something easy or inevitable. Building a mature human life and building the human city, precisely because it everywhere involves integrating real contraries, is a continually demanding challenge that *requires an equally strong and temporal or dramatic spirituality*. Since contrariety is a fundamental and permanent structure of the life of the city, as of the individual, that life should be characterized by vitality and drama, by (to use Aeschylus's terms) the action and suffering and learning of ongoing processes and patterns of integration. The ongoing work of the integrating mind and spirit requires real passion, but not the easy and seductive passions of totalism. Rather it demands a far more difficult passion for flexibility and patience and discernment, for what in his later books Lynch will more typically call a "realistic imagination," in contrast to simplistic fantasy. "What we need," he has already told us, "is an epistemology, a way of thinking, and a corresponding set of helps for the human passions that will match the [contrary] structure of reality itself" (6). And this means we need "the passion and strength" for "waiting, hope, the plodding, varying working out of a commitment, decision or insight" (5).

Faced as we are on so many fronts with the totalizing or polarizing temptation, we need (in the terms employed in the present book) a spirituality and a sensibility which will enable us to resist the tendency to escalate polar contraries into seductive but extremely destructive polarizations. We need, in other words, a set of habits and sensitivities and practices that will assist us in the continually necessary work of enabling contraries to "interpenetrate and be mutually creative," both in our individual experience and for the life of our city.

Contributing to the recovery and development of such a way of thinking and such sensibility was the goal of Lynch's book and the reason for
its subtitle. For a contemporary "exploration into western thought" should
contribute to a renewal of that "integrating" mind and sensibility which
has been one of the great achievements of western civilization. Lynch also
spoke, as we shall see, of this renewal as the development of an "analogical" habit of mind and sensibility, since the passion for univocal clarity is a
primary manifestation of the totalizing spirit.[8] In the terms of the present
study, then, *The Integrating Mind*, while but one of Lynch's many articula-
tions of the fundamental spirituality and sensibility to which he called us,
is in some ways the clearest in terms of its explicit articulation of that goal.

Self and World

Yet *The Integrating Mind* is not only, nor even primarily, a theoretical book
about responses (totalizing or integrating) to the many contraries which
structure human life in time. It is, rather, primarily a series of essays about
particular issues and arenas in "our contemporary national culture" where
totalizing patterns threaten and integrating responses are much needed.
The theoretical framework about contrariety, totalism, and integration is
articulated almost entirely (and only) in the book's opening chapter and
in its appendix. At this point, then, it will be most helpful to turn to those
particular essays, yet with the caveat that Lynch never attempts a survey of
the totalizing tendencies in our culture. He did, as we will see, return frequently to cases which he thought of fundamental importance—such as our
increasingly univocal understanding of freedom and a resulting opposition
to most forms of limitation, our related fear of passivity or receptivity and a
consequent national obsession with activity, and, perhaps most fundamentally, our increasingly privatized sense of self and a resulting loss of connection with the other of society and world.[9] More typically, though, he simply
refers to instances of the totalizing disease which are central to the topic at
hand. His goal was never an exhaustive analysis, but enough analysis to help
us begin to see the presence and danger of the disease and to understand
our need for a healing spirit and sensibility.

In *The Integrating Mind* such analysis begins already in the first chapter where, in explaining the totalistic temptation and its integrating alternative, Lynch makes "a few remarks" about "the interpenetrating relationship

---

8. See 55–62 (where Lynch even speaks of "the spirituality of the univocal man")
and 111–20.

9. This latter polarization is also a fundamental theme in *Images of Hope*.

between authority and freedom" (13), and about "our usual understanding" which sees freedom and authority as "external" to each other and thus as opposed—one the great inner desire of the person, the other the external "policeman or disciplinarian who sees to it that freedom does not overstep its bounds . . ." (13). Yet however often we experience such opposition, the deeper and more real structure of the relationship of freedom and authority is quite different. For whatever the many analogous forms in which we experience the contraries of freedom and authority (such as freedom and limit, self and other, or self and world), we are always dealing fundamentally with a both-and situation where we must learn to understand and to live into an interpenetration that is mutually-creative—authority giving actuality and substance to freedom, and freedom giving meaning and purpose to authority. Indeed Lynch says that "this is the most difficult of our interpenetrating contrarieties: to think that autonomy must come from authority, the inside from the outside" (14). Nor is this just a paradoxical assertion on Lynch's part. It is, rather, an argument that he makes throughout his book, most explicitly in what is probably best understood as the book's central or pivotal chapter: "The Problem of Freedom" (63–96). Before coming to that argument, however, let us watch this "most difficult of our interpenetrating contrarieties" take on a series of different but related forms in the essays of Lynch's book.

He provides what is probably his most general formulation of this fundamental contrariety in the book's final chapter, "Theology and Human Sensibility" (131–46). There his primary concern is to argue against a pervasive misunderstanding of both theology and art—the view which sees theology and art as essentially concerned with private and transcendental or imaginative things (in the pejorative sense of all those terms) in contrast to the "hard-nosed" and "realistic" mindset of business and commercial interests. Lynch turns this view on its head, arguing that it is precisely an over-reaching and today pervasive commercial mentality which, by falsely claiming that it really knows what humanity wants and needs, distorts the purpose of art, reducing it to entertainment or merely aesthetic experience, and simultaneously sidelines the significance of theology, reducing it to the sphere of privacy and merely personal preference. Yet in fact the primary purpose of both art and theology is to enable us to move more and more deeply and widely into contact with what is real—with the real world where we live and breathe and where alone our actual self and real freedom can develop. For the greatest need of human beings is to be in contact with (in touch with, connected to) the real world. "Of all the things we need," Lynch had said in his "East River" essay, "we need a world."[10] For self and world are the most fundamental contrariety governing our lives. They are poles of relationship and not of separation.

Earlier in *The Integrating Mind*, Lynch had argued that "human beings are on every level so essentially tactile that they have to reach out for the touch of something" (22). The human being is "a tactile creature who suffers to the degree that he is not in touch with the reality of himself and things and others . . . " (18). Later, in "Theology and Human Sensibility," he puts the matter this way: "the very deepest need the people have is the need for closeness to, union with, things and persons and God" (134). "Everybody knows, when it is put in his language, that real solitude is hell and that unity is peace" (135). "Let this be my growing theme," he later adds, "that what we need is reality and we cannot live without it" (140). Both theology and art are, each in its own way, responses to that need for contact and connection or union:

> It is the passionate vocation of theology, or religion[,] and art, real art, to satisfy, each in its own way, this tremendous need by putting men in touch with things and people and God. Theology and art are always searching for reality and always using different techniques to *uncover* it so we may be in touch with it. But the commercial instinct, as such, is not concerned professionally with reality, and its major instinct, as we know it in our day, is to *cover it up*. (135)

In *Christ and Apollo*, Lynch employs a biblical metaphor to refer to "real being outside of and real being inside the human person" as "the two pearls without price" (xiii). Here in *The Integrating Mind* he emphasizes that "we have to be close to ourselves, to have real self-identity, not to lose the taste of our own soul which is the pearl without price" (135). Yet the point of his entire argument in *The Integrating Mind* is that "the taste of our own soul" is only received in a growing contact and interpenetration of self and other, self and world, and ultimately (but with no steps skipped, no sudden leaping to transcendence) of self and God.

Thus one of the constant themes woven throughout the essays of *The Integrating Mind* is a critique of the many forms of privatization which tempt us with an increasingly totalized vision of solitary independence and freedom—a sense of self and freedom gained by many forms of withdrawal or separation from the world.[11] The goal of "Towards a Theater of Public

10. Lynch, "Me," 3. See p. 25 above.

11. The key word here is "totalized" since the experience of solitude is clearly a necessary component of an integrating sensibility.

Action" (121–30) is first to argue that our better or more serious theater has taken on an increasingly narrow and at times almost univocal focus on various inner or psychological explorations of the self. Lynch mentions not only Eugene O'Neill and Arthur Miller as examples of this tendency, but cites approvingly a description of Tennessee Williams as "the most typically 'internal' of contemporary American dramatists" (125–26).[12] Of course, exploration of the self should be a crucial part of the vocation of the artist (as of the theologian), and it is perhaps especially central to the vocation of the modern artist to put us in touch with the reality of the self. Yet, and this is the second part of Lynch's argument, a too-narrow, too univocal focus on the self finally becomes self-defeating. "For it is not possible ever to penetrate the private and the personal if we limit responses to the latter and do not see, as Dante did, the great analogies of the personal interior life on the levels of history, the social, the political, and the theological" (126).[13]

A few pages later Lynch refers not to Dante but to Plato and to the famous analogy employed in the *Republic* between the self (of the just man) and "the self writ-large" in the justice or injustice of the *polis*—in human society and the city. Lynch's point with both references, and with similar discussion elsewhere,[14] is not simply that there are many fundamental analogies (similarities within differences) between self and society, nor only that the self cannot be understood and cannot understand itself without continual reference to that larger image of the human. Rather his basic point is that the self cannot become itself, cannot develop and be educated and grow in breadth and depth, without continual interaction with the analogous human realities of family, society, language, and culture. "Of all things we need, we need a world." Absent a world, or with the increasingly thin and narrowed range of reference to the world in our modern theater, or especially with the kind of gnostic hatred of the world which we too often find in modern artistic sensibilities,[15] we end with an increasingly superficial and impoverished sense of the self.

Lynch makes a similar argument in his book's second chapter ("The American Adam") which analyzes our culture's tendency to reject or forget the past in almost every sphere of individual and social life. He notes what

12. Lynch references "an article in the *Swanee Review* by Henry Popkin" without giving volume or date.

13. In this book's next chapter (see pp. 109–10), we will see that Lynch makes an extended critique of *Equus* around precisely this point.

14. See especially the extended discussion of analogy earlier in *The Integrating Mind* (108–119) and in chapters 5 and 6 of *Christ and Apollo*. See also pp. 84–89 below.

15. Chapter 4 below provides an extensive discussion of such contemporary "Gnosticism."

many have noted, the obsession with change and novelty, and the corresponding lack of deep-rootedness so characteristic of life in the U.S.

> Is it not true [he asks] . . . that there has been a fantasy demand
> in the American air since the beginning of our history—a de-
> mand that we stand on our own in space, *without an essential
> sense of touch with history*, in a way and to a degree never or
> seldom placed so demandingly on a culture before? (24)

This question does not lead Lynch to deny the many goods in individual as
well as social and political life which have arisen from our cultural openness
to change, our determination to break with ancient tyrannies and taboos
and to try new things. Yet at some point, in fact at many points and in varying degrees, our constant and too totalized focus on the future becomes
a growing and dangerous loss of contact with the past. Lynch is here especially concerned with the gradual erosion of habits and practices and
forms of life which have sustained generations. Such erosion results from
our single-minded preoccupation with the future and our corresponding
lack of respect for and attention to what we have received from the past. Yet
however gradual its workings, this preoccupation constitutes a "totalizing"
failure to live within the contrary structure of human time. Past and future
are experienced not as interpenetrating contraries, but as antitheses because
we see ourselves, even if implicitly or at times reluctantly, as starting afresh
in a new land, set on a course of discovery and enterprise, action and success, and thus "totalistically" focused on the future.

We seek ever to be born again, as new as Adam, free from the evils
and restraints of the past. And this totalizing obsession is simply one of
the more pervasive and destructive forms of our fear of being passive and
receptive, of being open to authority and shaped by tradition. It exemplifies the still broader tendency to seek a new self by separation from the
already extant world. Yet the temporal contrariety of past and future (or
continuity and change, tradition and development, receptivity and activity)
is not so easily escaped. This tendency of the "American Adam" to "totally"
embrace novelty and progress, to exalt the freedom of enterprise and adventure, leaves him increasingly rootless and unconcerned about (indeed
largely unaware of) his need for continuity. It is a self-defeating tendency
for it finds our Adam with little sense of how to move sensibly and seriously
into the future and thus very susceptible to simplistic and conformist and
finally enslaving seductions. Conformist responses, in other words, become
almost inevitable on the part of those, not only the young, who have fewer
and fewer communal roots and customs, fewer and fewer shared aspirations
and restraints to guide them. They are, then, pushed by a deep need to keep

up with "the latest" and, on a related but far more serious level, by seductively simplistic ideological "solutions" (whether left or right) to our most serious and complex problems. Ironically, then, this passion for "freedom" from the past leads to the diminishment of actual freedoms, to a growing sense of isolation and the spread of artificial and stifling forms of externally imposed patterns which replace the internally appropriated habits of a free people. That, at least, is Lynch's critique of "the American Adam's" failure to be adequately sensitive to and responsive to the many forms of the fundamental temporal contrariety of past and future. It is another instance of the dangerous illusion of seeking one's identity by separating from the world.

The Intellectuals and the People

We tend, I suspect, to think of contraries in fairly abstract terms. That would seem to be true of the examples we have been discussing: freedom and authority, self and world, past and future. Yet we know that such contraries shape actual experience and the actualities of history. Thus it should come as no great surprise that one of the situations of contrariety that receives great attention in *The Integrating Mind*—and is again taken up in Lynch's later books—involves the fact that social classes often stand as contraries to each other in the life of the human city. In discussing this kind of embodied contrariety, Lynch did not focus on those classes (such as labor and capital) often discussed in political and economic analysis. Rather he was most concerned with growing polarization between the two cultural classes of "the intellectuals" and "the people." In later books he also speaks of them as "the artists and writers" and "the middle class."[16]

Put simply, Lynch's judgment, both philosophical and historical, is that there is (in the nature of things) and should be (in actual practice) both a

16. See further discussion of the "artists and intellectuals" below: Chapter 4 (passim) and pp. 171–74. Lynch did not intend to write a systematic analysis of "culture classes," nor did his writing ever fully clarify what he meant by "the middle class." He seems to have meant both blue and white-collar workers, including various professionals and managers—the vast majority of the people, for instance, who lived and worked in his beloved New York. Yet he also, as already noted, identified another group whom he calls "the culture engineers of our mass media" (132), "the engineers and exploiters" (133), and "the business and commercial mind" (137). It is clear to me that he was not "against" business and commerce, media and advertising. Rather he was fiercely opposed to those *elements* or *mentalities* in business and media which arrogantly pretended that they alone understood the real desires of the people and did not hesitate to use all their power and technique to manipulate people. When real intellectual leadership abdicates its responsibility by withdrawing from the people, these are the forces that rush into the resulting vacuum.

clear differentiation and yet an integrating relationship of mutual support between society's intellectual elites (artists, especially dramatic artists, writers of literature and serious commentary, some university people, important religious leaders as well as some civic and political leaders) and the larger body of "ordinary" people (whether white-collar professionals and managers or blue-collar workers). In fact he does not hesitate to speak of this relationship of cultural classes as "the relation between the Body and the Mind of society" (43–44). (We need to remember what respect Lynch had for the ordinary and for the body!) Yet his further judgment was that today, in our country, this fundamental contrariety has become increasingly polarized—the "Mind and Body" of society alienated from each other, filled with mutual distrust and even at times with hatred. *This* polarization of society's major cultural groups is, moreover, not simply another example of "the divisiveness produced by the philosophy of the clear idea." Rather it is "far more fundamental" than many other instances of the totalizing spirit since it "perhaps lies at the root of many of them" (45).

Lynch was, then, especially concerned to warn us about the danger of this division of culture classes and to work for recovery of a spirit of basic trust and mutual interaction between the mind and body of society. He was not naïve. Conflict between such culture classes is probably inevitable and quite often necessary and good. Yet *fundamental* alienation between such groups threatens to undermine the foundations of the human city. "I am thinking," Lynch says at one point in *The Integrating Mind*, "of the existence of two widely separated cultures among us, the intellectual and the popular culture, and the now long standing abyss that exists between society and those we might call the intellectuals" (45).

> As a matter of fact there *is* such a division of culture today. We are faced, and have for most of this century been faced, with the existence of two cultures in this land, the one diametrically opposed to the other and the two facing each other with something that resembles hostility . . . The one, the culture of the few . . . The other, the culture of the masses . . . Never, at any rate, has there been such an abysmal gap between the many and those who by vocation should be its creative and imaginative leaders. The two groups, like two armed factions, look upon each other with great mutual distrust. (46)[17]

17. Later he will say even more strongly: "We are in the middle of a vast cultural crisis and division. The real war is at home. It takes the form . . . of a complete collapse of faith between the two cultural groups that constitute the nation: the intellectuals and the middle class . . . [T]he lack of belief is intensified by a mutual contempt and fear such as has not often existed between two national groups in modern history" (IF, 66).

Again, these two groups are and should be really different in their cultures and their roles in society, yet they ought nonetheless to be somehow united or one. For they not only share a common humanity, but participate together, though each in its own way, in building the common life of the city. To do so, they need each other (as do body and mind) and must find many ways of being together—of interpenetrating and being mutually creative—even as they remain different. The intellectuals (Lynch's primary concern) have special need of regular and sympathetic contact with the life of the people because "it is impossible to find truth outside the human community" (102). Yet at the same time it is their vocation to be "creative and imaginative leaders," for "the central tradition of the intelligence in human society should be that of a kind of natural priesthood of light, communicating light and guidance to the people, leading the people and not itself to the heights of freedom and truth" (47).[18]

Yet today, albeit with notable exceptions, "the central tradition of many of our thinkers, writers, and university people" (47) can be "summed up by the well-worn word 'alienation'" (46)—alienation from society and from the life and culture of the people, an alienation frequently expressed by deep contempt for that vast "wasteland." There may, of course, be very good reasons for the intellectuals' critique of modern society. Articulating that critique forcefully and even fiercely is an essential part of their vocation. Yet when "the intellectual . . . begins to enjoy the subtle pleasures of his alienation [and] begins to turn the tragic *incident* of his isolation into a *metaphysical* value" (98), then something seriously wrong (both for the intellectuals and for the people) has occurred. Rather than being one of the major sources for an integrating spirituality, the intellectuals have themselves been seduced by the totalizing temptation. They withdraw to the purity of some higher realm, whether of art or thought or even "true" religion. Or, in rage at "the way things are," they allow their intelligence and sensibility to be reduced to some form of narrow ideological passion which wants to totally remake the city in its own image and likeness. And in reaction "the people" develop—typically with the encouragement of narrowly partisan interests—a deep disdain for intellectual life and for the "effete snobbery" of intellectual and artistic elites.[19]

The tragedy and danger of this situation is that both high and popular culture have, each in its own way, been seduced and distorted by totalizing tendencies. Their mutual distrust and polarizing contempt is perhaps the

18. Lynch's direct remarks to "the few" (48–50) about their responsibility for "the many" are well worth a number of readings.

19. It was, of course, Spiro Agnew, Richard Nixon's Vice President, who famously castigated "effete intellectual snobs." They, of course, returned the favor.

clearest sign of this seduction, the clearest manifestation in each of the reign of univocal thought and totalizing passion. And, as Lynch has said, this polarization "perhaps lies at the root" of many others.

What we need, then, is a recovery of mutual trust and fundamental confidence and thus a "good taste" of our shared world. Clearly each of us bears responsibility for that recovery. Thus the people bear such responsibility in their struggle for decent forms of family life and human work, and in the forms of art and culture, politics and religion to which they give their attention and support.[20] Yet Lynch held to the classical belief that intellectuals bore a special responsibility for such recovery and for the development of our society's "body of faith" and mutual trust. They were the readers he addressed and he continually challenged their at least to some extent self-imposed alienation. He called them to once again "enter the city" and take up their traditional vocation of leadership for the good of the people—to help the people, to take but one example, achieve deeper and more realistic understandings of freedom.

Freedom and Limitation

The people need such assistance because the development of integrating habits of mind and spirit is never quick, easy, or final. It is an ongoing task that requires at least "as much passion and strength" as the pseudo-magnificent totalizing spirit, but "a different passion and a different strength" (5). For, let us say it clearly, an integrating sensibility and practice is not something that is easy to understand. As the mutual interpenetration of real contraries, "contrariety" is precisely *not* a matter of clear and distinct ideas or actions. Rather, Lynch says, it constitutes a kind of "natural mystery" (67), especially for "the pure and logical intelligence" (76). "Only the doing, only the actual entering into the narrow real, will [finally] flood the whole intelligence, the whole being of man, with the light that two such disparate things can come together in one embrace" (76).

Yet some approach to understanding this "natural mystery" is both needed and possible, and we have already come some way with Lynch by understanding the contrast continually implied in his criticism of different contemporary manifestations of the totalizing spirit. Indeed, a critical awareness of totalizing tendencies and the developed ability to discern their presence in our lives is already a key component of the sensibility which we need. Thus the critical arguments and judgments of our "artists and

---

20. See, for instance, Lynch's direct remarks to "the many" (50–51).

writers"—Lynch not least among them—provide significant assistance for the life of the human city.

Let us now take a further step with him in understanding this "mystery" of contrariety by returning to the fundamental "problem of freedom" in order to see, in a series of examples, how real freedom, in contrast to various fantasies, is attained only in an ongoing encounter with many contrary forms of limit or law. Hopefully, by moving through some elements of Lynch's pivotal discussion of "this most difficult of our interpenetrating contrarieties" (14), we will also move beyond the simple assertion that we need integrating habits of mind and spirit, and towards a greater understanding of the reality of contrariety—of the fact that "many contraries . . . are mutually creative of each other and cannot live without each other" (v).

Lynch opens his discussion of "The Problem of Freedom" (63–96) by affirming, against the continual suspicion that Christianity (and especially Catholicism) is opposed to freedom, that freedom is a great human good, in some ways *the* great good. For freedom finally means the reality of self-possession, or what Lynch again refers to as that "good taste of oneself" which is the inheritance of the children of God.[21] So he does not hesitate to say:

> With all its heart *every* human heart wishes to be free, without
> let or hindrance of any kind, without obstacle, without limit,
> with fullness, abundance, and a total passion . . . Why should we
> in the least question this feeling? (65)

Thus the Christian (even the Catholic) "can share, and more than share, in *every human and secular operation in the modern world which moves towards individual, social, cultural or political freedom*" (65–66, emphasis added).[22]

Yet the real "problem of freedom" is not about the goal of freedom, but the far more difficult question of *how, in our actual lives and in the life of our city, we move to attain real freedom*—how, in other words, we understand the relation of freedom to the contrary reality of limitation. In response to this question, integrating and totalizing sensibilities are deeply opposed. Whatever its many forms, freedom "is always a kind of unbounded infinite and always involves a feeling of non-limitation" (67). Yet human

---

21. See 135 ("the need we have . . . to have real self-identity, not to lose the taste of our own soul which is the pearl without price") and also 142 ("the pearl without price, his own soul") and 72 ("the having, the feeling, the possession of the self, the *unum necessarium*, the one thing necessary"). As we will see below, in Chapter 6, achieving this "good taste of oneself" is the overarching goal of *Images of Hope*.

22. This is, I might add, a truly stirring affirmation even today. How much more so for the Catholic world when it was written!

freedom also always, inescapably, finds itself within a context of finitude and limitation, whether that limitation be a form of law or community or simply the very definite and particular limitedness of one's own existence. The integrating approach to such contraries, as we will soon see, involves understanding that the great good of freedom is attained only by the actual movement of life into those forms of limitation so that, in the end, freedom and limitation do not stand external and opposed to one another, but internal to and mutually creative of each other. Yet such an approach to freedom is not only difficult to understand but quite difficult to realize in actual life. Thus there is a constant temptation towards a simpler and more "pure" idea of freedom and of the path to freedom, no matter how fantastic or unreal.

It is perhaps sufficient simply to assert again that many, perhaps most, of our culturally dominant images and understandings of freedom tend to support that temptation—tend towards a totalizing emphasis on freedom *from* various forms of restraint or limit. Examples abound. And it is important to recognize that there are often very good historical reasons for that emphasis since so many of our modern freedoms did have to be won by opposition to outmoded or arbitrary and despotic forms of restraint. Yet it remains nonetheless true that we are generally not well served by such univocal images.

Let me, then, before turning to Lynch's examples of a more integrating understanding of freedom, provide just one of his examples of a pervasive totalizing misunderstanding and temptation. This example initially may sound odd, almost comic, though in fact it is deadly serious and in many ways fundamental to most of our dominant but deceptive images of freedom. It is the temptation to try to become free (to become ourselves!) by somehow leaping outside of ourselves. "Everything in us," Lynch says, "is specific and unique, our own and no others . . . [W]e are *only* ourselves and not everything else . . . [We are] bounded, limited, contained, determined to be one thing, and therefore not free" (72–73). Yet, again, along with such definiteness and limitation, "there is a second principle in us which is in some way the exact antithesis . . . something in us which wishes to be without bounds . . . some incredible will in us not to be something but *to be everything*" (73). So we "try to create some specious world in which to live and walk *outside of ourselves* . . . " (74, emphasis added). The limited reality of myself—or, in the case of some group, *our* specific actuality—becomes *the* problem, the cause of my (our) unhappiness and lack of freedom. To be free we must break from ourselves, leap out of our skins, be born again.

Of course, with the idea of being "born again" we begin to see just how prevalent this temptation is. For while there are important senses in which we must, indeed, struggle against ourselves (against vice and lethargy, prejudice and ignorance) and so be "born again," a totalizing mentality and imagination absolutizes this process. The self—the old self, the old way, this body, this family, this religion, this country, "this filthy, rotten system"—becomes *the* problem, *the* enemy. It is to be hated and vanquished, or totally remade by some kind of total conversion or revolution.

Nor is it just the adolescent or the mentally ill who hunger for such a total leap to freedom "outside of ourselves." As Lynch's discussion of the plays of O'Neill has already suggested,[23] our literature and theater, our films and popular culture, are rife both with such loathing of the actual self and its world, and also with romantic fantasies of total rebirth. Any number of celebrated films spring to mind: *2001: A Space Odyssey, Blade Runner, Thelma and Louise, Dances With Wolves, American Beauty, The Matrix.* The list goes on and on, and I am sure the reader can add many examples. How many, moreover, of our actual moral and political crusades (whether of the left or the right) bear the marks of this particular totalizing temptation. Not only do they frequently attract devotees who seek total release from the banality or the perceived evil of their actual selves, but their simplistic sloganeering continually reinforces this polarized sense of the demonic old order and the magnificent new alternative.

We have already seen how Lynch's analysis of "The American Adam" provides further instances of the pervasiveness of this simplistic understanding of freedom. So too is his discussion of the temptation of our "artists and intellectuals" to withdraw from the community of "ordinary people" into enclaves of artistic or academic freedom. Yet in all cases the seductive appeal of being "born again" or "free from the past" or "free from censorship" contains, at very least, the seeds of a totalism which aborts the actual development of real forms of human freedom. Here is how Lynch himself puts the matter:

> [A]s neither beauty, nor peace, nor God can be achieved save by a march through the concrete and the limited, the same thing is true of the . . . march to freedom. It is to be reached only through the finite, through facts, through limited facts, through the limits of moment after moment of time . . . (66)

And again:

> [O]nly in action, in the real taking up of the first principle (of limit, of Law) by the second principle (of boundlessness, of freedom) can the second really see itself in this moment as really

---

23. See p. 33 above.

born and changed from a purely speculative possibility to an
order of fact. (76)

The fact that we both achieve and come to understand this integration
of contraries only through action and experience may also help to explain
the importance for us of the dramatic imagination. For a well-wrought story
of human growth into freedom provides us with analogies to our own experience that we only come to real freedom and to a realistic understanding
of such freedom in the actual passage "through the finite, through limited
facts, through the limits of moment after moment of time". One instance
of that passage was suggested just above. The self can come to itself, to the
fundamental freedom of self-possession and a "good taste of the self," not
by any essentially impossible forms of leaping "outside of itself," but only by
entering into and moving within the actual contours of its own always limited and definite actuality. Many great novels and plays and films about self-
realization—the story of Alyosha in Dostoyevsky's *The Brothers Karamazov*
comes to mind[24]—help us to understand this realistic and "integrating" approach to the freedom of self-possession. They also help us remember and
recognize the perhaps more "ordinary" passages of our own lives toward
those forms of the freedom of self-possession which we may actually have
attained.

Yet the memory and imagining of such "passages" also helps us understand that the basic interior freedom of self-possession is never attained
without corresponding forms of "exterior" freedom that grow through our
movement into relation with "the other" of the world and (at whatever level
of awareness) with God. For we are, as we have heard Lynch argue, "tactile
creature[s] who suffer to the degree that [we are] not in touch with the reality of [ourselves] and things and others . . . " (18). "[T]he very deepest need
[we] have is the need for closeness to, union with, things and persons and
God" (134). It is by the movement of our lives into growing and deepening
connection with the definite *and limiting* actualities of "the other" that we
come to confidence and responsibility and the many other forms of real
freedom which characterize human life.

Think again of Lynch's discussion (in "The American Adam") of our
need to be "in touch" with the past. Without the benefit of many received
forms of life we grow in anxiety and in subjection to many externally imposed conformities. Of course "received forms" of custom and culture can
also be externally imposed conformities that suppress freedom. That they
regularly do so is, in fact, a platitude of our received wisdom and part of

24. I think of Alyosha perhaps because of Lynch's beautiful discussion of him at
the beginning of *Christ and Apollo*, 18–27.

the mythology of "the American Adam." Yet Lynch thought that the opposite was in fact more fundamentally true. Traditional forms of culture have themselves grown and changed over time, typically through the often-difficult, yet just as often fruitful interaction (or interpenetration) of the contraries of future and past, freedom and limit, individual and community. Lynch mentions, as one example, what he calls a "class," by which he means a pattern of thought and behavior which is "a long product of history and nature, the careful articulation of a group or an idea or a profession or vocation" (27). Such a class typically grows and changes *through* time and, ideally, through the *free, internal* appropriation (often after difficult struggles) of those who remain in some form of touch with its history and roots. The same can be said, in a much more generalized way, of all forms of tradition and community, whether they be geographic or ethnic, artistic or professional, religious or secular.

Language itself is perhaps the most pervasive and fundamental instance of such "received forms" and a good example of the complex interplay of freedom and limit. As anyone knows who has tried to teach reading or writing, or tried to learn a second language, language stands over-against us as a difficult and very definite limit. It is "other" than ourselves, frustratingly so when we don't know the word or don't know how to use it. And, of course, we know that this "other" mediates for us the many limiting "others" of the world. For the limits of our language really are the limits of our world. Yet we also know from experience that as we appropriate and internalize this limiting otherness of language, our freedom grows—our very self grows, as does the size and shape of our world and our ability to move into it with freedom and competence.

By way of contrast, Lynch refers in *Images of Hope* to George Orwell's description of "Newspeak" in *1984*.[25] The deliberate, gradual, externally manipulated reduction of language results in the growing enslavement of a people. He then, in further contrast, cites Igor Stravinski's experience of the fundamental need for a form of musical "language."[26] For when faced with the seemingly infinite variety of music he might compose, Stravinski has told us that he became paralyzed, trapped, hopeless. What broke the grip of paralysis and restored the freedom to compose was a return to the finite specifics of the language of music—first one note . . . then another . . . in a specific key . . . and so on. It was for Stravinski the very form of finitude that ended entrapment and released freedom. So too with both the ordinary speech of everyday and the refined achievement of the poet. With inevitably

---

25. IH, 65–66.

26. Ibid., 72–74. Lynch cites Stravinski's *Poetics of Music*, 66–69.

specific words, phrases, and sentences, and with definite (even if continually changing) forms and rules, language is always a form of limit and law. Yet it is clear that our very self and its many freedoms grow through internalization of the ability to use the otherness of language in order to move into and through the otherness of our world.

There is, then, a real freedom of openness to the future which typically operates in received forms of life. Such freedom has itself emerged through a complex interpenetration of past and future, memory and hope—through the kind of often difficult interpenetration which is most visible at points of major transition in individual lives or the lives of social groups. And the lives of such individuals and groups, because they operate within such received and shared consensus about many aspects of life, are typically further characterized by (at least) two other important forms of freedom: first, as already noted, by the deeper sense of freedom (that good "taste" of self and world) which arises from basic confidence in one's way of life and from the realistic trust that it is shared by others; and second, by the perhaps more casual, yet equally important sense of spontaneity, of openness to wish and whim, to wanting and doing, that flourishes in such an atmosphere of confidence.[27] Thus language and class and community are all forms of limitation which stand "over against" my freedom. Yet my real freedom grows by being "in touch" with them, by an internal appropriation of their limitation.

Let me note two final examples from Lynch's writings of the integration of freedom and limit—examples which contain the broader suggestion of our need for models and mentors, training and lived practice in the development of an integrating sensibility. In *Images of Hope* and again in *Images of Faith*, following the insights of developmental psychology, Lynch discusses the fundamental importance of the infant's relationship to its parents.[28] It is only through a limiting connection with this other (the parent), through its denials as much as its affirmations, that the primitive self of the infant begins first to emerge and then to develop. While we today take this fact of developmental psychology as obvious, we may not as readily notice that it is *the* most original and crucially important instance of the role of contrariety and limitation in the emergence of real human freedom. The successful development of this child-parent relationship becomes the basis of all such future passage of the self into the world, just as, of course, failings and failure in this relationship are at the root of much later difficulty and inability to grow into the mutually creative interpenetration of self and

27. The crucial importance of wishing for mental and spiritual health is a central theme in *Images of Hope*. Our need for a "body" of everyday trust is central to *Images of Faith*. See also the discussion of desire throughout Chapter 5 below.

28. See IH, 40 and 58, IF, 111–31, and Chapter 5 below.

world. It is our first training in a spirituality of integration, and we rightly understand it as love, both tender and tough.

In *The Integrating Mind*, Lynch comments at length on a related instance of such contrariety which comes later in the human journey—the relation of student and teacher, a relationship surely not limited to schools (76–84). Drawing briefly on Aeschylus, and at greater length on Plato and Ignatius, Lynch stresses how the teacher and the subject matter stand as very real forms of limit and law and discipline over against the student. Yet the growth of the student's freedom, of her ability to engage the world, and the consequent enlargement of both herself and her world, depend upon the successful interior appropriation of that which stands objectively over-against her freedom as a limitation. That process of appropriation or learning, often long and difficult, is greatly facilitated by the teacher's respect and love for the student's freedom. Thus Ignatius commands the director of the *Spiritual Exercises* to leave the retreatant free, to allow "room" for his personal encounter with the Gospel and for the inner freedom of his response. Similarly Socrates' famous method of teaching as a "midwife," by the skillful posing of questions, is predicated on the student's own inner "recollection" of the truth.[29] Before the mystery of the student's inner freedom, Lynch says, "the teacher must surely wish to become an extraordinary mixture of active impulsion and passive forbearance, knowing what is his task and what is none of his business, entering but not taking over, touching the free center, yet leaving the center untouched . . . "(81).

Our own memories of the typically complex and at times dramatic history of our relationships with parents and with various teachers and mentors, as well (again) as much memorable literature about such relationships, may help us to understand "the natural mystery" of the growth of freedom through its lived interpenetration with many forms of limitation. They may also help us more generally to understand the need we have for help—for ongoing education and formation or training, and for a developed "body" of humane culture—in developing, both as individuals and as a society, integrating habits of thought and sensibility. It is a need which is especially great today since so many forms of "the disease of the clear or pure idea . . . reign among us."

Among the many possible sources of such help, Lynch (as we have seen) emphasized the role of society's intellectual leaders, especially the artists and writers whose work shapes not just our significant literature and drama, but the imaginative life of our culture. Thus we need to ask about

29. Regarding the meaning of Plato's ideas on "recollection," Lynch suggests that Plato "is deliberately putting solid truths of the psyche into this strange, mythical form" (79).

the current state of the arts, especially the dramatic arts which depict, or fail to depict, the lived integration of contraries. More fundamentally, of course, we need to ask about the health of our shared images and of our power of imagining. Do our literary and dramatic arts provide us with a form of training in the development of an integrating sensibility? Or have they, too, succumbed to the disease of the pure idea? Are our images and ways of imagining such things as freedom and limit, self and world, and other contraries, are they themselves infected by that disease, or might they be part of the needed cure? Those are the fundamental questions Lynch takes up in the final chapters of *The Integrating Mind*, "Toward a Theater of Public Action" and "Theology and Human Sensibility." He had, of course, already wrestled with them in *The Image Industries* and *Christ and Apollo*, and he would return to them again, years later, in his *Drama of the Mind* project. They are the texts and questions we will take up in our next chapter.

Plato and the Integrating Mind

Yet before moving to that discussion of literature and artistic sensibility, there is one task that remains for the present chapter. As in *The Integrating Mind*, where Lynch placed his formal discussion of Plato in a lengthy appendix, I here "append" a discussion of Plato's significance for Lynch's understanding our need for an integrating mind and spirit. These pages may, then, be understood as a fairly technical recapitulation of what has gone before. They are, however, ridiculously brief and, I fear, quite superficial, especially given both the importance of Plato for Lynch's thinking and the relative difficulty of the ideas involved. Thus at the start I urge the reader who might be interested to turn to Lynch's own discussions of the ideas he took from Plato.[30] (It would also be possible for readers less interested in

30. As noted, the appendix to *The Integrating Mind* (147–81) presents Lynch's own summary of the argument of his book on Plato's *Parmenides*. Yet even that summary assumes a very good background in the thought of Plato and on the set of issues taken up in the *Parmenides*. Both the summary and the book, *An Approach to the Metaphysics of Plato Through the Parmenides*, are notoriously difficult for most of us. Fortunately, we have other places where Lynch himself takes us more gently through the book's argument. See especially CA, 119–22 (on Parmenides), and 140–48 (on Plato). More generally, see the entire argument of CA chapters 5 and 6. See also Lynch's discussion of Plato in his important article "Death," 462–63 and 466, and in IM 107–20. In addition, references to Plato, especially to *The Republic*, are scattered throughout his books (some of which, happily, have indexes). Finally, Lynch's earliest scholarly article was on "Plato and the Absolute State" (1938) and he wrote a short introduction "Plato: Symposium" for a 1951 text on *The Great Books* (16–21). See also Gerald Bednar's *Faith*, 43–119, for an extended commentary on Lynch's ideas about analogy.

Lynch's use of classical philosophy to simply skim through or even skip this final section of the present chapter.)

Lynch had told us in *Christ and Apollo* that Plato was one of his "abiding 'friends' and givers."[31] We have also heard him articulate there the important principle he took from Plato about not moving too quickly from the many to the one.[32] It is a fundamental principle to guide movement *through* the many complexities and contrarieties of life in this world, *through* the "two steps forward and one step back" of life in time, as the only adequate way to move *towards* any real experience of unity, and ultimately to move towards relationship or union with "the One." Thus it is a metaphysical principle about the structure of reality as both many and one, really diverse yet also really unified. It is also an epistemological principle about how we are to live with and integrate the many and the one, our need for real unity with our experience of and need for real diversity.

As noted, at the beginning of *The Integrating Mind* Lynch tells us: "What we need [in combating the totalistic temptation] is an epistemology, a way of thinking, and a corresponding set of helps for the human passions that will match the structure of reality itself" (6).[33] What we need, in other words, is *a philosophy* (or a metaphysics) which helps us to understand *both* that that contrariety is a fundamental reality, a basic structure of finite existence, *and* that unity is also a fundamental reality and a necessary goal of human striving. Consequently, we also need *a corresponding sensibility* or set of habits which will enable us to live fruitfully within the reality of contrariety as we move towards various forms of unity. We need, in other words, both ways of understanding and forms of practice that enable us to connect with or be in touch with reality—ways of integrating self and world (of attaining a good taste both of self and of world) that contrast fundamentally with the separation between self and world that is today characteristic of the experience not only of many intellectuals, but also of many "ordinary" people.

31. CA iv.

32. See above 0, 11 and CA 13, 146.

33. Lynch's use of the term "epistemology" here and elsewhere in *The Integrating Mind* (see, for instance, "The Epistemological Danger," 101–7) may seem a bit strange for those accustomed to think of "epistemology" as a fairly technical branch of philosophy concerned with the nature of knowledge. Lynch's usage extends that meaning to include "a way of thinking, and a corresponding set of helps for the human passions . . ." Thus there is for him an effective equation between "epistemology" and "sensibility" and "spirituality." We can, for example, speak not only of the "epistemology" of empirical science, but also of a "scientific sensibility" and even a "spirituality" of scientific endeavor. And thus of an "epistemology" as well as a sensibility and spirituality for public life, this book's focus.

In discussing this philosophy and its corresponding sensibility, we have thus far focused primarily on Lynch's use of the idea of contrariety. Yet Lynch, as noted above, also spoke regularly about "analogy"—again to refer both to the fundamental structure of reality (a metaphysics of analogy) and to a corresponding sensibility (a habit or an epistemology of analogy). Contrariety and analogy are correlative ideas which he derived primarily from his long study of Plato. Thus early in *The Integrating Mind* he reminds us that "In the case of Plato, the principle document for the study of the [metaphysics of] the interpenetrating contraries was the *Parmenides*; the outstanding document that analyzes [the epistemology of] the integrating process had been the Republic" (9). He clearly draws on both texts in developing his own ideas about contrariety and analogy.

One further suggestion before turning to a brief presentation of those ideas: attempting to imagine the abstract ideas discussed here as embodied in types of persons or forms of life may be of some help for understanding what follows. Lynch, for instance, on occasion speaks about "the univocal man" and the pseudo-magnificence of the "totalizing" leader.[34] At one point he also imagines Socrates as the complete embodiment of an analogical or integrating sensibility.[35] The method is similar to that employed by Kierkegaard in his detailed imagining of aesthetic and ethical and religious forms of life. For the habits of totalism, on the one hand, and those of integration and analogy, on the other, are not just abstractions. Rather they are actual forms of life, patterns of living in the world. Most of us, in differing ways and degrees, can find elements of both tendencies embodied in our own habits and patterns of living. Yet we also know or can imagine (especially with the help of good literature and drama) persons whose lives are dominated by and thus exemplify one or the other of these forms of life.

Now to Lynch's discussion of Plato which begins with Zeno and Parmenides.

Diversity and difference are constant facts of experience. In the history of Western thought, the early Greek philosopher Zeno is identified with that tendency of thought which has emphasized not only the facts of diversity and difference, but their irreducibility because of fundamental antinomies or contraries which always frustrate the attempt to find unity. In Lynch's words, Zeno "finds that, if we accept any kind of principle of multiplicity in being, *then certain oppositions or contrarieties will exist in the same entity*; the like will also be unlike; the one will also be a multiplicity" (54). Thus

34. See, for instance, CA, 114, on "the general spirituality and temperament of the univocal man."

35. Lynch, "Plato," 16.

the experienced fact of "the many" cannot finally be reconciled with a deep desire for unity or a "one."

Since Zeno, this fundamental emphasis on irreducible difference and opposition has found many forms of expression in human life and thought. It is, of course, often a legitimate protest against tyrannical or procrustean tendencies which seek to reduce the beauty and autonomy of many forms of difference into flat and narrow conformities. Yet it can also express another spirit or sensibility—one which deliberately and continually revels in endless difference, in paradox and opposition, and so continually rebels against all attempts to find unity, common ground, or community. Though he gives only brief attention to this tendency, Lynch describes it as "the spirit of the equivocal" for which "difference, and only difference, reigns everywhere" (CA 130). This "equivocal spirit" comes to expression today, for example, in some "postmodernist" critiques of "meta-narrative" and in a corresponding emphasis on endless differences of meaning and interpretation. It comes to far more fundamental expression in the pervasive demand for autonomy, in the many forms of individualism and the seemingly endless concern for difference of style and freedom of expression which permeate our culture. The "spirituality of the equivocal man" is, then, alive among us.[36]

Yet beneath or at the root of even such emphases on individuality and difference, Lynch nonetheless found evidence of the totalistic temptation.[37] We have already seen, for example, how he understood the almost desperate search for an *absolutely* separated or unique sense of self that characterizes much of the modern demand for autonomy as the expression of a totalizing sensibility. It was, moreover, the Greek philosopher Parmenides who, in the history of Western thought, first gave full-blown expression to such totalizing passion. For it was he, Lynch says, "who first discovered the Being of the philosophers," an intuition that "must be calculated among the great moments of human insight" (CA 119). Parmenides' great realization was that everything *is*, all things *are*, and this "is" which characterizes all things is *one and the same being* in all. Things are not simply themselves, in separate, locked in, atomic existence; rather the world is really and finally

---

36. Bellah, *Habits*, remains one of the clearest analyses of the different forms of individualism prevalent in the U.S.

37. Lynch clearly thought the univocal or totalizing spirit the greater danger. Perhaps he saw little need for a developed discussion of the equivocal spirit or personality because of the ironic fact that a truly consistent emphasis on absolute or *total* difference is, finally, simply one more form of the reductionist and totalizing sensibility. Absolute difference, in other words, effectively means (both logically and experientially) flat undifferentiated sameness.

One—not as it appears to ordinary experience but for the mind that is capable of clearly seeing what really is. (CA, 119)

Yet Parmenides great error came from his inability to move beyond a univocal or absolute understanding of this crucial "intuition of Being." For if everything that is "is" in the same way, then there is only absolute Being or (put more precisely) only absolute being and absolute non-being. There is only a fundamental ontological either-or. Any positive or actual sense of non-being is impossible, at least in the important sense of the relative non-being that is *and must be* present in all forms of finitude—in the many forms of difference and change which are inescapable in the world of actual experience; in the experience that this *is not* that, or *is no longer* the same; in the difference between one thing and another, between self and world, between past and future. In the abstract language of the contraries, then, there are for Parmenides (in reality, and despite appearances) no real contraries, no real situation of both-and. There is only the great either-or of being and non-being, each absolute in its way. There is only the one, not the many; only sameness, no real difference; only stability and permanence, no actual time or real change. All experience of difference or change is simply the illusion of appearance.

For many of us this may sound like so much philosophical mumbo-jumbo. Yet it is, Lynch argues, the clearest early manifestation in the realm of thought of that totalizing or univocal tendency which has continually, in many different forms and manifestations, seduced not only thought, but the passions of actual living. For we do—and quite legitimately, even necessarily, both in thought and in life—hunger for clarity, identity, many forms of unity, and finally for complete or ultimate unity. The central question of politics, for instance, concerns what forms of life will enable us to live *together* with real unity of purpose and harmony of practice. The central question of psychology and spirituality, at least in classical terms, concerns the reality of a soul which unifies one's sense of oneself and of one's life. In more modern terms, it is the quest for personal integrity and authenticity. And the central question of religion concerns the ultimate shape of such unity and the path(s) of salvation by which we might participate in it. Yet in all of these realms, whether in politics, psychology, or religion, and in many more, this search for unity is continually shadowed and often made demonic by the totalizing temptation and the univocal passion which would destroy all difference and reduce all unity to a "parmenidean" sameness, or more typically to absolute either-or polarizations.

Lynch's descriptions of the spirituality and passions of "the univocal man" are particularly strong since they were his constant target.[38] He stresses the great appeal and apparent brilliance of univocal thinking and, even more, of univocal passions and of the univocal personality—whether they be found in sweeping generalizations of thought (as in Parmenides' many offspring), in the powerful dynamics of ideological politics or advertising imagery, or in the pseudo-magnificence of the great leader and the Hollywood hero. The univocal is superficially characterized both by sharp clarity and a kind of immense energy, gathering all within its encompassing but totalizing unity. Yet beneath such surface brilliance is a spirit which is deeply reductionist and procrustean, driven more by will than thought, readily resorting to manipulation, exploitation and violence. It wills to organize and control or to eliminate and destroy what it cannot control. Thus it stands opposed to all forms of thought and sensitivity which seek to respect and respond to the complex diversity of the real. Parmenides stands for Lynch as symbolic forefather for all such patterns of thinking, passion, and practice.

The challenge for both thought and life, then, is to find "integrating" forms of understanding and patterns of practice which will enable us to resist such totalizing seductions and which will continually seek the unity we need, at every level or in every dimension of our lives, while at the same time respecting and, indeed, embracing the diversity without which any supposed unity will be a pale, empty, and even deadly thing. We must not, in other words, move too quickly from the many to the one! Put even more broadly, we must find ways of thinking and helps for our passions which will enable us to live within the many contraries that structure our existence. Not simply to live with stoic endurance of their inescapable tension, but to take up the difficult task of realizing in our thinking and our lives, and in our cities, their fruitful interpenetration and mutual creativity.

It was Plato, Lynch tells us, who "provided one of the great beginnings of the exploration of the Western mind" into the challenge to develop such both-and forms of understanding and living, the challenge first posed for thought by the opposition between Zeno and Parmenides.[39]

> Plato set up for us some of the correct and central procedures
> of human thought and some of the fundamental guides to the
> structure of reality. Like any philosopher, he was looking for

38. See above all CA, 113–29, and also IM, passim, but especially 3–4, 10–12, 55–62.

39. Elsewhere Lynch praises the Pythagoreans who "moved to a theory of the constant harmony" of the contraries (IH, 231).

unity, but he did not allow this passion for unity to push him into too hasty a drive from the many to the one. His supreme achievement was to modify, control and discipline the severe rigidity of the Parmenidean divisions between absolute dichotomies. In his own dialogue, the Parmenides, which Hegel called the finest masterpiece of Greek philosophy, his powerful mind wove all the contraries together, so that they were there but inseparably there, creating each other, depending on each other: the one and the many, being and non-being, like and unlike, motion and rest . . . and so on . . . He had made thinking that much more difficult, but he had made it truer. (8–9)

Plato himself only came gradually to such an understanding of the co-existence and interpenetration of the foundational contrariety of the one (Parmenides) and the many (Zeno). His first attempt to reconcile them by means of his theory of ideas still left unity (the idea) and diversity (the facts of experience) external to one another.[40] In time, though, he developed a logic and metaphysics of "participation" whereby he saw that any unity or one "is" only by the participation in its unity of its many constituent elements, and those many elements "are" only because of the "structural and structuralizing principle" of their one (CA, 145). The Parmenides, Lynch argues, gives Plato's fully developed argument for and explanation of this idea of participation.[41]

For Lynch, "analogy" is another broad way of understanding the Platonic notion of participation and thus the idea of contrariety. For the idea of analogy is a way of understanding how the actual structure of contraries (in reality) is such that they are "mutually creative" and "cannot live without each other." The medieval doctrine of "the analogy of being," which developed from Plato and from subsequent wrestling with the fundamental problem set by Zeno and Parmenides, is "a metaphysical explanation of the structure of existence" which, on the one hand, rejects any fundamental separation of beings (whether atomist or nominalist, dualist or idealist or, for that matter, "postmodern"), and, on the other hand, also rejects any form of monism or totalism which eliminates real difference.[42] It posits, rather, a fundamental structure of both real similarity and real difference in all finite existence, such that our discovery of "analogies" between different existents is not simply a matter of loose comparison, but real insight into the basic structure or actuality of things.

40. See CA, 143–44.

41. Again, see the appendix to *The Integrating Mind* for Lynch's condensed and difficult summary of the logic and metaphysics of the *Parmenides*.

42. See CA, 143–52, especially 149–51.

Let me quickly give three kinds of examples of such analogical structuring or metaphysics.

There are real analogies between "things" in the world, between classes of existents (plants and animals, for instance, or human civilizations and animal communities). All such classes are really "the same" insofar as all are actual existents (all "sharing" or participating in real being). All members of each class are also really "the same" since all really "share" or "have" the being of that category (plant or animal or human). Yet each class as a whole and each individual within each class is also really unique and different. Individual persons, to take a fairly easy example, are analogously both one and many. Each person is both unique and yet the same (in being a human person) as every other person. Nor are such sameness and difference separable, as if we could somehow subtract the "shared personness" from the distinct individuality. As persons, we are at once really the same and really different, and this allows us, for example, both to talk about universal human rights and to respect and love unique individuals.

In *Christ and Apollo*, Lynch used this idea of analogy to argue (this is my second example) that a good work of dramatic art is unified not by some clear (and thus separate) idea which is then exemplified by repetition in character after character or plot situation after plot situation. Such "external" unity might be legitimate for allegory, but a great work like the *Oedipus* achieves its unity by the fact that every character and every twist of the plot, while sharply differentiated and in a real sense unique, at the same time contributes to and shares in the unified meaning of the whole. Nor is that unified meaning separable from the many parts, by means, for example, of some plot summary or some abstract statement of "the theme." Rather, one can only really "get" the meaning, come to understand the unity, by staying with and moving through the many parts.[43]

As a final example, let me note, with Lynch, that there are many real analogies between self and world, and these analogies allow for the interpenetration and mutual creativity of self and world. We come to be our actual and unique selves by participating in and growing ever more deeply into the worlds of our family, country, culture, religion, and language. We have above seen this process exemplified in Lynch's analysis of "the problem of freedom" and will soon see it exemplified again in Plato's discussion of education in the *Republic*. There is both a real difference and a real sameness between self and world. Nor is this just loose and perhaps comforting talk. It is, strictly speaking, an ontological fact—a complex fact, but a fact

43. See CA, 155–56, on *Oedipus* and the entire sixth chapter for its discussion of analogy and the literary imagination.

nonetheless, and one that we come to know (at least implicitly) as we grow simultaneously in a good taste of both self and world.

Here, then, is how Lynch at one point describes the metaphysics of the analogy of being:

> [It is] a world where everything is chock-full of its own reality and importance but also able to participate in larger communities of reference; where all things have meaning and transcendent reference and actuality in their own right. (115)

Said differently, this metaphysics is an understanding of the fundamental structure of reality which seeks to account for the expansive diversity that we experience, while at the same time affirming the fundamental unity of all that is. It is, moreover, an understanding that this fundamental unity (of being) is itself comprised of many different and analogous forms of unity. Reality, in other words, is not the flat, everything-is-the-same-One which Parmenides' discovery of Being suggested and which, each after its own fashion, every form of the totalizing spirit hungers for and seeks to impose on the world. But neither is it the equally (and ironically) flat oneness of those who think that everything is purely and simply different. Rather the real is a very complex whole (or unity) of many different kinds of unity, each a whole (or one) realized only in its own diverse "constituent members" (in the diversity of its many).

Yet if something like this complex and analogical "unity of diverse unities" characterizes the structure of reality, then we need habits of mind and spirit which will enable us to understand and live within that reality, habits which lead us not to move too quickly *through* our experience of many actualities towards many forms of unity or oneness. In now speaking about how we might understand and live within the analogous structure of being, we move philosophically from metaphysics to epistemology, and to habits and practices, sensibility and spirituality. And those of us who, to this point, may have had real difficulty with Lynch's discussion of metaphysics may find at least some relief in turning to his discussion of those analogical habits of mind and spirit which prepare us to resist the totalizing temptation and enable us to live in ways that correspond with and respond to the actual structure of reality. For, again, Lynch's goal in writing (other than in his *Parmenides* book) was not to provide any detailed explanation of the Platonic-scholastic metaphysics which he understood to be true, but rather to retrieve and develop, for our times, the forms of practical wisdom which flow from that analysis of the structure of reality.

Lynch, then, calls for the development of a "habit of analogy" (113) as the central form or embodiment of an integrating mind and spirit. He also speaks of an "analogical instinct" and of analogy as a "mentality" and a form of "sensibility," and even calls "the capacity for analogy" a "blessing" (112–15). It is the habit or aptitude for finding real unity (in our lives, in the world, in the life of our city), but only by respecting and moving through and learning from many real differences. Thus it is the habit and aptitude of working to integrate the many differences and contraries of the actual. Obviously, then, the habit of analogy is not just an intellectual method for discovering a certain kind of unity between body and spirit, self and world, individual and society, and so on. Rather it is a fundamental and necessary spiritual "instrument" or aptitude for the work of a lifetime as we seek to realize a complex personal unity in the many diverse experiences and dimensions and stages of our lives.

Yet the achievement of such unity or integration by the ongoing exercise of a habit and sensibility of analogy is not only the work of each individual's life. It is also the educational, cultural and political task of the human city. As an example of this broader social and political exercise of the habit of analogy, Lynch refers more than once to the educational system outlined in the seventh book of Plato's *Republic*. It required the future leaders of the city to learn "all the analogical unities in mathematics, astronomy and the other sciences," to also undergo "a thorough moral and ascetical training," and to gain a complex sense of integration by participation in "the great analogue of human society."[44] Here are some of the quite beautiful words that Lynch had used much earlier in his life to describe the process and goals of such education:

> [T]he ideal will ultimately be a discovery of all the unities in the universe, all its different "stories." Finally . . . philosophy will discover the kinship between these various sciences, will come to see that they all form but one pattern, that there is a single strain sounding throughout this universe. And . . . the perception of this single song of the sciences is the clearest picture we can form of the transcendental Idea of the Good.[45]

Such learning develops an analogical habit of mind and sensibility that enables the student to understand the many complex forms of unity, or of order and integration, achieved by Athenian culture and politics. Perhaps even more significantly, it makes it possible to discern the difference between such forms of order or unity and all univocal or totalizing

44. 118; see also 101, 112 n 2, and 128.
45. Lynch, "Plato," 15.

alternatives. It also prepares the student to then contribute to the ongoing political and cultural task of maintaining and enlarging such integrations.[46]

Yet Lynch was not trying to deify Plato or somehow return to ancient Athens. He refers in similar terms to the earlier "world" of complex analogical unities explored by Homer and to the later, medieval "cosmology and society" which came to expression in *The Divine Comedy*.[47] His point is not that we today should somehow attempt to return to the earlier and simpler worlds of *The Odyssey* or *The Republic* or *The Divine Comedy*. It is, rather, that Homer and Plato and Dante, each in his own way and for his time and place, represented in his great writing a certain epitome of the habit of analogy. For the goal of that form of thinking and living is to "look for a form of order that orders indeed, but leaves reality, every iota of yours and mine, intact—multitudinous, different and free, but together at last" (CA, 108). *The Odyssey* and *The Republic* and *The Divine Comedy* gave expression to such "a form order" that grew from the science and politics, the psychology and theology, and all the "multitudinous, different, and free" aspects of early Greek, Athenian, and Medieval Christian culture. As works of both art and thought, they enabled people of those cultures to learn and grow into the many integrating analogies between self and world. Lynch's point is that we need to learn from such models (and many others) as we today take up the immense challenge of achieving such inclusive or analogical forms of order and unity within the vastly expanded horizons of the modern world.

In making that point, Lynch may seem to have moved a long way from the abstract metaphysical problems wrestled with by Zeno, Parmenides, and Plato. And I, at least, must in the end leave to those more qualified the question of whether he is correct in drawing such personal and political implications from the thought of these earlier poets and philosophers. I assume that he was largely correct and that, rejected or disregarded though it be today, the metaphysics he sketched is also broadly true.[48] What is in any

---

46. Of course the ultimate goal, in the *Republic*, of such an education is not simply practical. Rather the development of such an analogical sensibility will enable the future leader to begin to grasp the fundamental analogy between immanence and transcendence, and so to understand the fundamental "principle of unity and goodness in and behind the universe" (118) which is the ultimate ground of justice.

47. 100.

48. The literary scholar Denis Donoghue is one (among not a few, I suspect) who finds Lynch's ideas about analogy unsatisfactory. See his chapter-long discussion of Lynch's use of analogy in *Adam's Curse*, 69–92. Yet I am more impressed by the fundamental consonance between Lynch's ideas and those developed by his friend and fellow-Jesuit David Toolan in *At Home*, a book about science, religion and the environmental crisis. There Toolan argues that Newtonian science has largely been responsible for the environmental crisis since its fundamental image of the physical world as a

case clear is that he did draw out such implications and that they were the primary concern of his writings.

It is also true, as already noted, that Lynch undertook a serious critical analysis of our own literary arts in order to ask whether we can find in them the kinds of resource provided for earlier times (and still for ours) by Homer and Plato and Dante. It is to that aspect of Lynch's work that we now turn.

---

mechanism created a centuries-long separation and opposition between human and natural worlds—between self and world. Yet contemporary or "post-modern" physics has revealed a more dynamic and living universe, a cosmos where, for all its unpredictability, we humans can again find ourselves at home. Toolan even compares the discoveries of contemporary physics to "the medieval doctrine of the analogy of being" (*At Home,* 179) since they open for us again a universe where many forms of connection or analogy are possible between the human and the cosmos.

4

Apollo–The Dramatic Imagination

W hat is the role of the arts in the development of human sensibility and spirituality? What, especially, is the role of those dramatic arts (theater, cinema, narrative poetry and fiction) which tell the stories of our lives and provide fundamental images of life in the human city? What kind of sensibility and spirituality are in fact at work in the dramatic arts of our culture? Are conflicting sensibilities "at work," so that we live today not only with deeply divided ideas about the role of the arts and of the imagination, but with actual warfare between opposed sensibilities? If so, where do we stand in this cultural war? Where should we stand? What kinds of arts and imagination do we need and how might we support their development? Is it, finally, even thinkable, in times of such artistic diversity and freedom, and of such overwhelmingly secular content, that Christ might contribute to that development, might even be central to it?

Such broad, even daunting questions were ones Lynch addressed throughout his career. From his early doctoral work on Aeschylus, through the "breakthrough" publication of *The Image Industries* and *Christ and Apollo*, to the later years of work on *The Drama of the Mind*,[1] Lynch's concern with the literary and dramatic arts is woven like a bright golden thread through all of his writing. With the classical writers and theorists, he con-

1. See above p. 8, n. 18. The manuscripts in Fordham University Library's Archives indicate that Lynch intended to use fourteen published articles, spanning his entire career, in *The Drama of the Mind*. Eight articles published between 1975 and 1984 were clearly written specifically for the project. For the record and because of their relation to the topic of this chapter, I note those articles here in chronological order: "Euripides' 'Bacchae'" (Summer 1975); "The Imagination of the Drama," (1975/76); "The Task of Enlargement" (Dec. 1976); "A Dramatic Making of the Human" (May 1978); "Foundation Stones for Collaboration between Religion and the Literary Imagination" (June 1979); "The Drama of the Mind" (Fall 1980); "The Life of Faith and Imagination" (March 1982); "Easy Dramatic Lessons" (Spring 1984). "The Drama of the Mind" (1980) provides the best overview of the whole project.

sidered drama the highest of the literary arts since it involved both sight and sound, and (at least in its classical forms) it integrated narrative movement with lyric beauty, the rhythms of action and dance with those of poetry and song. Thus he wrote mostly about theater, both ancient and modern, and about cinema. Yet he also referred regularly to other major achievements of the dramatic imagination such as Dante's *Divine Comedy*, Cervantes' *Don Quixote*, and the novels of Dostoyevsky.[2]

So central is his concern with drama and the literary imagination that many remember him exclusively as a literary critic. "Yes, a critic well-versed in philosophy and theology, but not really a philosopher." Or so I was told by one academic philosopher who knew Lynch. For his part, Lynch would have understood the specialization implied by such a judgment. Yet he would have vigorously opposed the implication that literature and the dramatic imagination are not fundamentally concerned with the same things as philosophy, theology, and even the sciences. He argued constantly against any understanding of the arts and of human imagination which saw them as something separate and somehow special or esoteric, as primarily devoted to some "purely aesthetic" or "imaginative" function. For him, the primary form of imagination is what he called "the realistic imagination," and it is one of our most basic and necessary ways of coming to know and understand what is real. Thus literature, and especially the works of the dramatic imagination, not only can but should be "both cognitive and ontological."[3] In other words, their primary and most central function is "ontological"—to engage what is real—and thus "cognitive"—to enable us to really understand it.[4] "The [dramatic] artist," Lynch said, "carries us rhythmically and by the force of a constructed action right into the heart of reality and not into the heart of a dream" (IM, 141).

Lynch's interest in the dramatic arts, then, was of a piece with his larger project. For he saw us (if I may recapitulate) as swept up in one of the truly momentous periods of transition in human history, threatened by traumas of rapid change and much tempted by flight to fantastic dreams or

2. In what follows I will, simply for reasons of style, use the terms "literary imagination" and "dramatic imagination" interchangeably, with the understanding that Lynch's major interest was drama, but that he did not limit the idea of drama to theater and cinema.

3. This phrase becomes a central refrain in his *Drama of the Mind* articles and is the central theme of that book project. See, for instance, "Foundation Stones," 329–44.

4. Lynch certainly knew that the literary imagination served other purposes. It can play and dream, spin out tall tales of romance, action or adventure, or simply produce beautiful sound and image. These are all legitimate and even important functions of literature. Yet they remain secondary, even though many today believe them to be the primary functions of both art and human imagination.

into totalized causes and so into "absolute and walled cities." He wished to contribute to those fundamental forms of practical wisdom which would both enable us to resist such temptations and to move humanly into the many dimensions of this transition—to build anew the human city within the greatly enlarged horizons of our world. He called for the collaboration of many talents and skills in the development of those habits of mind and spirit required for this task. Yet he always believed that "artists and writers" had an especially important role to play in nurturing the forms of sensibility and spirituality which would carry us "into the heart of reality and not into the heart of a dream."

Mimesis

As we have already seen,[5] Aeschylus and the other classical Greek dramatists had played such a role for Athens during a similar period of momentous change. They have, moreover, continued to play this role for us ever since. For while the functions of literary art in the history of the West have been many, the central tradition of literature, and especially of drama, is most clearly indicated by Aristotle's term "*mimesis*," perhaps best translated (with Eric Auerbach) as "the representation of reality."[6] In this tradition of mimetic or representational realism, the primary role of the literary imagination (as of the human imagination more generally) is to "imagine the real"—which may well mean not only discovering, but also inventing and thereby enlarging the scope of human reality. By seeking, in a variety of genres and styles, to "imitate" or "represent" the reality and action of human life, the artist herself explores and comes to know the real. And her knowing deepens and enlarges our sense of the real. Even more, she helps us develop the habits and sensitivities that enable us, in our turn, to resist temptations to flight or retreat, and to take up the task of building fuller and more human lives. Thus by imagining stories of human life—by plot and character, by the rhythms of word and action, and at times by song and dance—the dramatic arts can nurture and develop the many "analogies of action" which sustain our efforts, as individuals and as societies, to move fruitfully into ever larger and more real worlds of fact and meaning.[7]

5. See pp. 41–46 above.

6. Lynch referred frequently to Auerbach's immensely important study *Mimesis: The Representation of Reality in Western Literature* in support of his understanding of the centrality of the "realistic" or "mimetic" function of literature. He correctly notes that it "remains one of the classics of modern criticism" (IF, 94).

7. The term "analogy of action" is taken from Fergusson, *The Idea of a Theater*,

Already in 1939, in only his second published article, Lynch had given clear expression to this understanding of literary realism. "Art," he there says (and he is speaking primarily of the literary arts), "concerns itself with an object," and the human soul "only discovers itself by the growth of the object it knows . . ."[8] Thus the goal of all education, but especially of education in the arts, is to develop the human capacity for attention to objective realities. In a subsequent article that same year he spoke specifically of poetry's ability "to shock the mind into seeing something" and thus to contribute to the "slow building up of the power of admiration and love."[9] Yet art can thus educate and enlarge the human spirit only because "the mood with which it approaches the world [is] not the transcendental gesture of contempt for things; nor is it weary of this world. Rather its enthusiasm is a natural declaration of faith in the value of things, of matter, of the perfect imposition of form."[10]

In many ways those two fundamental ideas—the artist's "natural declaration of faith in the value of things, of matter," as well as her struggle to achieve "the perfect imposition of form" to re-present those realities—are an apt summary of the foundations of the tradition of representational realism. For in that tradition, the primary vocation of the artist is grounded in this "natural declaration of faith" or confidence in the things and human realities of this world. And that vocation is exercised in the continual search for "the perfect imposition of form" as an expression of that faith.

For Lynch, once again, Aeschylus stood at the beginning, as the first great figure in this tradition of literary realism. Yet Christ stands at its center. That, of course, is the meaning of the title of *Christ and Apollo*. As the book's "Introduction" explains, Lynch takes "the symbol of Apollo as a kind of infinite dream over against Christ who was full of definiteness and actuality . . ." (CA, xii).[11]

> Even if a little unjustly, let Apollo stand . . . for that kind of fantasy beauty which is a sort of infinite, which is easily gotten everywhere . . . On the other hand, I mean Christ to stand for the

---

another of the major sources on which Lynch drew.

8. Lynch, "Art," 77–78.

9. Lynch, "Value," 328.

10. Lynch, "Art," 80.

11. As noted previously, there is a two-page difference in pagination for prefatory materials (*but only there*) between the 1975 University of Notre Dame Press edition of *Christ and Apollo* which is cited here and the original 1960 Sheed and Ward edition (where the present reference would be to page xiv). Because of the assumption of its greater availability, the UNDP edition (which remained in print well into the 1990s) is regularly cited in the present work.

> completely definite, for the Man who, in taking on our human nature (as the artist must) took on every inch of it (save sin) in all its density, and Who so obviously did not march too quickly or too glibly to beauty, the infinite, the dream. I take Him, secondly, as the model and source of that energy and courage we again need to enter the finite as the only creative and generative source of beauty. (CA, xii)

This assertion of Christ's centrality to the Western tradition of literary realism is, for Lynch, both theological and historical. Theologically, of course, the real, historical Christ of the Gospels (and of Ignatius' *Exercises*) is the absolutely central figure of the entire human drama and the ultimate ground for belief that goodness and beauty are found, in art as in life, not by flight from history into some dream, but by moving "incarnationally" into all the definite actualities of matter and time. Yet this is not only a matter of Christian belief. Rather such belief has borne tremendous fruit in the actual history of our literature. For, and this is fundamental to the argument of Auerbach's *Mimesis*, the realistic tradition of Western literature grew not only from the heritage of Greek theater, but even more from the narrative realism of the Bible. Said differently, it was the stories of the Bible, with their continual focus on actual and often quite ordinary people and situations, and above all the sharply and realistically focused story of Christ in the Gospels, that in fact have given a primarily realistic or mimetic focus and direction to the development of Western literature over the past two millennia.

Lynch, then, in all of his writings about literature and cinema, called for a recovery of this central literary tradition so that "the artists and writers" might again play their crucial role in the development of those forms of sensibility and spirituality which we so greatly need. He called, in other words, for "Christ" to again come to the assistance of "Apollo."

Apollo

For the sad reality today is that "Apollo" has more and more become devoted to "a kind of infinite dream," to "that kind of fantasy beauty which is easily gotten everywhere." Such, at least, was Lynch's overall judgment of the state of our dramatic arts—a judgment spelled out in detail for cinema and popular culture in *The Image Industries*, and for the literary forms of high culture in *Christ and Apollo*. Instead of serving our great need for those strong and realistic habits of thought and imagination which might help us to move into the new realities of our times, the arts, at least the dramatic arts, have generally succumbed to their own forms of the totalistic temptation. They have, in the term Lynch first employs in *Christ and Apollo,* become increasingly "gnostic,"[12] turning in contempt from the perceived wasteland of the world and seeking refuge either in some romantic or aesthetic haven, or in some ideologically pure "walled city" of separation from the mainstream of the human city.

Thus our dramatic arts both express and contribute to a pervasive sensibility which has not only lost touch with (or is alienated from) the shapes and rhythms of ordinary human life, but more fundamentally has lost confidence in such actuality. Our literature and cinema, even (perhaps especially) that which prides itself on being most realistic and worldly, is shown by Lynch's probing to be captive either to various forms of contempt for the world and time, or enchanted by the dreamy appeal of visions of romantic transcendence and by the pseudo-depth of various forms of aesthetic intensity, and often by all these forms of escape from the actual. Nor is it simply contemporary works of the dramatic imagination which are thus held captive. For contemporary *theories* about the nature of the literary imagination so emphasize the utter autonomy of the literary work that they too effectively serve "as masks to avoid the question of that true and fundamental relevancy of the literary organism to reality" (CA, 10).

Of course I need to be careful here, lest by brief summary I turn Lynch himself into a totalizing, either-or thinker. He clearly knew that "the current state of our literature and cinema" was complex, not a matter of simple black and white. He found much to admire, much indeed that itself constituted a critique of the world-hating and world-escaping tendencies of the contemporary imagination. He knew, as well, that there must always be a balance of trust and distrust in our attitude towards the world; for there are many real evils which we must guard against. Yet "the balance is crucial," and "it is probable that today the balance [in both the arts and the wider culture] has swung over to distrust of people and the world. This is one of the strongest features of gnosticism [and] it permeates our world, at this moment" (IH, 161). Thus his overall judgment was that the *prevalent* or *predominant* expressions of the dramatic imagination today, in both high and popular culture, help to spread a fundamentally gnostic sensibility, a sensibility trapped by constant dialectical swings between disgust and dreams.

12. Lynch expressly locates the argument of *Christ and Apollo* within "the long war" which began "with the first battle between the gnostic and Hebraic imaginations" (CA, 3). His most detailed explanations of what he meant by "Gnosticism" are found in *Images of Hope,* especially 160–69, but also 55 and 119–21. It is a perennial set of "attitudes and feelings towards the world," "an imaginative tendency" which sees the world "as alien and an enemy," as something which "cannot be trusted" (IH, 161). "The evidence is strong," Lynch adds, "that whenever reality is or looks too difficult there is a tendency to fly into some gnostic and private version of reality" (IH, 165).

A New Heart and a New Spirit

Everything Lynch wrote about the arts and artistic imagination sought to combat that pervasive sensibility. "[I]n our time," he wrote in the introduction to *Christ and Apollo*, "we need a new movement toward the definite and away from the dream" (CA, xii). *The Image Industries*, intended for a much wider audience, concluded on a prophetic note of even greater urgency:

> [W]e are dealing with a question of the largest national moment when we talk of the present and future state of the mass media among us. We have arrived at a great crisis in our history . . . We are a great people, capable of very great things, but the fact is that the truth of what is being asked of us is being concealed from us in very large measure. We are engaged with a great enemy, and we will find ourselves increasingly engaged in every corner of our souls. The conflict is more than military and economic. It is and will be primarily intellectual and spiritual. It will be ultimately *a conflict between two states of the imagination*. (II, 157–58, emphasis added)

Lynch himself came to this conflict of imaginations and sensibilities armed with his love of Aeschylus and the mimetic traditions of Western literature, and grounded by Ignatian faith in the significance of Christ for the imagining of time and human action. Thus he was, both by faith and intellectual formation, a partisan in the "long war between the gnostic and Hebraic imaginations" (CA, 3). His critical discussions of the dramatic imagination, in other words, were never "value-free" or "merely academic." For he saw a crisis and a challenge that went well beyond any narrowly-conceived literary or aesthetic domain.

In *The Image Industries* he explicitly called for the collaborative effort of artists and critics, theologians and the universities—each group with its proper competence and sphere of action—to work for the development of a national cinema and television worthy of being called "art," and for an educated populace which might demand such art.[13] Yet even the more scholarly discussion of *Christ and Apollo* was clearly meant to serve the

---

13. See especially II, 6–20. This was also Lynch's indirect response to the moral crusade for "decency" that had been mounted during the 1950s, especially within Catholicism, to "clean up" the cinema. He worried that such pressure would leave the more fundamental problems of the image industries untouched. The commercial masters of the industry will "clean up a particular sequence of two minutes" and then be free "to let the other ninety-eight minutes of morally indifferent [but spiritually destructive] trash remain" (II, 15). See II, 126–42, for Lynch's broader discussion of art, censorship and morality.

same urgent civilizational purpose. In his "Introduction," Lynch referred to Auerbach's analysis of how "the development of the literary imagination in the West" had meant the "development of 'a new heart and a new spirit.'" Then he added:

> "A new heart and a new spirit." This would indeed seem once more to be the great desideratum. What we need is the restoration of confidence in the fundamental power of the finite and limited concretions of our human life. But not a cheap confidence. (CA, xiii)

What we need, in other words, is not the "cheap grace" of gnostic-romantic disgust and dreams, but the difficult recovery and development of those forms of the dramatic imagination which would exemplify and contribute to a fundamental spirituality ("a new heart and spirit") of basic confidence in the movement of human life through time ("the fundamental power of the finite and limited concretions of our human life").

Of course, such a literary movement "toward the definite and away from the dream" must itself be no dream. It will not happen quickly. It will need the sustained, long-term work of critics and literary theorists, of the schools and universities, and of artists who will themselves unmask the many ways in which the literary imagination has lost confidence in the definite and been seduced by the dream. It will require, in other words, a long-term effort of criticism to laugh from the stage of consciousness and culture the fantastic nonsense that has become common fare not only in the mass media but in more sophisticated artistic forms as well—and to call to account the commercial monopolies which have increasingly achieved such hegemony over the imaginations of our people.[14] It will also require the equally long-term and even more difficult constructive work, above all by artists, but also by critics and the schools, to develop a renewed sense of the realistic imagination as the formative ground for our dramatic literature and cinema.

In this context, Lynch also called (especially in the just referenced essay on "Theology and Human Sensibility") for the crucial role that might be played by theology—both in a critique of the gnostic tendencies prevalent not only in the national imagination, but also in the Christian imagination, and even more by a sustained re-affirmation and development of Christian (or "incarnational") faith in the importance of the definite and temporal dimensions of human life. Yet this call for a theological role in the

14. While it is an implied theme throughout *The Image Industries*, Lynch's sharpest critique of the commercialization of the dramatic arts is found in the essay "Theology and Human Sensibility" (IM, 130–46, especially 132–40).

transformation of the national imagination was not an attempt to baptize the arts. Rather it was a call for the collaboration of theologian and artist, *each with their own specific competence*. For "It is the passionate vocation of theology . . . and art, real art, to satisfy, each in its own way, this tremendous need [for reality] by putting men in touch with things and people and God" (IM, 135). They are "two natural allies . . . for that drive back into reality which is so essential for modern man" (IM, 137).

Some Clarifications

In the years since Lynch wrote those words there has been much discussion about religion and the arts, and (at least in certain circles) about the idea of a Catholic or sacramental imagination. Thus, before turning to the task of illustrating Lynch's concern about the current state of the dramatic imagination, I should like to add some further clarification regarding (1) Lynch's focus on mainstream or secular literature, (2) his understanding of literary "realism," and (3) his understanding of "imagination."

(1) Lynch was always primarily concerned with "mainstream" and increasingly secular forms of literature and drama, and he consistently affirmed the legitimate autonomy of this artistic imagination. He certainly knew and respected the fact that many of our better artists and writers are not Christian, often not religious in any way, and at times openly antireligious. For literature is not the servant of theology or religion any more than of political programs or crusades for moral uplift. Nor, of course, (and this is the real contemporary issue) can we allow it to continue to become more and more a slave to narrow commercial interests. Rather the autonomous expressions of the literary imagination are crucially necessary ways whereby we humans struggle to understand and to enlarge our (increasingly and legitimately secular[15]) sense of ourselves and of our world. In serving this "cognitive and ontological" purpose, literature is certainly subject to criticism, yet it remains a distinctive and appropriately autonomous form of discovery.

Lynch, in other words, was not particularly concerned with what might be called "religious literature." He clearly knew and appreciated literature which focused on specifically religious topics and themes. He would hardly be inclined to deny that directly religious questions and experiences are crucial aspects of that reality which is the artist's concern. Yet his few detailed discussions of contemporary works with explicitly religious themes all focused on their failure to stick with the definite actualities of the

15. This is the theme of Chapter 7 below.

human—their tendency, in other words, to effectively identify the religious with the dream.[16] These works were important for Lynch, in other words, primarily because they exemplified the same problem that he found in the much wider realm of secular literature.

Yet it is true that he did on several occasions speak about "the Catholic imagination"[17] and, had he lived longer, may well have followed with interest recent efforts to discern the influence of such an imagination on the work of Catholic writers and cinematographers. He was, however, never interested in the search for "Christ figures" or in efforts to identify symbols of grace and salvation in secular literature. I am, moreover, fairly certain that his primary concern in any discussion of a "Catholic" or "sacramental" imagination would be that it stick with the real and the human, not jumping too quickly or easily to transcendent or ultimate meanings.[18] Renewed interest in a sacramental imagination is, I suspect, an inevitable and legitimate protest against the oppressive reductionism of many aspects of contemporary secularity. Yet Lynch would urge us to be wary of any quick and cheap religious "victories" in our current culture wars. The real contemporary challenge of an incarnational and authentically sacramental sensibility is to recover those forms of realism which will enable us to find and follow the lines of the truly human into the expanding and appropriately secular horizons of our present and future.[19]

(2) It is important to note, however, that in speaking about "realism" Lynch never envisioned some narrow form of artistic expression, certainly not those gnostic forms of contempt for the world which are today often referred to as "realism."[20] He knew what Auerbach had amply demonstrated,

16. We have already noted his critique of O'Neil's "religious" plays (see above p. 33 and CA, 85–88). See also his scathing dismissal of the empty sensationalism of DeMille's *The Ten Commandments* (II, 45) and his more nuanced criticism of religious themes in the work of both Graham Greene and T.S. Eliot (CA, 167–75).

17. See II, 155–56, CA, 154, 164, and CP, 49.

18. See pp. 215–16 below for additional discussion of the Catholic and sacramental imagination. The central argument of *Christ and Apollo* is that the literary imagination comes to insight and meaning of any kind *only* by sticking with and moving through the real lines of the actual and human. The book's final chapters on "The Theological Imagination" and "The Christian Imagination" make explicit the implications of this general argument for the religious dimensions or the religious reach of the literary imagination.

19. As Lynch says at one point towards the end of *Christ and Apollo*, "it is a reasonable certainty that an art which really follows the lines of human experience will be following the lines of light and the Holy Spirit, and will willy-nilly get to God" (CA, 181). It will, in other words, become "sacramental" by remaining real.

20. For Lynch's most pointed comments about the unreality of these dark forms of modern "realism," see his essay "Reality."

that the mimetic tradition of Western literature gives evidence of a rich diversity of "realistic" forms, from the choral formalities of classical drama, through the symbolic realism of medieval theater, to the many forms of modern and post-modern realism. Lynch loved and wrote about writers as different as Dante and Cervantes, Dostoyevsky and Dickens, Thomas Mann and Samuel Beckett. He knew that farce and satire, the grotesque and the picaresque, symbolism and even fantasy could all serve the broad purposes of the realistic imagination. He also knew that there undoubtedly are an almost endless number of as yet undiscovered forms and styles by which the artistic imagination might seek to encompass, express, and enlarge the reality of the world and of human action. The limits of realism are given only by the immensely rich diversity of the actual and the almost endlessly fruitful power of different artists and artistic movements to develop forms and styles for the imitation and enlargement of our sense of it. Thus his constant appeal was not for some narrow "realism," but for the flexibility and freedom that the imagination needs if it is to continue to open our attention to and admiration for the real.[21]

(3) What, then, did Lynch mean by "imagination"? He meant, as he says at one point, "all the resources of man, all his faculties . . . and his whole heritage, all brought to bear upon the concrete world . . . to form images of the world and thus to find it, cope with it, shape it, even make it" (CP, 23).[22] Such an extremely broad "definition" at first seems very strange since we tend to think of imagination as a special faculty which typically enables us to transcend the ordinary in order to "create" a separate realm of the artistic or the fantastic. Lynch, however, did not understand imagination as a single faculty of any kind. Rather he thought of it as the sum of *all the resources of man, all his faculties* of seeing and feeling, speech and story, memory and intelligence whereby we receive and in turn shape the images which enable us *to find the world, cope with it, shape it, even make it*. The first and most fundamental task of imagination, he never tired of repeating, is "to imagine the real" (CP, 23, 64). For "The imagination is really the only way we have of handling the world. It is at the point of the imagination, at the precise point where an image is formed, that we meet the world, deal with it, judge it" (CP, 23).

In case these assertions seem exaggerated or esoteric, Lynch asks the reader to simply think of the images she has of "a man, a woman, a child, birth, life, death, morning, night, food, friend, the enemy, the self, the

---

21. See his "The Task."

22. For a similar "definition" see IF, 18. Lynch's most detailed discussions of "image" and "imagination" are found in IH, 243–56, and CP, 23–27.

human . . . " (CP, 25). These words (and thousands more) are not simply signs for abstract concepts. They are more fundamentally the bearers of images—and not simple images, not snapshots of reality. Rather such images are the result of an immense accumulation of experience and thought, most of which we have received. And they are indeed the precise point of our contact with the concrete and actual world of experience.

If such reference to the many ordinary images which daily mediate our contact with the world remains confusing, then I would ask the reader to focus just on the first two images from Lynch's list—those of woman and man. Think of the rich complexity of those images, of their deep roots in tradition and in art, in culture and personal experience. Think of the many subtle and not so subtle ways in which they accompany us as we move through daily life. Or consider the poverty of daily life when our images of man and woman are narrow, fixated, adolescent or ideological. Then think of the immense (and immensely important) contemporary and world-wide struggle we all are engaged in, whether we wish it or not, to criticize and enlarge our images of woman and man so that we might live more fully and humanly in this inevitably gendered world. Perhaps then Lynch's emphasis on imagination and his very broad understanding of it will not seem strange or esoteric.

For Lynch was not simply concerned with artistic or literary imagination, but with the more general power of imagination to enable us to move into and through the actuality of our world and our lives, *and* with the power of inadequate, distorted, fixated and totalized images to inhibit such movement. The imagination, in other words, whether of an individual or of an entire culture, can relate to the real in two fundamentally antithetical ways, though in many different forms and degrees. It can choose to move (or allow itself to be led) either into or away from the real and actual.[23] It can be an immensely important way of knowing the real, of being "cognitive and ontological," or it can be a form of escape to fantastic walled cities or romantic dreams.[24]

There is, then, a very close relationship between "imagination" and "sensibility"—between, for example, a realistic imagination and an analogical sensibility, or between fantasy images and a totalizing sensibility. Lynch

23. For a quite explicit statement of this antithesis see Lynch's "Drama of Mind," 22–23.

24. It perhaps bears repeating that there are also many legitimate and important forms of fantasy, of play and entertainment and escape. Yet such secondary forms of the imagination remain healthy only where there is a clear sense of the primacy of the realistic imagination.

does not equate the terms "imagination" and "sensibility," but at times seems to use them interchangeably.

The "artists and writers" who collaborate in the production of our cinema and theater or who write our stories and songs are, then, immensely important because of their power to influence the imagination of individuals and of the entire culture. They can help us to imagine and engage the real or lead us to remain with the superficial, with stereotype and cliché. Or (worse still) they can cause us to be traumatized by fear, or fixated by totalized passion and whipped into ideological frenzy. Thus we must, with Lynch, ask about the current state of our dramatic arts. For the state of our images and imaginations is utterly central to the condition of our sensibility, to the adequacy or inadequacy of those habits of mind and spirit which constitute our actual, lived spirituality. If, then, as Lynch argues, our dramatic arts are largely held captive by an essentially gnostic sensibility, then we do indeed need "a new movement toward the definite and away from the dream," a movement in our arts and in our entire culture.[25]

Habits of Critical Discernment

In many ways the most basic aspect of such a movement involves the development and deepening of critical habits of mind and spirit. Of course it might be said that our culture is already far too skeptical and critical. Yet Lynch would want us to distinguish between a pervasive and all too easily attained spirit of critical contempt and the far more difficult skills of critical discernment which are an essential element of the spirituality he called for.[26] Indeed, all of his writings, not only those about literature and drama, call for and exemplify the fundamental need for such critical discernment—in politics and religion and personal life as much as in the arts. Here, in a lengthy citation from the beginning of *The Image Industries*, is how he put the fundamental issue we face in all the dimensions of our lives:

> Together the terms *fantasy* and *reality* summarize everything
> which is not and everything which is. With *fantasy* we associate
> such words as *dream, illusion, unreality, the distortion of reality,*

25. See pp. 193–94 below for further discussion of Lynch's understanding of imagination.

26. *Images of Faith* (subtitled "An Exploration of the Ironic Imagination") calls for the development of an ironic as an essential component of the life of faith. Yet throughout the book (especially in Chapter 3, "The Structure of the Irony of Faith"), Lynch continually challenges us to discern the crucial difference between today's prevailing "ironies of contempt" and what he does not hesitate to call "the irony of Christ." See pp. 149–58 below.

unrooted thought, escape. With *reality* we associate all things from common sense (as long as it is not cowardice) to daring (as long as it is rooted in the realistic and the possible); it includes the whole range of the truly human over against everything that is phony, absurd, illusory or "angelic." The range of both words is, therefore, truly enormous. They include the two possible directions that all human insight, character, and action can take either at one moment or over a long span of time. Either of the two words can mark the quality of a whole culture or nation, and it is crucially important to know which is having the largest effect on us at any one moment . . . The proper balancing of these two forces is always the most serious question confronting any civilization . . . We must always be asking whether . . . we are taking the stance of fantasy or are facing reality with wisdom and courage. (II, 21–22)

Ideally, of course, the artist herself can be one of our greatest allies in the development of an authentically critical sensibility. For her work can and should help us develop, at levels of our spirit far deeper than simple ideas, the ability to recognize the difference between the real and the phony, the definite and the dream. Lynch, for example, points to the way in which now-classic films like *Rashomon*, *La Strada* and *The Bridge on the River Kwai* challenge us to understand how readily illusion and fantasy can, with tragic consequence, take hold of the human spirit.[27] Such films, which often also depict a "saving" recognition and recovery of contact with reality, challenge us and simultaneously enable us to develop such critical discernment.

As more literary examples of the artist assisting our development of critical sensitivities, Lynch notes the importance of the ironic sensibility cultivated by the work of Thomas Mann and Samuel Beckett, and, of course, by Cervantes' "immortal attack . . . in *Don Quixote*, on all the all-believing and all-concocting romances of chivalry . . ."(IF, 121–22).[28] It is, moreover, certainly possible that Lynch himself first fully appreciated the tremendous importance of the dramatic artist for a culture's development of habits of critical discernment through his own early study of the *Oresteia*. For there Aeschylus challenged Athens, and has continued to challenge us, to see the terrible ways in which individuals and an entire culture can be trapped by rigid or totalized fixations—in this case, a narrow, hate-filled and escalating need for revenge.[29]

27. See II, 31–34 (for *Rashomon*) and 73–74 (for *Bridge*), and CA, 41–42 (for *La Strada*).

28. See the index of IF for Cervantes and Mann, and the index of CP for Beckett.

29. For Lynch's analysis of the *Oresteia*, see the index of CP. See his essay "Euripides

We are, then, fortunate when our arts themselves help us in the development of an appropriately critical sensibility. Yet it is today more often the case that we need such critical habits and skills precisely to defend ourselves from the spiritual seductions purveyed by both our image industries and our supposedly more sophisticated dramatic arts. Thus we especially need the help of the critic—whether the professional critic (if he has not simply become another cheerleader for those seductions) or those authentically critical spirits we may at times be fortunate to meet in our universities, among our writers, in our churches, and among family and friends.[30]

I am, of course, arguing that Lynch was (and remains) one of those "authentically critical spirits." For he not only called for the development of an appropriately critical sensibility, but his writings continually exemplify it. He was a superb critic, and not only of the arts, but of the many different dimensions of life taken up in his writings. Indeed, his books and essays, by their typically circling, repetitive and gradually enlarging style, actually become a form of training in critical sensibility for those willing to undertake more than a quick read.

In terms of the dramatic arts, *The Image Industries* is his most pervasively critical work. It is a sweeping attempt to awaken us to the imaginative and spiritual poverty behind the pseudo-magnificence of Hollywood's "dream factory," and to the seriousness of the fact that today's massive image industries are not just an often unseemly blemish on the surface of our culture, but have invaded our interiority, the souls and sensibilities of our people.[31] Thus it calls all of us to develop those critical habits which are fundamental for a sensibility that knows the phony and the unreal for what they are, and will hoot or hiss them from the stage of our lives.[32]

'Bacchae'" for a related analysis of Euripides' exposition of the terrifying consequences of escalating fantasies. See also pp. 146–48 below for Lynch's discussion of the *Bacchae*.

30. See II, 15–8 and 22–28 for Lynch's comments on the much-needed role of the critic.

31. At one point Lynch says that "these media are now a supersubstantial force in the formation of the imaginative life and the culture of our nation" (II, 9). Yet it is again important to add that Lynch's critique was not totalistic. *The Image Industries* itself praises many examples of fine cinematic art and one later essay, "Counterrevolution," called special attention to elements in the image industries which ran counter to the dominant tendency.

32. Some might be tempted to say that such criticism of TV and Hollywood, however necessary at the time Lynch wrote, is now passé. Today "we know all that!" That's why we refer dismissively to "the dream factory." Perhaps; yet I would argue that Lynch's slender book remains important for the perceptiveness and detail of its critique. Indeed the real danger today, perhaps especially among intellectual and cultural elites, is that, in wearily "knowing all that" about TV and cinema, we have already succumbed to a kind of gnostic dismissal of popular culture. When we do not indulge the passive

Christ and Apollo, of course, is in its turn an even more developed argument that imaginative failure is not limited to the mass media, but is found every bit as much in the dramatic forms of high culture. It, too, calls for and constantly exemplifies the kinds of critical habits we need. As do all of Lynch's later writings about literature and theater.

Yet it is simply not possible here, within the limits of the present study, to attempt even a superficial summary of the critical analyses presented in *The Image Industries* and *Christ and Apollo*, to say nothing of Lynch's other writings about the dramatic arts. Nor would it be desirable were it possible. Far better that the reader take up Lynch's own writing. Rather, in what follows I will simply indicate some of the major topics and themes discussed in *Image Industries* and *Christ and Apollo* and then take up his very important discussion of the contemporary dramatic imagination's failure to deal with the reality of time. I make no attempt here at completeness, any more than Lynch himself would claim any form of comprehensiveness for his own far more detailed critical work. He wrote to alert us to central weaknesses in our dramatic arts, and to invite us into the kinds of critical thinking and debate which might deepen our own sensitivity to these and other weaknesses. The topics and themes on which he focused do not attempt to present any sort of typology of major critical issues. Rather they overlap and are interwoven, again like crisscrossing the same field from different angles, in an attempt to raise the reader's own level of critical awareness. In what follows, then, I will crisscross that field with him, occasionally adding more recent examples of my own, in an effort simply to suggest both the richness of his criticism of our dramatic arts and our own need for such a discerning mentor.

Fantasy and Reality

As noted, the most fundamental critical issue for Lynch is the ability to distinguish fantasy from reality. There is nothing wrong with fantasy so long as we know and enjoy it for what it is. The critical challenge is to recognize fantasy when it pretends to be reality. Thus *The Image Industries* presents a series of overlapping analyses of ways in which our mass media substitute fantasy for reality: by the regular reduction of complex emotions to simpler and supposedly more intense forms; by fixating the imagination on certain

---

part of our own souls in the seductive superficialities of the dream factory, we simply shrug and withdraw to some particular sphere of "higher things." Thus the separation between intellectuals and the people which so concerned Lynch only becomes greater. And the spiritual vacuum opened by this separation is ever more quickly filled by the commercial forces of an industry which is, if anything, far more powerful and pervasive today than when Lynch wrote.

narrow clichés (of love, for instance, or of violence); and by continual reliance on "magnificent" images (the constant close-up, the big scene, the huge climax, the latest technologies for endlessly magnifying sight and sound). *Christ and Apollo*, in its turn, opens with chapters on "The Definite" and "Time" which indicate some of the ways in which many of our poets and writers not only fail to engage these two most fundamental dimensions of human actuality, but actually conceive the task of the "truly creative" imagination to be that of deliberately "transcending" such paltry and limiting realities. From that foundation, Lynch then traces different forms of the substitution of fantasy for reality in both contemporary tragedy and comedy, and, at the end of the book, in efforts to depict religious realities. At the very center (both literally and substantively) of *Christ and Apollo* stands Lynch's basic argument that reliance on "univocal" forms of imagination (reducing the diversity of actuality to some single and typically intense or magnificent image) is the common root of all such failure to penetrate and move through the actual.

The Gnostic Imagination

One of the more prevalent forms of the substitution of fantasy for reality to which, as already noted, Lynch continually called attention is the stark Gnostic or Manichean division between light and darkness, good and evil. Since there are real evils and real goods, one of the artist's great challenges is to provide adequate images of such realities. What we too often get, however, is simplistic conflict between "the dark side" and "the force," black hats and white, monsters of horrific moral or physical evil and heroes and heroines almost without blemish. The gnostic imagination is not concerned to understand the actual and subtle workings of evil in the human heart and in society, nor the many complex forms of good. It already knows how bad things are and spreads its univocal blanket of darkness and denunciation over everything, reducing all difference—all the many forms and rhythms of evil, as well as the typically messy mixing of good and evil—to dark sameness. Except, of course, for the equally univocal "blanket of the beautiful" (CA, 125) with which it covers the few who are good and their soaring moment of romantic love or of ultimate victory. Gary Cooper and Grace Kelly ride out of town at the end of *High Noon*, just as Susan Sarandon and Gina Davis fly from this ugly world in *Thelma and Louise* and Harrison Ford escapes to a "wild green yonder" in *Blade Runner*. The much-praised film *American Beauty* provided a similarly gnostic combination of fleeting glimpses of beauty against a pervasive backdrop of middle-class banality, a tension which, as in *Thelma and Louise*, is resolved only by death's leap to some ethereal beyond.

This gnostic-romantic pattern is, moreover, not limited to lesser, more popular cinematic works. Though Lynch, to my knowledge, only once mentioned the work of Stanley Kubrick, who is widely reputed to be one of our truly great cinematographers, that one reference (IH, 166) concerns the gnostic sensibility which pervades *Dr. Strangelove*. I would add that nothing in Kubrick's subsequent career, up to and including the much-ballyhooed posthumous release of *Eyes Wide Shut*, would have led Lynch (or me) to alter that fundamental judgment. As prime instances of Kubrick's essentially gnostic imagination, I note not only his depiction of the world as pervasively violent in *A Clockwork Orange*, but even more the suggestive antithesis between deadening technical mechanism and the dreamily transcendent innocence of the "cosmic child" in *2001: A Space Odyssey*. Of course what makes that antithesis especially ironic is Kubrick's own well-deserved reputation for technical brilliance and innovation. Yet such reliance on technical virtuosity unfortunately (and certainly not only in Kubrick) disguises a poverty of real imagination, the kind of imagination which might better follow the smaller and more subtle lines of the actual.

Nor is this gnostic substitution of fantasy for reality found only in contemporary cinema. We have on several occasions noted Lynch's analysis of the plays of Eugene O'Neill which bounce back and forth from dark depictions of the world to dreamy evocations of some alternate form of redemption.[33] Lynch, we remember, chose to focus on O'Neil because he was "an accurate reflector of much of the contemporary dramatic temper" (CA, 81). Indeed, the entire chapter on "Tragedy" in *Christ and Apollo* (where Lynch discusses O'Neill) is a sustained argument that "the older and more accurate idea of tragic movement has been completely reversed both in the theory and practice of the modern theater" (CA, 70). For if there is one place where the dramatic imagination has sought to enable us to understand human limit and failure, it has been in the long and immensely important tradition of tragedy which follows the descent of the human to a final act in real darkness and death. Yet modern tragedy, Lynch argues (with reference to writers as diverse as Ibsen and Strindberg, Shaw and O'Casey, Arthur Miller and Archibald MacLeish), has refused to follow the actual stages and rhythms of that descent. It depicts evil, but only because "the tragic protagonist . . . is cursed by the necessity of walking, victim and innocent, through an insane world," a world of "worthlessness, threat, evil, absurdity" (CA, 77). Then, in the face of such external darkness and threat, the modern

33. See p. 33 above and CA, 81–88.

tragedy substitutes a new kind of final act, where the all-but-finally-defeated protagonist suddenly finds the strength of heroic (but unfounded) resistance or is suddenly embraced by a miraculous "new dawn." Thus the new tragedy has become "incurably romantic, abandoned the finite, and grasped desperately at some kind of infinite" (CA, 70). It provides, in its own way, the same leap from darkness to light, the same replacement of reality by a gnostic-romantic fantasy that Lynch had found in contemporary cinema. Thus it, too, fails to help us understand real good and real evil. Rather it plays on our own fantastic wish for some pure and simple escape from the mud and messiness of the actual.[34]

The Magnificent Imagination

So pervasive in our contemporary dramatic arts is "the magnificent imagination"—the substitution of the fantastically "big" or "intense" for the actual—that it may need little comment. In *The Image Industries*, for example, Lynch noted Hollywood's general inability to imagine religion other than in magnificently (or magically) phony terms. There he used DeMille's then-current *Ten Commandments* as a prime example.[35] Unfortunately, examples of such resort to smoke and mirrors to depict the spiritual or the holy can be multiplied almost endlessly.[36] Even more obvious, of course, is the constant resort to various forms of magnificence in "action" films. Magnificent chases, escapes, explosions, impacts, sights and sounds are all outdone again and again as each new "generation" of action films makes use of newer and "better" technologies for image making. Always there is action, action, action; always bigger and more intense. Yet in fact there is typically very little real human and dramatic action. There is simply the univocal repetition of the same, again and again in the course of a film, building only in intensity and magnificence to some "can you top this?" finale.

Nor (again) is this substitution of magnificence for reality limited to the popular arts. Lynch reminds us that "the intellectual can indulge in his

---

34. Lynch does not much discuss the presence of the gnostic imagination in contemporary fiction, but one does not have to go far to find evidence of its presence. I point, as but one example, to enthusiasm for the dreary and endlessly repetitive darkness of Cormac McCarthy's novels (though his more recent *The Road* seems in the end to break with that pattern).

35. See II, 45–51, as well as all of Chapter 5 on "The Magnificent Imagination."

36. Thankfully there are notable exceptions such as *Dead Man Walking* and Robert Duval's *The Apostle*, as well as Kristof Kieslowski's magnificent made-for-TV series *Dekalog*. More recent examples would include *Of Gods and Men*, *Philomena*, *Ida*, and *Calvary*.

own forms of the spectacular though they always appear more refined . . . [They take] the form of what we may call a dedication to the supereminent importance of 'virtuosity' . . . " (II, 47). Years later, in his final essay on contemporary theater, Lynch gives two then-current examples of such "virtuosity" whereby magnificent technique becomes a substitute for real dramatic imagination.[37] Tom Stoppard, Lynch notes, is one of the leading lights of the London stage, perhaps then best known for *Travesties* and *Rosencrantz and Guildenstern Are Dead*. Yet just these plays, Lynch says, "wipe out or obscure human existence . . . by the all-conquering, all-smothering virtuosities of brilliant, fiery, infinitely speedy intellectualism."[38] Others, Lynch continues, have praised Stoppard's verbal and intellectual virtuosity with terms like "intoxicating," "brilliant," "dazzling," "exuberant and freewheeling."[39] In sharp contrast, Lynch himself asks us to see that what we actually get in these plays is "the incomparable seduction of the human spirit by a parade of overwhelmingly rich words, words, words, that allow no moment in which we might be brave and cool enough to ask about the relation of any two words." The final result of such intellectual magnificence is, in Lynch's damning judgment, a "distancing from existence [that makes it] impossible to have any contact with people and things as really there."

Far more common, and thus even more dangerous, than Stoppard's intellectual magnificence is the kind of emotional intensity exemplified by Peter Shaffer's *Equus*, which received the New York Drama Critics award for 1975.[40] As Lynch describes the play, "from a rather calm yet fantastic beginning, [*Equus*] builds rhythmically to a point and then a plateau of ecstasy and, finally, to a feeling in the audience that it has had contact with secret places of beauty and glory."[41] At the literal level, the play is a story of the psychiatric analysis of a disturbed young man who has driven spikes through the eyes of six horses in a stable. As the boy and his doctor try to

37. Lynch, "Easy." This essay contrasts the "magnificent" virtuosity of Peter Shaffer's *Equus* and of several plays by Tom Stoppard ("How to Miss Reality") with the far simpler, but much more realistically dramatic work of Athol Fugard ("How to Hit It").

38. Ibid., 15. Lynch earlier had written that while Stoppard is "the reigning master of the theater in England . . . his greatest enemy is the constant, never ending brilliance of mind, and vocabulary of mind over against human fact and feeling . . . [It causes] leaping into unearned insights or into a charlatanism of exploding ideas . . ." "Dramatic Making," 169–70.

39. Ibid., 16. Subsequent citations in this paragraph are from pages 14 & 15 of the same essay.

40. Ibid. Lynch had earlier reviewed *Equus* when it first played in New York. See "What's Wrong?" The *New York Images* essay cited here repeats the same basic critique.

41. Ibid., 14. Subsequent citations in this paragraph are all from the same essay, pages 14 & 15.

understand his action, their imaginations are "stirred to points of ecstasy." The youth's imagination floats "'creatively' through the equestrian images of the Old Testament" to the point where a horse becomes "nothing more nor less than the Son of God" and "the lines of *a horse* have been wiped out by autonomous ecstasy." There is, moreover, "the same breakdown of relationship between root fact and waves of vision" for the psychiatrist. His imagination revels in "vast dreams of ancient Greece, to such visions as will overwhelm the audience and prevent it from preserving the memory of truth." And the rhetorical presentation of these visions of glory builds in constant rhythmic juxtaposition with "the universal contempt with which the doctor . . . moves in what we call the real world." What Lynch calls an "ontology of contempt" for all ordinary life—for "reason, analysis, ordinariness, the middle class . . . his own wife"—builds in the doctor's speeches in constant contrast with his (and the boy's) visions of ecstasy.

Yet as the play progresses even the specific elements of ecstatic vision and contempt for the ordinary cease to be important. The rhetorical rhythms themselves take over and are "granted exclusive importance,"[42] separated not only from the few facts of the medical case, but from all facts and all reality. Here is how Lynch, in his original review of the play's New York opening, described the final point of ecstasy achieved in the doctor's curtain speech:

> He crowds every fraudulent cliché of the play into speech that no longer has any responsibility for articulating a single word or meaning. As given by Anthony Hopkins (and as, i think, the whole dramatic structure demands), the speech was a wild, rhetorical flood of sound giving the clues of only a few audible words . . . These few words are meant to be a final signal to the audience that it is time for passion and time for a standing ovation. For the truth would never measure up to the mad rhythm and must therefore be concealed by the power of autonomous incantation.[43]

Thus does the magnificent imagination draw applause and critical acclaim by the virtuosity of its rhythmic evocation of emotional intensity. Yet it is an intensity which, as is the case for all such magnificence, is not only unrelated to actual facts and real human action, but typically embodies gnostic contempt for such actualities.

42. Ibid., 15.
43. "What's Wrong?" 420.

Time and Sensibility

Finally, at the risk of verbal excess of my own, let me "crisscross" the field of Lynch's criticism once more by relating what *The Image Industries* calls "The Problem of Sensibility" (42–67) to *Christ and Apollo's* discussion of "Time" (CA, 31–64). Lynch opens that discussion by noting that "Of all the finite, limited things with which the imagination is confronted, time is perhaps the most limited."[44] Yet "it is perhaps not too much to say that on the attitude we take toward time . . . , on our decision either to strain against it or accept it, depends all our peace." In making such fundamental claims, Lynch is not talking only or even primarily about literature. Rather, he says, time "is nothing but *ourselves*, as we move without pause through all the phases and stages of our lives . . ." He then adds his most fundamental concern: "though time is always in motion, it is a motion that has a structure and . . . only by staying within this structure of temporality and moving with it can one gain access to real insight."

Lynch means nothing esoteric by such statements, simply that human life itself, as well as the dramatic literature which seeks to imitate and understand it, are both "basically actions, achieving themselves in the growth, the moving structure, the flowing pattern." Put even more simply: "true understanding [in both art and life] is gained only through . . . an illumination that comes out of a passage through *experience*, this illumination leading to another experience, and this to further illumination, and so on, even unto death." This, of course, explains the central importance for us, and for our culture, of *dramatic* literature and the *dramatic* imagination's "Aeschylean rhythm" of action, suffering, and insight. For we are much helped in coming to real understanding of ourselves by the dramatic artist's imagining of the rhythms and stages of real human time. As we are much hindered when our dramatic arts fail to meet the challenge of imagining time and begin instead to offer (as in *Equus*) a fantastic sense of time or a fantasy of transcending time's structure and limitation.

This fundamental significance of time, and of the adequate or inadequate imagining of time, is perhaps nowhere more evident or more important than in what *The Image Industries* calls "the problem of sensibility,"[45] the problem or challenge presented by "all those elements of feeling and pas-

---

44. The running citations in the remainder of this paragraph and in the next are from CA, 31–33.

45. Citations in this and the subsequent paragraph are from II, 42–45 and 52–53. Lynch's use of "sensibility" here to refer to human passion and emotion is simply a specification of the more general use to which I have put the term throughout this book.

sion which we have always denominated under such names as joy, affection, grief, hate, envy, loneliness, regret, longing, jealousy, love, and every other emotion which has moved the souls of men and women from the beginning of time until now."[46] For such feelings and sensibility are, Lynch reminds us, "the gift of God" and one of the more important ways, indeed sometimes "the only way," by which "man relates his whole being, well or badly, accurately or inaccurately, to reality." And while emotions may either arise suddenly, with the force of a storm, or persist subtly over long periods, the actual development and deepening and transformation of our feelings and sensibility—to put the crucial matter here quite simply—"takes time" and is subject to the structures and stages of real human time. Thus the dramatic artist, as one who "is *really* interested in the state of human sensibility"—indeed, Lynch says, this "is his whole vocation and preoccupying task"—must be especially sensitive to the reality of time as it affects the rhythms and movements of human feelings.

Yet (and here is "the problem" of sensibility) precisely because "the world of human feeling is a very complicated, subtle, and powerful world," there is that in each of us (and in our artists) which would like "to flatten down or ignore the emotional life," to reduce it to "non-bothersome proportions." At present, moreover, our image industries nurture and expand that part of us that wishes to keep things uncomplicated, to have our feelings touched, but only slightly, only in small and sentimental or sensational doses. For Hollywood, Lynch says, "has devoted the better part of a whole industry to the production of pieces which either ignore the true inner reality of man or reduce it to petty proportions." It "substitutes flatness of perception and tawdry sensationalism" for real sensibility and makes sure that "very little occurs with real depth of feeling or insight into the heart of man."

In *Christ and Apollo*, Lynch argues that there is a similar and related "instinct in all of us which rebels against time," which tries "desperately to hold onto . . . a moment of goodness or peace," or else tries "to make all movements run together into one fine moment, a single static thing which will . . . resemble some kind of eternity" (CA, 32). This perennial temptation, moreover, is especially strong at present. Thus Lynch can say: "It is evident that modern man, particularly modern man in America, wishes to escape from the rigors of time" (CA, 46). And again, even more forcefully:

46. The listing in that sentence is deliberately long, deliberately detailed and diverse, because Lynch wishes to suggest the range and importance of human emotion as he begins a discussion of how our image industries have not only failed to help us explore that range and importance, but have actively caused the reduction, the flattening and narrowing of human sensibility.

[I]n the modern imagination . . . there has been a collapse of confidence; we have no faith in the dense reality of time. The search for all the forms of intensity in our civilization is a sign of the rebellion against the finite moment of time . . . (CA, 92)

As evidence of this "collapse of confidence" in time, Lynch points to philosophers, especially Descartes "who first put forward the notion of a pure intelligence within us which is not subject to time" (CA, 37), but also "Leibniz, Spinoza, and Kant, among others, [who] have held that temporal things do not lead to a deep, possessive awareness on the part of the mind" (CA, 47). Yet Lynch is even more concerned to note the fact that for "many writers of the last few literary generations, time is not only an enemy, but *the* enemy" (CA, 34). For such writers—Lynch mentions many, but gives special attention to Proust and Poe, each exemplary in his own particular way—art, especially the literary imagination, becomes a privileged instrument for defeating time.[47]

In much contemporary literature, then, the dramatic imagination not only fails to help us understand the real rhythms and structures of time, but has actually sought to become "at once the conqueror and the destroyer of time" (CA, 38). Yet precisely by thus seeking to transcend time, serious literature effectively joins Hollywood in its failure to deal with "the problem of sensibility." It, too, contributes to that "search for all the forms of intensity" which testify to our culture's loss of confidence in time and in the goodness of those rhythms and structures whereby time educates and deepens feeling and sensibility.

Let me give one fairly easy example of this conjunction of a loss of confidence in time with the failure to deal adequately with human feelings and sensibility. It is the all-too-typical substitution of fantastic intensity for real imagination in the dramatic depiction of love between woman and man, though the same substitution can readily be found in depictions of any of our strong and central emotions, whether anger or grief or joy or regret.

Lynch himself does not often speak about romantic love or sexual desire, but his few comments in *The Image Industries* go to the heart of the matter. He refers to the moment when "a well-known torch singer steps out

47. See CA, 34–35 and 42–44 for comments on Proust, and 36–37 for Poe. As further examples, I note the startling images of immobility and escape at the end of recent works by two major U.S. novelists: the man sitting alone, ice fishing on an isolated forest lake, at the end of Philip Roth's *The Human Stain*, and, even more striking, the protagonist's wife sitting alone at night on the high, cold catwalk of the Mount Palomar observatory, totally absorbed by the distant beauty of the stars, at the end of Saul Bellow's *The Dean's December*. In both books the concluding image represents a deliberate escape from the cluttered and messy action of the entire preceding story.

upon a TV stage" (II, 25).[48] Today we'd speak of a "pop-star," any of dozens
of "sexy" ladies and men whose rock-videos and concert performances (and
roles in advertisements) fill our TV screens. What does she sing? "Nothing,"
Lynch says, "or the closest approximation to nothing ever heard." He means
that quite literally. Her song typically is "Something about love, for which,
we remember, men have died according to all the rigors of reality." But the
words "cannot be heard, are not intended to be heard." For if we *really* heard
them, it would "give the joke, the farce, the insipidity away." To insure that
we don't hear, and don't think about the reality, the other "artists involved
must jump off into further illusion." The continual quick cutting of the
cameras, the dizzying manipulation of smoke and lights, the constant cre-
scendo of supporting instruments (do they play anything but crescendos?),
the rapid and provocative rhythms of the dancers—all must contribute to
the impression that these inane words and mechanical (Lynch says "sickly")
rhythms "are capable of producing this glory." Yet such technical production
of various forms of visual and musical intensity actually hides rather than
reveals the reality of love.[49]

Somewhat later, in commenting on Hollywood's substitution of "fixation" (or the riveting of mind and imagination to one focal point and one
moment) for real imaginative freedom, Lynch speaks of "the close-up work
of the camera in many cheap films" with "endless scenes of minor mawk-
ishness" where "we are forced to look into somebody's swooning, love-sick
eyes" (II, 70).[50] As further examples of such fixation he notes, "the endless
depicting of the single moment [of love] and the restriction of so much
love to boudoir scenes." Such techniques, he says, "represent safe fixations
of time and space in [depicting] love." They exemplify less a lack of morality
than "a lack of imagination." "The camera *refuses to move on into the wider
environment of the force of* love because the artist's imagination is immo-
bilized and cannot move on." The artist cannot (or will not) "venture for a
moment out of the cheap dream into the real world of people and things
and *that real world of rhythms where love might be found moving on and
on.*" "This sort of treatment of love," Lynch concludes, "has the incredible

---

48. Subsequent citations in this paragraph are from this same description of the
torch singer.

49. Of course "the technical production of intensity" is at least as old as the endlessly repeated "chase scene." Increasingly, though, the technical substitution of forms
of intense "speed," in both sight and sound, for a more human pace and rhythm characterizes all of our media, even (remember Stoppard) the most sophisticated.

50. Subsequent citations in this paragraph are from II, 70–71, with emphases
added.

effrontery to masquerade under the name of freedom, at the very moment in which it seeks to seduce our imaginations into pin-pointed slavery."

The moment of romantic intensity, then, is typically an artistic form of cheap grace. It is a cheap trick prostituting art. It contributes to the degradation of our sense of that fundamental relationship between love and time which Lynch had so aptly described as "the real world of rhythms where love might be found moving on and on." It does so, moreover, not at the level of ideas, but at the far more damaging level of sensibility. Yet it is but one of many ways by which our dramatic arts, failing to stick with the actual rhythms of time, fail miserably in their representation of human feeling.[51]

A New Movement Toward the Definite

Criticism always involves a kind of two-step—a negating movement which exposes the phony and fantastic even as it simultaneously points us to and gradually enlarges our sense of a more positive alternative. Thus Lynch's critical analyses of the contemporary dramatic imagination, and his broader call for us to develop critical habits of mind and spirit, are always pointing towards and contributing to a "new movement towards the definite and away from the dream," and not simply in our arts. Indeed the development of "a new heart and a new spirit" by "restoration of confidence in the fundamental power of the finite and limited concretions of our human life" (CA, xiii) is one of our must fundamental civilizational tasks—if not *the* most fundamental—as we take up the challenge of moving into the vastly expanding horizons of present and future. That task will be very difficult, given the levels of fear and alienation and the dialectic of disgust and dreams which characterize so much of contemporary culture, whether social and political or artistic and intellectual.

There is, then, something problematic about Lynch's hope that both the arts and faith and theology (both "Apollo" and "Christ") might provide leadership and resources for such a "new movement." For at present neither the arts nor theology and faith occupy a central place in our society, and each in its own way is held at least partially captive by the prevailing gnostic sensibility.

---

51. The chapter on "Tragedy" in *Christ and Apollo* (65–90) provides another extended analysis of the contemporary imagination's failure to deal with death as the final stage and "structure" of human time—both with the actual time of death, and with the many small "moments" of suffering, loss, failure and other kinds of "death" which are inescapable aspects of the rhythm of time.

Yet Lynch was always clear about the role he saw for the dramatic arts in the movement to "restore confidence in the fundamental power of the finite":

> True art helps us to move out of the dream and into reality, and it helps us to endure the movement. (IM, 143)

> [T]he literary process is a highly cognitive passage through the finite and the definite realities of man and the world. (CA, xi)

> [The dramatic artist] says to us equivalently: "Put your hand in mine and I will lead you, by process and stages, into human worlds you would never have suspected, and if suspected would have never dared."[52]

One could multiply such citations almost endlessly since Lynch continually called for (and worked for) a broad recovery and development of the central mimetic tradition of western literature. A *recovery* which is no retreat to the past, though it must inevitably draw from the roots and resources of the past. And a *development* which opens new pathways of imagination into the expanding reaches and depths of the world. Such recovery and development of the forms of the dramatic imagination would help us to move humanly, with renewed habits of mind and spirit, into these reaches and depths, healing our many alienations and allowing us to find ourselves again by again finding ourselves in touch with the realities of our world.

Lynch was equally clear and insistent in affirming the role of faith and theology in a "new movement towards the definite." Indeed, the final ground of his confidence in the possibility of such a movement is given with the name of Christ. As he says at the beginning of *Christ and Apollo*:

> I mean Christ to stand for the completely definite, for the Man who, in taking on our human nature (as the artist must) took on every inch of it (save sin) in all its density and Who so obviously did not march too quickly or too glibly to beauty, the infinite, the dream. I take Him, secondly, as the model and source of that energy and courage we again need to enter the finite as the only creative and generative source of beauty. (CA, xii)

Yet it must be admitted that, put so starkly, this affirmation of the role of faith and theology may seem just the sort of religious magic and leaping that Lynch himself again and again disavows, especially since he clearly wants to speak not only to the choir, but to the mainstream of secular literary intelligence. A more adequate discussion of what Lynch meant by

---

52. Lynch, "Dramatic Making," 168–69.

"Christ" will have to await this book's final chapter. For the moment, let me end this chapter simply by indicating three dimensions of the ground on which Lynch stood when he issued his call, in the name of Christ, for a recovery in our times of the mimetic vocation of the dramatic imagination.

(1) Though it may appear surprising, given the frequent severity of his criticism, the first ground of Lynch's confidence that his call can be answered is the artist herself, or more generally the very nature of the dramatic imagination and its fundamental need to return to the real. For Lynch, as already noted, believed that the art is essentially grounded in "a natural declaration of faith in the value of things" and is moved by the desire to achieve "the perfect imposition of form" to represent such things.[53] In *Christ and Apollo*, he gave a theoretical explanation of that "imposition of form" in terms of the idea of analogy.[54] There he argued that successful dramatic imagination always moves analogically, not univocally by the cheap grace of easy ecstasies. It seeks a unity of meaning, in other words, not by reducing the many parts of its artistic work, or the many realities they represent, to simple instances of one controlling idea or feeling (as in Schaffer's *Equus*). Rather it achieves unity and meaning *by respecting, engaging, and moving through the diverse elements of the real*—finding a real but analogical unity in that diversity, and re-presenting that unity in the many different but analogically-related parts of its artistic work.[55]

Take, again, the example of a love story. Whether in book or on stage or in cinema, the movement of a good love story (artistically speaking) does not stay fixed on, or move relentlessly towards, one magnificently dreamy (or steamy!) image. Rather it follows the smaller, more definite lines of actual love as it develops in different situations and stages over time, or in the related but different stories of different characters. *War and Peace*, for example, is (among many other things) an analogously developed love story in just this sense. It moves towards an understanding of human love by building a complex unity out of a number of different characters and relationships, each with many changes and developments over time. Each character, each situation, is allowed to appear with the clarity and definiteness of its actuality and difference. There are no sudden leaps to unearned romantic glory, no dominating magnificence which forces a narrow unity of tone or insight on all difference. Yet the movement of Tolstoy's imagination (and our own) through these many differences leads to a real and enlarged

---

53. See p. 93 above.

54. CA, 108–60; see also pp. 84–89 above.

55. See Lynch's reprise of Francis Fergusson's classic analysis of the analogical unity of *Oedipus* in CA, 155–56.

understanding of love. That achievement is, in Lynch's terms, the work of an analogical imagination. The power of such dramatic imagination is that it enables us, in turn, to move with some greater understanding and sensitivity into the analogously same-yet-different experiences of our own lives.

Of course Lynch does not base his confidence in the artist and her craft on this theory of analogy. Rather it is the reverse. His confidence is in the fact that some artists have continually managed to "get it right," to produce "the real thing," and will continue to do so. The theory of the analogical unity of the work of art is simply an explanation of how the imagination of such artists has actually "gotten it right" by moving further and further into the real. The artist herself does not need the theory. What she needs is real imagination, freed from the paralysis of disgust and dreams, as well as her own constant desire to "get it right." For the development of such imagination and desire, she above all needs keen attention to the actualities of the world and of human action. She probably also needs regular study of the achievements of other artists as well as the regular help of critics. Nor do the critics necessarily need the theory. Yet they certainly must have a taste and sensibility schooled both by experience and by the history of artistic achievement. The value of the theory of analogical unity is that it may help both artist and critic to better understand what they are seeing in their continued apprenticeship both to tradition and to the real, and thus what they themselves are attempting in their creation or criticism of new work.

(2) The second ground on which Lynch stands in issuing his call is, then, implied in the first. It is the long mimetic achievement of Western literature and theater, beginning with Aeschylus and continuing unto the latest successful and increasingly global achievements of the dramatic imagination in our own time. Whatever the historical skepticism of some contemporary critics, Lynch at least was convinced that this tradition is at once still accessible and still ours. Sustained attention to its achievement would enable today's artist and the rest of us to move again, with our own imagination and freedom, into the challenging realities of our time.

Lynch's last major writing project involved just such an attentive "return to the sources" of our dramatic tradition. Most of the articles written specifically for the *Drama of the Mind* project[56] focus in detail on specific classical plays: on Aeschylus' *The Persians* and the *Oresteia*, on Sophocles' *Oedipus*, and Euripedes' *Bacchae*. One essay describes how the very architecture of Greek theaters was deliberately designed to keep the mind of playwright, actor, and audience in continual contact with those larger

---

56. See p. 90 n. 1 above.

natural and divine realities within which human action occurs.[57] The titles of some of these articles give a clear sense of Lynch's purpose: "The Drama of the Mind: An Ontology of the Imagination" (since the human mind is essentially temporal or dramatic and must, if it is to know, move imaginatively through time into the real); "The Imagination of the Drama" (since it is especially the imagination of dramatic artists which models for us that movement through time which traces the real lines and rhythms of human action and experience); and finally "A Dramatic Making of the Human" (since the dramatic imagination of 5th Century Athens actually shaped a new and enlarged form of life for the human city, and a renewed dramatic imagination today might again help us in this same task).

Yet these essays, and Lynch's many other writings about the dramatic imagination, did not focus only on ancient theater. Rather they move freely from that point of origin, noting and on occasion pausing to comment on the many achievements of the mimetic tradition. I have already noted Lynch's considerable interest in Dante, Cervantes, and Dostoevski. To that I should add his discussion of more recent dramatists like Synge, Beckett, and Fugard.[58] And, of course, his already-noted interest in the achievements of contemporary cinema.

(3) Yet this tradition of dramatic realism was not shaped only by its Greek origins. It has been shaped even more fundamentally by the impact of the Bible on our narrative and dramatic imagination.[59] Thus for Lynch, the third and most fundamental ground of his confidence that a recovery and development of the tradition of dramatic realism can be realized is Christ. Lynch was convinced that this name can and should speak, albeit in different ways, to both Christian and non-Christian, believer and non-believer. It can be, in the words of an already-cited passage from *Christ and Apollo*, "the model and source of that energy and courage we [all] again need to enter the finite as the only creative and generative source of beauty" (CA, xii).[60]

In *Mimesis*, Auerbach had focused on how the concreteness of biblical narrative contrasted with the high style of classical antiquity by bringing the story down to the life of the ordinary person and everyday events, and how that contrast had gradually transformed the "representation of reality in Western literature." Lynch, tutored by Ignatius, focused more narrowly on "the actual life of Christ" and "the great fact of Christology that Christ

---

57. Lynch, "Drama of Mind," 23–28.

58. For Synge see CA, 41, 146, 149, 156, 193–94. For Beckett see CP, 67–70 and "Imagination of Drama," 4, 6–7. For Fugard see "Easy," 18–19.

59. See especially 14–23 and 40–49 of Auerbach's *Mimesis*.

60. See p. 116 above.

moved down into all the realities of man to get to his Father" (CA, 12). For it is above all the stories of Christ's life, of his fully human movement through time, even unto death—stories repeated continually over centuries in word and image and ritual—that have shaped the dramatic imagination of the West.

Of course for Lynch the significance of Christ is far more fundamental than this empirical fact of literary history. For "Christian belief is in its essence belief in a Man who, having 'created' time, could not possibly be hostile to it; who had directed it from the beginning by His providence and . . . who finally entered it and grew into it with such subtlety and power that He is not the enemy of but the model for the imagination and the intelligence" (CA, 50). In the movements of His life, Christ "re-explored the time of man," taking "as his instrument . . . the whole temporal process . . . [and traversing] the whole length and breadth of the human adventure" (CA, 176). Thus "He who is the Lord of all things is the lord of the imagination" (CA, 157).

Clearly these highly rhetorical phrases from various points in *Christ and Apollo* deserve further explication. For the moment I can best provide an indication of their meaning *for the believer* simply by citing a sermon Lynch gave in 1954 at a Mass for a Catholic poetry society:

> [O]ur God is a God of Existence, and not of dreams . . . He is the God of Abraham, Isaac and Jacob; and being this kind of God, being a God of existence, then He can only be found in existence, in the things that are, in real people, real situations. This God is not to be found in the past, nor in the future, nor in a dream, but in the present, its people, its mud, its obscurities, its need for pain and decisions . . . What else has Christ wished to indicate to us save that this human way of ours is not a curse or condemnation, not an evil to be escaped from by men or by poets, but is the way into God and glory, whether for the soul or the poetic imagination.[61]

Yet what of the non-Christian and the non-believer? What of many in that secular literary mainstream Lynch wished to address for whom Christ is not "the Lord of all things"? It is at least quite clear that for these too Lynch also proposed Christ "as the model and source of that energy and courage we again need to enter the finite." Early in *Christ and Apollo* he says:

> What I am attempting to formulate throughout this book is an ideal attitude for the imagination in relation to the finite . . . [T]he attitude I am proposing . . . is exemplified in Christology . . . [W]e need go no further than the earthly, concrete, limited

61. Lynch, "For Redeemed," 84–85.

Christ . . . *Whether we believe in Him or not,* He represents an ideal point at which the imagination can relax the strain of its double aspirations [for both concrete existence and larger meaning] (CA, 15, emphasis added).

Even for the non-Christian, in other words, Christ is a legitimate and culturally powerful symbol ("an ideal point") for that movement into time and the definite which the artistic imagination itself, in its own proper autonomy, necessarily seeks in its quest for larger meaning and beauty.

It is, then, this sense of the utter importance of the movement through time and the definite, a movement embodied in Christ for one and simply symbolized by Christ for the other, that is the basis of Lynch's hope that Christian and non-Christian might cooperate in working to heal the imaginative and spiritual diseases of our time. It is also the fundamental basis of his continual call for the collaboration of theology and the literary imagination in this urgent cultural task.

Perhaps Bill Lynch was naïve even in hoping for serious collaboration between theology and literature, much less in thinking that such collaboration could contribute to a significant transformation of our dominant forms of sensibility and spirituality. For it seems that, despite various efforts since he wrote to build bridges between literature and theology, there remains a deep chasm of distrust. It seems even more clear that our dramatic arts, again despite many notable achievements, remain too often just instruments of entertainment, producers of dream and fantasy, far more controlled by commercial interests than when Lynch wrote. Both faith and the arts still seem fundamentally relegated to the sidelines of society, each assigned an essentially private and therapeutic function by the usually benign and occasionally even pious dismissals of the "realists" who manage our ever-more dominant economic, political, and cultural systems.

Perhaps it has always been so. Yet it is also possible that such judgments are too easily misled by surface appearances. Perhaps those of us tempted to think Lynch naïve remain, in fact, captive to forms of gnostic sensibility which have reduced our sense of the real and narrowed our understanding of imaginative possibility. Perhaps, too, a residual Gnosticism leaves many of us Christians with a too highly "spiritualized" and "disincarnate" understanding of Christ.

This much, at least, seems certain. Lynch himself, student of Aeschylus and Plato, and disciple of Christ, never envisioned any easy victory in the long war between fundamentally opposed forms of imagination and sensibility. Nor did he ever cease to enlarge the scope of his own engagement in that war.

5

Dionysus–The Education of Desire

L et me put it clearly and simply at the outset: this chapter takes up three of Lynch's books: *Images of Hope* (1965), *Images of Faith* (1973), and *A Book of Admiration*.[1] It is about the long, indeed the life-long journey whereby the foundational human force of desire or *eros*, that source or ground whence flow faith and hope as well as admiration and love, is gradually educated into ever more human and virtuous forms of life. [2] It will also be about irony which plays such a central role in that education, and about the equally central role of imagination, particularly about the ironic imagination and the development of an appropriately ironic sensibility.[3]

At first glance, the publication of *Images of Hope: Imagination as Healer of the Hopeless* in 1965 seems to represent a major shift in Lynch's work. Its focus on mental illness and hope is quite different from the broader philosophical, literary, and political writings which preceded it. The book grew

1. A 111-page typescript of *A Book of Admiration* (with many hand-written corrections and additions) can be found at the Fordham University Archives, along with correspondence about that typescript (dated May 22, 1974) from Ann Rice, Lynch's editor at the University of Notre Dame Press. As it stands, the text clearly still needed much editing. There are, moreover, definite indications within the text that further sections were envisioned, though there is no evidence that Lynch ever got to them. Bednar (*Faith,* 96 n.46) says that "Lynch was still working on this remarkable book at the time of his death."

2. It will become clear that, at least for Lynch, faith, hope, admiration, and love are not neatly separable "things," like bricks in a wall or building blocks in a moral system. Rather they are, as concepts and as realities, analogous—that is to say that they are both the same and different, each a "different" aspect of or way of embodying "the same" basic reality. In Lynch's writing and in what follows here, they are like so many threads continually interwoven in the depiction of that reality. For my purposes, then, I will typically be speaking of them together and somewhat interchangeably, without overly cautious distinctions.

3. Lynch's discussion of irony is so central to *Images of Faith* that he subtitled the book "An Exploration of the Ironic Imagination."

not from Lynch's years of work in those areas, but from his own experience of mental illness, and from subsequent study of psychoanalytic literature and "a year in residence among the actualities of the mentally ill" at St. Elizabeth's Hospital in Washington (IH, 15). It's "Forward" by Leslie Farber, then a leading figure in psychiatric circles, also suggests that it was intended at least in part for those concerned professionally with mental health issues.[4]

Lynch himself admits that at first *Images of Hope* "seemed a departure . . . from work I had been doing over recent years on the life of the imagination. It took me a long time to see . . . that there was so strong an equation between hope and the life of the imagination." "I mean," he then adds, "the life of the imagination in the widest possible sense, not only its life as it is more narrowly if wonderfully contained in the arts" (IH, 13).

The book finally involved, in other words, not a basic shift in the focus of his work, but an *enlargement* of that focus to include the journey of the individual (of contemporary Everywoman and Everyman) into our world and therefore into a life of realistic hope. For without hope there is no movement into reality, and that is one good way of understanding mental illness. Yet as the book makes clear, the therapeutic journey of the mentally ill from hopelessness to hope is simply an especially pointed and poignant instance of the human journey of every woman and man.[5] *Images of Hope*, then, represents a more sustained analysis of the individual spiritual journey than one finds in Lynch's earlier books. Yet that analysis brings Lynch back to fundamental themes developed in those books.

Lynch would again take up this focus on the individual's odyssey in *Images of Faith* and in the never-completed *A Book of Admiration*. He even notes, in the draft pages of that latter project, that friends suggested that the three works were a kind of trilogy about the great foundations of the Christian life: faith, hope, and love.[6] It is clear, however, that Lynch was primarily concerned, to put the matter in traditional theological language, with the "natural" forms of these virtues. Or, perhaps better put, his concern was the

4. The book has stayed in print for more than fifty years, presumably because of use in such circles, perhaps especially for studies in pastoral psychology.

5. My concern in this chapter is with that common human journey. I suspect that the analytic ideas in *Images of Hope* remain quite relevant today to the treatment of mental illness even as pharmacological treatments have increasingly taken precedence. Yet I leave discussion of the book's significance for the treatment of mental illness to those better qualified.

6. BA 5. While he there expresses hesitancy to attempt a book about so grand a theme as love, Lynch is nonetheless clear that "admiration" is one of the fundamental forms of love. In what follows I will speak about both admiration and love, since admiration is the topic on which Lynch wrote, but always with the understanding that it is a basic form of love.

human development of these great and fundamental forms of life, with the education and shaping of the basic energy of desire into ever more human forms of hope and faith, admiration and love. He clearly was concerned to elaborate what he saw as the central contribution of Christ to that education. Yet he was little concerned with older theological distinctions and debates, whether about the interplay of nature and grace in that education or about the specific content of classical treatises on the theological virtues.

Images of Faith, by far Lynch's most complex and synthesizing work, is at once concerned both with the calamitous hemorrhaging of shared faith and mutual trust from the life of our body politic, and with faith's development in the life of the individual. Indeed the discussion of faith's development is so central in *Images of Faith* that the book will provide something of an overarching framework for the present chapter. In his *Book of Admiration*, by contrast, Lynch says he wants to write autobiographically about some "specific and very actual things I have in my own life admired and still do," yet he simultaneously makes very clear that his more fundamental theme is the "birth and genesis of admiration" itself (BA, 1) and our need, both as individuals and as a culture, to recover and develop many forms of admiration to counter the many forms of alienation and contempt which pervade private and public life.

> [For admiration] is basically a motion from the self, out of the self, into reality . . . This is a book of the journey of the self, especially of the sick self—and we are all a little bit sick—into the world. I do not think that it is modern; in fact it is anti-modern if you take as one of the many definitions of modernism the movement from the world into the self. (BA, 1)[7]

This chapter, then, focuses on the education of desire. It uses, as did Lynch, above all in *Images of Faith*, the figure of Dionysus as symbol for that primal energy which must be educated into forms of faith and hope, admiration and love. It traces the spiritual journey of such education in the life of the individual—of Pilgrim or Everywoman and Everyman—just as the next chapter will focus on this "same" journey or drama from the wider perspective of society or the human city. Yet while unavoidable, this distinction between the individual and society (and between self and world) is somewhat misleading. Adapting Gospel imagery, Lynch as we have seen

---

7. Shortly thereafter Lynch suggests that he should perhaps call his book "a little journey to the exterior" in deliberate contrast with "Eric Heller's *Journey into the Interior*, a good book for those who want to know how in the first place much of the world got caught in the void of the self" (BA, 4). The incomplete reference is to German critic Erich Heller's still important book *The Artist's Journey into the Interior*.

spoke of both "the power of real being outside of and real self-identity inside the human person," what he often referred to as "the good taste" both of oneself and of the world, as "the *two* pearls without price" (CA, xiii, emphasis added). Yet he knew and continually stressed that self and society (or self and world, or inside and outside) constitute a fundamental contrariety.[8] "For the taste of the world is the taste of me. They go back and forth, the two tastes, determining each other" (BA, 39). The self comes to itself only as it enters the world. "Of all the things we need," we have heard Lynch say, "we need a world."[9] But the world is the world that we know and make, and only that society or city which nurtures the journey of the self into the world can truly be called human. In this chapter, then, we look at this basic contrariety from the perspective of the self and the journey outwards, in the next from the perspective of the human city which today both nurtures and distorts that journey.

What follows, then, draws on all three of these books, though most heavily on *Images of Faith* and then on *Images of Hope*. Yet it is (again) not an attempt to summarize Lynch's books, nor is its particular outline drawn from any of them. Rather I have simply selected key ideas from them in order to imagine and suggest the individual's journey into the kind of spirituality and sensibility Lynch called for as a response to the hopelessness and contempt, the deep fear and lack of fundamental trust, which are so characteristic of life in the human city, perhaps especially today.

For, to reiterate a constant theme, the vastly expanded and still expanding horizons of human life in our times present very difficult challenges for hope, faith, and love. Lynch begins *Images of Hope* with a lengthy section on the many forms of hopelessness which pervade our culture. *A Book of Admiration* also begins with the fundamental problem that so many contemporary human beings have turned within themselves in fear, depression, or contempt. *Images of Faith*, for its part, is centrally concerned with the crisis caused by the erosion of so many forms of basic trust or faith in our society and the consequently growing climate of contempt.

There are, of course, many particular causes for such loss of faith, such contempt and hopelessness. Yet perhaps the most fundamental cause is a loss of firm footing, of basic contact with and good taste of both self and world. In *A Book of Admiration* Lynch returns repeatedly to the thought which he had articulated more fully in *Christ and Prometheus*—that we live during an era shaped by a momentous release of energy, something comparable to

---

8. See Chapter 3 above for the details of Lynch's discussion of contrariety.

9. See p. 25 above.

the "promethean" developments of 5th Century Athens.[10] Much in us has responded to modern developments with hope and expectation. Yet a good half of us responds with fear, guilt, and retreat. Our problem, as Lynch puts it in *Images of Faith*, is that the vast horizons of "this new world" seem to be "ironizing every limited, definite thing [even our very selves], ironizing it out of existence, dissolving it, dissolving all" so that "Yeats' phrase returns to the ear: The center cannot stand" (30).[11] Our temptation, and all too frequently our actual response, is withdrawal into various forms of distrust and hopelessness. We build, to return to that basic image with which Lynch had opened *Images of Hope*, various walled cities to exclude all that is threatening and different.[12]

Yet both Christ and our own Dionysian energies call us instead to build inclusive cities where renewed forms of contact with the realities of our world will both embody hope, faith, and love, and nurture their continued development in individual lives. At one point Lynch says, quite simply, "reality . . . existence itself . . . is the great object of hope and is curative in all its wide forms" (IH, 139). Yet he was not naïve. There is much real evil. Contact with the real involves serious challenges and often immense struggle. It requires an Asechylean rhythm of moving forward and falling back, acting and suffering. Yet for all the struggle and suffering, or perhaps because of it—by moving *through* it—the odyssey of growth in hope and faith and love is fundamentally an odyssey into and not away from this world.

I must, finally, warn that the degree of selectivity in what follows far exceeds even that of preceding chapters. How else but by extreme selectivity might I "cover," in one chapter, three complex books and their great themes of faith, hope, and admiration? So too, then, the danger that I will here, against Lynch's repeated warnings, be moving far too quickly from the many to the one, from a few selected ideas and examples into an abstract or merely notional form of understanding. Yet my purpose, again, is simply to introduce. Thus I will be tracing only one path across that field which Lynch continually crisscrossed in many different ways in these books—in the hope that the reader might be led by my simplified version to take up the slower movement of Lynch's far richer texts.[13]

10. See pp. 15 & 16 above for CP, and BA, 7–8, 17–19, 53.

11. The reference, again, is to Yeats' poem "The Second Coming," and Yeats' actual words are "the center cannot hold."

12. See p. 17 above and IH, 26–27.

13. I realize, of course, that few will have the opportunity or perhaps the interest to read the manuscript of *A Book of Admiration*. It seems nonetheless important to include at least occasional reference to it in this chapter since Lynch himself clearly saw it as part of his continuing exploration of the human journey. It is, moreover, a

Dionysus

I begin as does Lynch in *Images of Faith* with Dionysus as symbol both for the great good of primal human energy or desire, and also for the many temptations and dangers involved in that very great good. I will sketch an image of the movement of that primal energy in the making of an individual life, a movement whereby desire must continually be educated into more and more adequate forms of hope and faith, admiration and love. In doing this I am following Lynch by trying to imagine the spiritual journey, to imagine realistically how faith and hope and admiration actually develop, and to distinguish their authentic forms from destructive but also quite pervasive substitutes.

Imagine, Lynch says, the deepest origin of the human potentiality for faith—*and with it also* that "same" fundamental energy that is the root of hope and the original source of admiration and love. Imagine this depth as "the most primary, the most elemental force in human nature . . . " (IF, 9), as "a giant, universally operative force that is seeking proper objects, definitions, form, shape, people . . . " (IF, 36). It is, Lynch does not hesitate to claim—and I deliberately emphasize the scope of his claim by my bracketed additions, for he means nothing less—"so mighty a torrent that it becomes the primal and originating force in (1) [all] human politics, (2) [all] relationship, and (3) [all] thought" (IF, 35).

One could use ancient words like "*eros*" or modern terms like "*id*" to try to describe this primal force, and we might benefit thereby from insights developed in philosophical, theological, and psychiatric thought. Yet, while clearly informed by such insights, Lynch was always somewhat wary of theory-laden terms, primarily because of the hunger for notional and univocal clarity which too frequently operates within their use. He preferred more concrete forms of description and explanation and so turned to mythology and classical theater for fundamental images which grounded his analyses. In *Images of Faith* Lynch actually refers first to Euripides' character Medea for an image of faith, or actually an image of the immense and terrible fury at faith's betrayal, to the point of killing her own children. She gives us an initial sense of the depth and, in its original form, the irrational power of faith in human lives.[14] For a fuller image, though, Lynch subsequently turns to Dionysus, "one of the most brilliant metaphors the human imagination

remarkable, albeit very unfinished writing.

14. See IF, 38–39.

has forged to describe that universal and primal force . . . which is so much larger a part of man than we have reckoned with" (IF, 45).[15]

Above all, Dionysus provides a dynamic image for the original form of that force when it is "not yet educated" and "has as yet only initial relation to . . . the world" (IF, 41).[16] As such, in this barely discernable form, "It is beautiful, ecstatic, as yet unironic; it is mad and visionary . . ." Dionysus' devotees "seek him upon the mountains . . . in wild and lonely ritual" where they "break out of the limits of any embodiment, for the sake of pure experience." Each becomes (here Lynch is quoting Lewis Richard Farnell's *The Cults of the Greek States*[17]) an "'enthusiast' [who] is *entheos*, 'full of the god' [and] possess for the time the power and character of his deity," whose "method is in the madness . . . the whirling dance . . . the frantic clamor . . . the drinking of certain narcotics or stimulants . . . the drinking of the blood and the eating of the raw flesh of an animal . . ."

Yet the incarnations of Dionysus are not all so "wild and lonely." In ancient tradition, "He is the god not merely of wine, but of the flower and the tree and every coursing, growing vein and thing in the earth. He is the god of life and ecstasy, of the bull and the goat and the phallus, of all fruitfulness and productive vigor." He is fundamentally, then, not an enemy but a friend of the human as the source of "all fruitfulness and productive vigor." In Christian terms, this demigod is a foundational element in God's good creation of life, and especially of human life.

Clearly, then, Dionysus is not simply an imaginary figure of ancient myth, ritual and theater. He is, rather, very much with and within us today, evident in so many dimensions of contemporary culture that few are not (at some level of awareness) "especially interested in this beautiful god . . ."[18] Thus he may well stand for us as a powerful image not simply for the most original and irrational source of faith, hope, and love, but also for the subsequent ways in which that energy becomes incarnate in the story of our lives and in the real history of our times—for the ways (to repeat) that "it

---

15. References to the figure of Dionysus occur throughout *Images of Faith* (see especially 41–45). Lynch's exploration of the contemporary significance of Dionysus came to subsequent expression especially in his 1975 *Cross Currents* essay "Euripides' 'Bacchae,'" then in his *America* review of *Equus* ("What's Wrong"), and finally in an abbreviated version of the *Cross Currents* essay published in *New York Images* in 1986 ("The Bacchae").

16. Subsequent citations in this and the following paragraph are from IF, 41–43.

17. Farnell, *Cults*, 5, 161–162.

18. Lynch, "What's Wrong," 420. In this review of the Broadway production of *Equus* Lynch does not hesitate to call Dionysus "the presiding God" of recent U.S. culture. See pp. 109–110 above.

becomes the primal and originating force in (1) human politics, (2) relationship, and (3) thought."

In the terms of developmental psychology, then, Dionysus is present not only in the necessary first form of the infant's "faith in his own omnipotence," but also as the energy for his gradual emergence "into the articulated world of objects and of time . . . " (IF, 62).[19] For most of us, such Dionysian energy is probably even more clearly evident during adolescence and young adulthood—in the dreams and ideals, the struggles and suffering so characteristic of these subsequent developmental stages. Yet, as both the daily news and the social sciences continually remind us, Dionysian passion is also clearly evident and continually operative in so many social, political and cultural causes and crusades, whether for God and moral purity, or for peace and human liberation, or for conquest and vengeance.[20]

The Structure of Desire

Through the figure of Dionysus we, with Lynch, have begun to imagine what might be called a, or even *the* basic structure of faith, hope, and admiration (though this is my terminology, my attempt to provide an overview of Lynch's more complex imagining). Each flows initially as a mighty torrent from a primal source within our being. So central is that source to faith that in *Images of Faith* Lynch simply calls it "faith," by which he means that it is the most original form of faith and the source of all subsequent forms. He then argues that this sense of faith's origin should become our primary image for faith—an image of faith as operative prior to all knowledge and experience, not just as something subsequent to them as we find in other, more prevalent images of faith. Yet such primal faith, as also the hope and love which course within it, immediately and necessarily seeks experiential contact with real objects and persons in this world. Thus we also need to stress the "horizontal" character of this image of human faith—to see that primal faith's most immediate outreach is to this world, an outreach that is foundational for those later forms of faith which we more typically imagine as "vertical," both as subsequent to knowledge and experience and as transcending this world. The basic structure, then, of human faith—the basic

---

19. For Lynch's detailed analysis of the infant and child's first forms of faith see IF, 111–25.

20. As we shall see in the next chapter, *Images of Faith* was, among many things, an extended and sympathetic, but critical dialogue with the various progressive and revolutionary crusades that especially marked the time when Lynch wrote.

structure of desire—is that of a primal energy which, in stages and phases, moves gradually but ever more fully into and through the actual world.[21]

That same basic structure is also operative in the broad argument of *Images of Hope*, even if Lynch there presents it in slightly different terms. The mentally ill, he argues, are trapped within themselves by various forms of hopelessness, as are we all to some degree. Yet the root of all such hopelessness is the inability to wish. For it is the simple but utterly fundamental ability to wish, to have and make ordinary but real wishes, that grounds hope. Thus, when we are hopeless, it is the ability to wish that gradually restores health by connecting us ever again to the real world of objects and persons. What, after all, is a wish but a movement of desire from the self to some aspect of the world? And we wish only if we have some real hope that our wishes might be realized, only if prior wishes have been realized. Thus the seemingly simple and most ordinary act of wishing is, on Lynch's analysis, central to understanding mental illness. The real root of illness is not, as some theories and images might have it, too much wishing and excessive anxiety, nor is it the mad and hopeless wishes which at times do indeed characterize the behavior of the ill. Rather it is some frustration of the simple but utterly fundamental ability to wish.

> I speak that strongly [Lynch says] because wishing and wanting, and the energy involved in these operations, must come very close to defining what is best and most necessary to man . . . *What makes him ill when he is mentally ill are all the things in and out of him that prevent him from wishing.* When these things rise to a certain pitch of the inhibition of wishing, he begins to be without hope and to be sick. He is in prison. Only the triumph of wishing will bring him release. (IH, 130)[22]

So central is wishing to human well-being that Lynch also says (in language which, as we've seen, later becomes central in *Images of Faith*):

---

21. This argument for a more primary and realistic image of the nature of faith is the first meaning of the title, *Images of Faith*, and the subject of the first half of the book. See especially IF, 3–4, 9–13, and the entire second chapter ("Reimagining Faith").

22. Emphasis in original. A "triumph of wishing," let it be emphasized, is not a "triumph of the will." An exaggerated emphasis on will ("just do it!"), and especially on some absolutized "triumph of the will," is a sign not of hope but of hopelessness and even madness. The modern emphasis on will, in contrast to ordinary wishing, is itself a typical sign of illness in our culture and a source of many pseudo-heroic images which lead us ordinary mortals into depression and other forms of hopelessness. See also the chapter on "The Absolute Wish versus the Willful Act" in IH.

Let us conceive then of a single human energizing and wishing faculty that comes close to being man himself . . . It is a free, generalized energy or love or capacity for wishing . . . (IH, 140–41)[23]

Yet, once again, what most characterizes actual wishing is its immediate relation to an object, to something that it wants. And the healing power of our wishes is found in the reality of their objects. Thus, Lynch calls special attention to what we too typically take for granted:

> To enter the presence of objects is an extraordinary experience. The mentally ill experience them as though they had never been there before; as though for the first time there is nothing wrong . . . The mind is at rest. It senses a relationship of mutuality with objects, as though they were made for it and it for them . . . These are rare moments, for the well or the sick, these pure moments of quiet contact with objects. (IH, 198)

In more general terms, Lynch never ceases to reiterate that "reality—that is, existence itself—[is] the great object of hope and is curative in all its wide forms" (IH, 189). "For reality is the very atmosphere of men. They must breathe it or perish" (IH, 201). "It is all the forms of separation [from reality] that cause all the degrees of hopelessness. It is all the degrees of contact that give us the degrees of hope" (IH, 191). Thus "a restoration of different contacts with reality . . . is the great need of [both] the sick and the well" (IH, 189).[24]

Clearly, of course, for Lynch as for all believers, the reality of God (in "the beatific vision") is the ultimate object of wishing and of hope, the ultimate reality we need contact with. Clearly, too, such ultimate hope is a crucial source of an individual's (or a culture's) ability to wish for objects and relationships in this world.

> [For] there is a double movement of the human spirit, a movement toward God and a movement toward the world. The successful maintenance of the movement toward God is the very thing that makes possible the free, uninhibited movement of man into the world in every possible form save sin: in work, in the family, in politics, in science, in the literary imagination, in literally doing whatever one wishes. (IH, 152–53)[25]

23. Emphasis in original.

24. The second part of *Images of Hope* centers on wishing and is called "Towards a Psychology of Hope." The third and final part centers on reality as the object of hope and is titled "Towards a Metaphysics of Hope."

25. As we shall see below, in Chapters 7 and 8, the concluding "Epilogue" to *Christ and Prometheus* makes a similar argument that all the autonomous wishes, great and

Yet once again, and perhaps especially for the believer, we must be constantly wary of moving too quickly from the many to the one. For our God is not some distant "Transcendence,"[26] but a God of existence, of incarnation, of time and the definite. Thus while it is true that "successful maintenance of the movement toward God is the very thing that makes possible the free, uninhibited movement of man into the world," it is *also* and from a developmental perspective *more fundamentally true* (and more true to the overall argument of *Images of Hope*) that successful maintenance of movement into the world is the continually necessary ground for developing an ultimate hope and faith in God that is something more than fantasy or illusion.[27]

The basic structure of hope, then, as of faith (and love), clearly reaches to ultimate reality. Our hearts are indeed, as Augustine famously prayed, "restless until they rest in Thee." Yet throughout our lives it is a structure that first moves us "into the valley of the human" (IH, 117). It requires, to return to the key passage with which we began this book, "the concrete movement of faith and the imagination through experience, through time, through the definite, through the human, through the actual life of Christ" (IF, 81).

For Lynch, moreover, as that passage clearly indicates, this concrete movement is one of both "faith *and the imagination*." The structure of hope, as of faith and love, requires not just the movement of desire into this world, but *a companion movement of the imagination* without which there can be no contact with the actual world. For finally only the realistic imagination makes experience of this world possible.[28] Thus the imagination enables and guides hope's wish-filled movement into the world, just as it is also essential to the basic structure of faith and admiration, not simply some helpful addition for the creative few or the artistically inclined. Indeed, so essential is the imagination for the life of hope that Lynch does not hesitate to claim that there is a fundamental "equation between hope and the life of the imagination" (IH, 13).

---

small, that are constitutive of the great contemporary project of human secularity, finally need the full energies of religious faith if they are to be sustained in their autonomous, secular integrity, and are to defend themselves from their own mad and absolutized surrogates.

26. As, for instance, in the philosophy of Karl Jaspers.

27. This, it may be remembered, is the central argument of Lynch's important early essays "Culture" and "Saint Ignatius." See pages 39–41 and 32–37 above. It is also one of the central strands in the complex argument of *Images of Faith*.

28. In a fascinating section of *Images of Faith* (112–19) Lynch discusses the intermediary role that fantasy, like that found in most children's literature, plays in the gradual introduction of the child's faith into the harder edges of the actual, and in the gradual development of more realistic forms of imagination.

The mentally ill do not wish adequately or sufficiently, and thus do not hope, in large part because their imaginations are inhabited by ghosts and giants, fixated on illusory absolutes, or, alternatively, because they are shriveled by trauma and lost in confusion. Their wishing is constricted by the absence of an imagination that discovers or builds an adequate sense and good taste of the world, an imagination that leads thereby to a correspondingly good taste of the self and to simple confidence in the good of one's own wishes.

> An ideal human wish, a wish that is effectively human and humanly effective, is imaginative and accompanied by a correspondingly full act of the imagination in relation to what it wishes . . . Where there is no imagining there is no wishing; where there is no wishing there is no imagining. (IH, 148–49)

Imagination, then, is a further aspect of the basic structure of faith, hope, and admiration. It is midwife and mentor to their development from Dionysian origins into reliable and sustainable forms for living in this actual world. Thus it is indeed fortunate, Lynch suggests, that "Imagining things rightly is among the most human of gifts. Most of us, while not artists or poets, are better at it than we think" (IH, 149). Still, the adequate development of this gift of realistic imagination "takes time and is not an easy process for anyone, much less for the ill who have a thick undergrowth of shadows [of fantastic or fear-filled images] to march through" (, 195). It takes time, and typically much struggle and suffering.

It also takes help. For despite what may be suggested by romantic understandings of the imagination (and of hope), the actual development of imagination (as also the corresponding development of hope, faith, and love) is not a solitary or purely interior process. Rather, as Lynch insists, "the act of the imagination . . . [must] be or become an act of collaboration or mutuality. Hope not only imagines; it *imagines with*" (IH, 23). The child begins by imagining with her mother and father, sisters and brothers; the patient learns to imagine again with the help of his therapist; we all develop our imaginations with more than a little help from our friends, and with help from our artists and from the broader culture of our city which, at its best, *is* nothing other than an extended and continually renewed "body" of realistic images and imagining. Thus imagination (and hope, faith, and love along with it) "cannot be achieved alone. It must be an act of community, whether the community be a church or a nation or just two people struggling together to produce liberation in each other" (IH, 24).

The human journey, then, while it will inevitably and necessarily have many moments of solitude, perhaps especially during dark nights of suffering and hopelessness, but also during needed periods of withdrawal and reflection, is always simultaneously both personal and "an act of the city of man" (IH, 24). That too is part of the basic structure of hope, faith and love. For they depend continually on the help of others, on the adequacy of their imagining, and even more fundamentally on the adequacy of the forms of imagining or "the state of the images" which prevail in our culture. Indeed so central in the structure of desire is this role of help from the images in our culture that Lynch would have us include it in our basic image of faith. We need to see, he says, or to imagine that faith "has a body; indeed it has many bodies" (IF, 13). He even goes so far as to say that "Human society is faith itself" (IF, 57). For society is the result of the continual, historic action of primal faith moving into the world and quite literally embodying itself in relationships and institutions, in patterns of action as well as patterns of thought and imagination.

Further elaboration of this aspect of the basic structure of desire—its embodiment in social and cultural forms and the role of those forms, for good and ill, in the development of faith, hope, and love—will better await subsequent sections of this chapter and the next. As also will consideration of irony as a final element of this basic structure. For the education of desire depends upon a strong element of irony among such cultural forms, or, what is much the same thing, it depends on the specific cultural development of adequate forms of the ironic imagination. Yet explanation of the role played by irony will be easier once we have paid greater attention to the many problems and temptations which accompany the movement of Dionysus into the world.

For the moment, then, I can perhaps best conclude this initial consideration of the basic structure of desire with a simple observation about the way that structure is exemplified by admiration. For thought about admiration (and love), in contrast to thought about faith and hope, is helped rather than hindered by the dominant images of our culture. In seeking to recover a sense of the basic structure of faith, Lynch had had to work against prevalent images of faith as subsequent to knowledge and experience, and as essentially vertical or world-transcending in its orientation. So, too, in writing about hope he'd had to counter dominant understandings of hope as a resource of last resort, *after* all else had failed, and as a purely interior strength unrelated to help or to ordinary wishing or to the actual world.[29] By contrast, our prevailing images of admiration, and more generally of love, are more clearly "horizontal." What do we admire? Some object, of course, something or someone "out there" in the world. What, then, is the

---

29. See especially IH, 31.

structure of admiration? Clearly it "is basically a motion from the self, out of the self, into reality" and Lynch's *Book of Admiration* "is a book of the journey of the self . . . into the world" (BA 1). Thus the "structure" of admiration recapitulates what has already been said about the basic structure of faith and hope.

Yet it may here be important to add a further note. Throughout the manuscript of *A Book of Admiration*, Lynch continually warns against the tendency, indeed the great temptation, to think of admiration primarily in terms of great and lofty things. Thus early on he says:

> But one thing I do not mean necessarily is the great, the spectacular or the perfect; I will, above all, be thinking of *the earthly admiration of earthly things* and not of ideals or ideal human beings. Let me leave these great things to others and betters. Though I am not too modest; I have really chosen the better part. (BA, 2)

Nor is this emphasis on the ordinary and earthy, even on the small and the poor, important only for Lynch's understanding of admiration. The small and the ordinary are typical objects of our faith and hope. What do I wish for? The good taste of bread, a place to sleep, a simple smile of recognition, the floor under my feet. The small and ordinary are, moreover, as we will especially see when we come finally to a consideration of irony, the most fundamental pathway to that which is really great and lofty. Of course the great and spectacular do have their rightful place in our hopes and admirations. Yet too often they are obstacles rather than helps in the education of desire.

The Plot Thickens–The Dramatic Structure of Desire

As already noted, Lynch himself never gives any simple or neatly focused description of the basic structure of desire.[30] His writing is always deliberately more complex since it both aims at more realistic description and simultaneously tries to wean us from our desire for just one or a few (absolutely) clear ideas or images. For as we know, the emergence of the force of primal desire in our lives and into the world is invariably accompanied by complexity, by twists and turns, by opportunities and obstacles, by many problems and continual temptations. It stands in continual need of educa-

---

30. The closest he comes to such straightforward description is in his writings on the structure of drama as part of his *Drama of the Mind* project. See, for example, his essay "Imagination of Drama."

tion and correction precisely because of, but also by means of, such opportunities and problems. Thus its movement is never the kind of linear
progression I may unintentionally have suggested by speaking thus far
about a "basic structure" of the movement of desire. Rather its actual movement is typically circuitous and always dramatic, marked by an Aeschylean
rhythm of action and suffering, by the steps back as well as forward which
Lynch in his East River essay used to describe the progress of his own life
into "muddy fleshed out dreams."[31] Only through such dramatic rhythms
is there real education and the development of adequately human forms of
faith and hope, admiration and love.

To help us better understand the actual movement of desire into the
world, Lynch stresses that all of the classical descriptions of Dionysus are
deeply ambiguous.[32] He is beautiful and powerful, ecstatic and visionary.
He liberates his devotees, filling them with overpowering energies of love
and hope and faith. Yet by himself he is simply energy, absolute and pure
and un-ironic. Thus he is also wild, uneducated and uncivilized. He en-
genders faith that is dangerously blind, hope that is easily delusional, and
furious hatred as much as ecstatic love. He has no time for the rhythms of
reversal and patience, deliberation and discernment.

> The clue to understanding the spirit of Dionysus is the brilliance
> and magnificence of its love and its hate, its capacity for both en-
> thusiasm and destruction, together with its total ambiguity, its
> inability to keep these two forces together [in any self-limiting
> balance]. It is always one or the other. (IF, 45)

What counts is passionate intensity. Remember Lynch's comments on the
mad and continually escalating rhythms of *Equus*![33] Nor does such intensity
remain on lonely mountain heights or confined within ritual moments and
movements. Rather Dionysus, with all his magnificent hunger and thirst,
comes roaring into the life of the city, into personal life as much as politics,
and brings with him destruction every bit as much as creativity.

I recently had occasion, after many years, to again see the film version
of Nikos Kazantzakis' *Zorba the Greek*, that much celebrated early 1960s
dramatization of the Dionysian spirit. This time I was struck by the elements
of dark passion and violence that I'd simply ignored in the enthusiasm of my
youthful viewing. It then also struck me that Bernardo Bertolucci's justly
celebrated *Last Tango in Paris*, released as if symbolically and ironically a

31. See pp. 24–26 above.
32. See IF, 41–45.
33. See pp. 109–110 above.

decade later, at the end of "the 60s," provided a much darker and far less ambiguous depiction of the destructive aspects of Dionysian passion. Indeed much of Marlin Brando's fame as an actor, not only in *Last Tango* but all the way back to *On the Waterfront* and forward to *Apocalypse Now* and *The Godfather*, rests on his ability to embody a smoldering, Dionysian ambiguity—with love and loyalty, anger and fierce hatred, all inextricably interwoven. The key, again, is intensity, but an always ambiguous intensity.

Thus we need to understand and to actually imagine that the movement of primal faith and hope and love into the world is deeply problematic and dramatic. For it always means that the soaring energy of dreams and great ideals, what Lynch at times refers to as "the larger line" within which our lives are inscribed, must move into the "smaller line" of our actual lives.[34] One can understand the problem, as well as the pain and suffering involved, by imagining again the infant's movement from an original sense of omnipotence and unlimited desire into the increasingly narrow confines of relationship to *this* food and *this* warmth, *this* mother, *this* family, and eventually into the emerging confines of *this actual* if still very primitive self.[35] Again, though, it may be easier for most of us to imagine in greater detail the (remembered) sufferings, the frequent missteps and misfortunes of the young who struggle to bring passionate desires and hopes into the actual and always limited relationships and careers and politics of adult life.

Yet this fundamental problem of relating passionate idealism to the real, the energy of Dionysus to ordinary life, is not simply part of the early developmental stages in life's journey. It is, Lynch stresses, "the problem of every man at every stage of life: how shall he relate his longing for happiness to reality; how shall he prevent an impossible gap between his wishes and the real world, belief and reality" (IF, 118). This challenge of relating the ideal to the real and our wishes to the limits of the world *always* remains *the* fundamental problem and challenge for faith, hope and love. And we may perhaps better understand its daunting and dramatic character if we briefly, albeit somewhat artificially, attend to its component elements.

First, then, the "objective pole," so to speak, of this drama, the actual world into which desire must move. We know well that this world is no simple and unmitigated good, not a simple aggregation of all the benign realities towards which wish and desire move. Rather the world is immensely complex, not only structured by continually challenging contrarieties,[36] but

---

34. See IF, 31 and 118.

35. As noted, Lynch (IF, 111–25) provides a detailed analysis of these initial movements, drawing especially on developments in the field of "object psychology."

36. See the entirety of Chapter 3 above.

also darkened by shadows and scarred with sin. It is typically both confusing and confused.[37] It is often unwelcoming and just as often actively hostile.
Think again, for instance, of the life of the child. Even in the best of situations, the outreach of the child's desire will regularly be met by inadequate
response, by parental fatigue, by misunderstanding, by confusion and occasional anger. And it often seems that "the best of situations" is almost the
exception. We know that many infants are homeless and hungry and hurt.
We know the appalling statistics about many different forms of child abuse
both here at home and around the world. We find in the physical, mental,
and spiritual illnesses which plague the lives of so many children abundant
evidence of the world's deep and often violent opposition to faith and hope
and love.

(Here I must pause to warn against my own rhetoric. There is always a
fine, often hard to distinguish line between a much-needed, even appalled
attention to the darkness of the world, and a univocal or absolutized and
Gnostic sense of that darkness. My attempts at brief summary, here and
below, may well cross that line, for myself as for the reader. Lynch, as we
will again soon see, continually criticized the absolutized contempt evident
in the sensibility of too many contemporary artists and intellectuals. Their
dialectic of disgust and dreams is the facile but false way of dealing with
Dionysian desire. They touch "the world" only enough so that they may leap
elsewhere to some pure and transcending form of love or faith or hope.[38]
Far more difficult is the sensibility to which Lynch calls us, one that sus-
tains the passage of desire *through* the world, through action and suffering, through real darkness always intermixed with real light, into "muddy,
fleshed-out dreams.")

Yet children are only the most obvious victims of the way the world
wounds and even kills the primal energy of desire. Think of the many ways
that the deep and legitimate dreams of youth are frustrated by inadequate
systems of schooling, work, and civic life. Think of *Catcher in the Rye*, but
then also of *The Death of a Salesman* and *A Raisin in the Sun* in order to
remember that such frustration is hardly limited to the young. Finally,
though, think of "the poor" who are so often victims of the world's pride
and greed; think of the homeless and underemployed, of the mentally ill, the
oppressed, victims of war, refugees, the growing masses of those yearning
for even the most modest freedoms and the most basic good taste of self and
world. Though here, again, we must be careful since there may be more of

---

37. See Lynch's chapter on "Hopelessness and Confusion" in *Images of Hope*
(81–104).

38. See Lynch's discussion of such "leaping" in CA, 8–10.

such simple taste among "them" than among "us." Still, the massive world-wide reality of poverty, imagined realistically and not romantically, can and must stand for us, as it did for Lynch, as a fundamental sign of the world's indifference and hostility to the yearning outreach of hope, faith, and love.

Yet even such a sweeping rhetorical evocation of ways in which "the world" despoils the primal energy of desire would be seriously incomplete did it not further emphasize how the world conspires not simply to oppose, but also to "welcome" and then seduce and misdirect our hope and faith and admiration. Such misdirections were typically Lynch's greater concern because of their pervasiveness in our culture. We have seen how in *Christ and Apollo* and *The Image Industries* he gave detailed expression to his conviction that our dramatic arts regularly mislead the energy of faith, hope and love, drawing it away from the actual lines of the real and into a hopeless dialectic of disgust and dreams. Recall, too, his concern throughout *The Integrating Mind* with the many forms of totalizing temptation prevalent in our wider social and political culture. Yet Lynch's analysis of the pervasiveness of such seduction and misdirection is perhaps nowhere more probing than in *Images of Hope*. There, his exploration of mental illness helps us understand that the world's evil is manifest not simply in its outright hostility to hopes and ideals, but perhaps even more in the many manipulations and seductions of hope at work both in our personal relationships and in powerful social currents of fantasy and fanaticism.

It is, moreover, in the detail of such analysis in *Images of Hope* that Lynch also provides what is probably his clearest explanation of what it is within us—in the "subjective pole," so to speak, of the structure of desire—that makes us so susceptible to such seductions. For it is not only "the world" (in the pejorative sense we have just been using), but also something deep within that distorts and damages the movement of primal desire. Here we return to that deep ambiguity in the spirit of Dionysus that so concerned Lynch. For pure or primal Dionysian energy not only *wishes* to move into the world, but simultaneously *wills* to oppose any limitation in such movement. In fundamental self-contradiction, it seeks both "the triumph of wishing" (for real objects) and a "triumph of the will" (that would transcend all finite and real objects). In so doing, moreover, it feeds as much on fury as on love. It wants to hope and believe, but wants hopes and beliefs that are absolutely pure and clear and final. No doubts, no hesitations, no complexity, and certainly no irony about itself (though plenty of contemptuous irony for all limitation and finitude). Just absolute purity and pure intensity.

In *Images of Hope* Lynch names this destructive dimension of desire "the absolutizing instinct."[39] His own words probably provide the best explanation of his meaning:[40]

> By the absolutizing instinct, I mean something very literal and nothing complicated. I mean the instinct in human beings that tends to absolutize everything . . .

> The instinct's whole drive is to make absolutes out of everything it touches and to pour floods of fantasy into the world about it. It is the father of all hopeless projects and of hopelessness. It is the enemy of the human and of hope.

> [It] reveals its own nature by marching with its habitual magnificence into its many concrete forms. It will not be shy about revealing itself. For it is never subtle, but always loud and boisterous, always magnificently present on the scene. It is also a world of false hopes which counterfeits the reality of hope.

> Whatever is seen (or wished) as an absolute through the glasses of this instinct receives an enormous discharge of phantasy [sic]. The absolutizing instinct magnifies. In its presence each thing loses its true perspective and its true edges. The good becomes tremendously good, the evil becomes the absolutely evil, the grey becomes the black or white, the complicated, because it is difficult to handle, becomes, in desperation, the completely simple. The small becomes the big.[41]

> . . . it is a magnifying, and over-ebullient, over-enthusiastic principle, never content to leave anything in its plain human setting. I for one have difficulty in deciding which it is, a completely ridiculous and childish exaggerator of things that always moves towards nonsense—or a distorted, distorting and misdirected part of a powerful movement of the soul towards the absolute. Perhaps it is something of both, with the worst features of both, and it is not necessary to choose between them.

---

39. See above all his chapter on "The Absolutizing Instinct" (IH, 105–25).

40. Subsequent citations are from IH 105, 106, and 108.

41. It is at this point that Lynch refers to that bar of soap which I mentioned in my "Preface" (p. xvi above). Under the influence of the absolutizing instinct it is so magnified that "there is precious little soap left." It "has become all things that the instinct desires: the creator of beauty, the winner of friends, the sharer of the life of Marilyn Monroe . . . A powerful stream of phantasy [sic] has rushed into—and destroyed—the soap" (IH, 107).

Such is the ever ambiguous spirit of Dionysus operative within us, yearning to reach out to the world, yet always ready to connect with the many seductive and absolutized forms of that spirit already operative in the world.

"Get Real"–The Flight From Possibility

I have hopefully begun to sketch a more complex and more dramatic image of the basic journey of faith, hope, and love. Let me now, in this and the next section, take two further steps in such realistic imagining before turning to the role of irony in the education which Lynch saw as necessary for that journey. I want in these sections to indicate, again with no attempt at completeness, some of the forms of absolutized seduction and misdirection that Lynch thought especially characteristic of the present moment. (I hope it will be evident that today's "present moment" is *fundamentally* the same as when Lynch wrote, even if surface preoccupations and polarizations may have somewhat shifted.)

We can begin by recalling Lynch's sense that ours is an era of such momentous change that it is comparable with only two earlier periods of epochal transition in the human story.[42] One fairly simple way of suggesting the character of the contemporary sense of change is to indicate the immensely expanded horizons—Lynch actually says "infinitely" expanded—within which we now struggle to find our bearings. Referring to Alexander Koyré's *From the Closed World to the Infinite Universe*,[43] Lynch notes how "space and time widen at both ends of the picture. Infinite time, infinite space, endless history, endless change emerge," and "Yeats' phrase returns to the ear: The center cannot stand" (IF 30).[44] Later in *Images of Faith* he takes up in greater detail this sense of living within vastly expanded horizons and stresses that "There is nothing that modern sensibility is more aware of than that it has moved into a world of infinite possibility" (IF, 144).[45] Then he also reminds us, with reference to E. R. Dodds' *The Greeks and the Irrational*, that "at least once before, an ascendant human culture, faced with new magnitudes of possibility and a new freedom, turned instead in fright into paths of superstitious passions and irrelevant imitations of the true idea of revolution" (IF, 145).

---

42. See pages 15–16 above.

43. Koyré, *From Closed World*.

44. See IF, 177 n. 8 for comment on Yeats' "The Second Coming."

45. The entire section is titled "The Movement through Infinite Possibility" (IF, 144–56).

For that, as Lynch saw it, is a crucial aspect of our actual situation. We are indeed faced with "new magnitudes of possibility and a new freedom," and thus with the possibility of a "true idea of revolution." Yet those magnitudes have so incited the absolutizing instinct, both within ourselves and in the imaginative life of the culture, that we often (perhaps even typically) feel ourselves surrounded by menacing giants. Thus we do frequently turn "into paths of superstitious passions"—either by gnostic retreat from the world or by throwing ourselves into equally absolutized forms of passionate activism (taken up in the next section of this chapter).

Lynch himself did not want to suggest that there is or even can be any one clear description of our situation, or any one adequate form of response. In fact, the very act of grasping for some one utterly certain description and response is itself a primary manifestation of our actually having "turned . . . in fright into . . . superstitious passions." And we will inevitably be betrayed by what we think we have grasped. For "The mind and imagination is crippled by the gathering intensity of the single approach, the approach that finally reaches a pinpoint in its range of visions [and] grows rigid and dark from the intensity" (IF, 78). Rather we must, for the healing of our fears and the restoration of real hope, return again and again in thought and imagination to the actual present, seeking more human avenues of understanding, never allowing ourselves to be trapped by some absolutized image.

Yet even with such caution in mind, we still find that our expanded sense of "infinite space, infinite time, endless history, and endless change" is often accompanied by the deep fear that there really no longer is any center, nor any human path ahead. We may feel bombarded from all sides by a seemingly endless and thus also quite random whirl of information, by vague appeals and indistinct shouts in the night. Or our present may again appear flat, robbed of significance and direction, like the typical setting for a Beckett play. We could describe *this* sense of the present by saying that "modernity's 'culture of optimism' . . . is giving way to a postmodern 'culture of ambiguity.'"[46] Yet Lynch himself prefers more concrete description. Ours, he says, often seems "a present that is empty and bare, that has no good taste at all" (IF, 133). Responding to such a sense of the present, the absolutizing instinct casts a univocal blanket of barrenness over the entire world. We are tempted to echo that resigned "Whatever" or the cynical "Get Real" that have become catchwords today for far too many.

It also happens, moreover, that the fragments of news and opinion that bombard us seem exclusively bad—new threats of disease; wars and rumors of wars; economic crisis, environmental depredation, growing poverty and

---

46. Volf and Katerberg, "Introduction," x.

inequality. Then this sense of a flat and empty present readily slides into a companion feeling that the present is cursed and evil, not simply a wasteland, but so filled with threat and violence that it provokes the reciprocating dynamics of deepening guilt and growing despair. Writing in the early 1970s, Lynch thought that we had become "nationally obsessed with [such] a sense of the curse and its accompanying guilt, an obsession that has its own kind of joy" (IF, 159).[47] Unfortunately it often seems that little today would lead him to change that judgment. Too many of our artists and writers, as I have repeatedly said, having lost confidence in the world, now seem to revel in their expressions of alienation and contempt. And so it also is with so much of popular culture.[48]

One almost classically modern pattern of response to this pervasive sense of a present that "has no good taste at all" and is even "cursed" is to turn from the world and retreat within. We can have no faith in or hope for this world since there is nothing left to admire. Thus all the energies of hope, faith, and admiration turn desperately within to find some pure and unspotted refuge. As noted previously,[49] Lynch deliberately contrasted his effort in A Book of Admiration with what, paraphrasing Erich Heller, he described as the modern artist's "journey into the interior," the intellectual's retreat "from the world into the self" (BA, 1)—or, as I have put it, into a world of dreams. In fact Lynch's basic purpose in writing about admiration was to counter this retreat by imagining many dimensions of admiration's journey of the self into the world. For the forms and practices of admiration, perhaps especially the most ordinary, are so many types of a "good taste" of the world, so many forms of therapy (indeed Lynch does not even hesitate to call them forms of salvation[50]) for the times and ways we become lost within ourselves and within our various walled cities.

Images of Hope, of course, had previously provided a similarly sustained reflection on the healing movement of simple wishing. For it is especially the mentally ill who have become lost within, mired by various forms of hopelessness and entrapment. Yet once again, the mentally ill are but a particularly poignant instance of a far more general tendency. For we have

47. Shortly before, in Christ and Prometheus, Lynch had been so concerned with this growing national sense of guilt that he had devoted a whole section to "The Search for Innocence" (99–120).

48. At one point in Images of Faith (107), Lynch provided a lengthy list of then-recent films which gave expression to such contempt. It would not be in the least difficult to provide a similar list today.

49. See above p. 124, n. 9.

50. BA, 4. He suggests as a "secondary title" that his is "a book on the many forms of Salvation." See also BA, 99.

all, in greater and lesser degrees, sought escape from the vast challenges of our world by many readily available forms of the turn within.

In *Images of Faith*, as previously in *Christ and Apollo* and *The Integrating Mind*, Lynch had focused particularly on the tendency of so many of our "writers and intellectuals" to view the world with ironic contempt.[51] There he provided a detailed analysis of the different "ironies of contempt" that characterize and polarize so much of our public discourse.[52] Yet the contemptuous sound and fury of our culture wars, whatever its particular practical intent, typically served also, perhaps even primarily, to reinforce a prior retreat into walled cities of ideological or aesthetic purity, cities of separation from the other, indeed from the whole ugly mess.

Nor are such sophisticated expressions of contempt necessarily the most worrisome contemporary forms of retreat from the world. For there are many more ordinary forms of such irony continually at work to unmask and reject all nobler ideals and hopes for engagement with the world. Archie Bunker is still very much with us, as are his younger counterparts who deliberately lose themselves in the trivial pursuits of consumption and entertainment and the occasional pursuit of some private form of ecstasy. As, too, is the despair of many of the poor who daily experience, in ways most of us can barely begin to understand, the actual vanishing of the "American Dream" and the callous emptiness of much public rhetoric which continues to evoke it.

Of course, Lynch's primary goal in *Images of Faith* is to differentiate all such ironies of contempt from a fundamentally different kind of irony, one that restores hope and thus enables again the movement of faith into the world. Yet he also wanted to stress the difficulty of developing that latter irony because of the pervasiveness of the former. For it often does seem that today the word "irony" has become virtually synonymous with cynicism and contempt.[53]

---

51. Paul Fussell's *The Great War* was published shortly after Lynch's *Images of Faith*. It's analysis of the transformation in sensibility among British and American writers caused by World War I provides abundant confirmation for Lynch's discussion of our men and women of letters. Here is Fussell's thesis: "I am saying that there seems to be one dominating form of modern understanding; that it is essentially ironic; and that it originates largely in the application of mind and memory to the events of the Great War" (35). The deep difference between Fussell and Lynch is that for Fussell only one kind of irony is possible for "political and social cognition in our time" (35), an irony so filled with contempt that it precludes hope, faith, and admiration.

52. See especially IF, 96–108.

53. See, as just one example, the univocal use of the term by Jedediah Purdy in *For Common Things*, a book written with laudable intent as "a response to an ironic time" (xi). "Irony," Purdy says, "has become our marker of worldliness and maturity. The

Apocalypse Now

Retreat from the world, whether contemptuous or resigned, was not, however, the only response to the challenges and fears of the present that worried Lynch. He was as much if not more concerned with what, on the surface at least, seems its polar opposite. I mean, of course, the kind of passionately and supposedly radical thrust into the world that is manifest today in many different forms of angry activism—whether on the right or the left, reactionary or revolutionary. For what characterizes many such movements is their typically Dionysian mix of fanatical hatred and apocalyptic hope. One might with some justice say that where *Images of Hope* and *A Book of Admiration* focused primarily on the contemporary retreat within, *Images of Faith* was more concerned with the equally seductive appeal of those ideological absolutisms that again came to the fore in "the 60s" and have characterized political and cultural polarizations ever since.

I say that this aggressive activist response "seems" the opposite of retreat within because in fact both responses continually reinforce one another. Each is a form of the same hunger for an absolutely clear path. One irony of the withdrawal response is suggested by the image of "walled cities" that Lynch used in his introduction to *Images of Hope*. For an absolute retreat must be defended from enemies who always seem to grow increasingly dangerous and hostile. Thus rigid retreat turns to violent defense, which in turn readily leads to pre-emptive attack. The same absolutized contempt and fear that caused flight from the world now re-enters the world to conquer and destroy.[54] Later, of course, or perhaps even simultaneously, it will again be driven from the world by guilt and fear at its own ferocity.

It is perhaps easier for us to share Lynch's concern about such Dionysian incursions into the world since we too have witnessed their terror in recent history—from the magnificent delusions of "the Great War," through Nazi and Stalinist totalitarianisms,[55] to Cold War polarizations and the recent localized horrors of Pol Pot and Rwanda, Darfur and Syria, Al Qaeda and ISIS. Thus, of course, we also face the absolutized delusions of the suicide

---

ironic individual practices a style of speech and behavior that avoids all appearances of naiveté—of naïve devotion, belief, or hope" (xi). His opening chapters describe this ironic style as "Avoiding the World" and especially "Avoiding Politics."

54. "The citizens [of walled cities] spend their time reassuring each other and hating everyone else. Actually they will never be safe and the final irony will be that they will have to make war on each other" (IH, 26–7).

55. "We have no stronger example of the modern emergence of Dionysus in the political order than the emergence of the mystique of total ecstasy, force, and the cult of the absolutely purified blood strain in the Führer's *Mein Kampf* and his creation of the National Socialist German Worker's Party" (IF, 44).

bomber as well as the extremes of our own rage against all such fanatical crusades. (I write this having just heard news of more terrorist horrors and finding myself once again wrestling in spirit not only with the hateful evil of terrorism, but also with the madness of my own outraged response.)

Of course, we also face analogous tendencies much closer to home in domestic forms of religious and political absolutism—whether those of the right which revive aspects of earlier forms of fascism, or those on the left which once again feed as much on utopian hatreds as on fantastic hopes.

Lynch was concerned to understand such passions since he saw them as so much a part of our present situation. Yet he sought to remind us, lest we also become traumatized by an absolutized image of present dangers, that the outbreak of apocalyptic expectation and anger are perennial human tendencies. He regularly recommended study of classic histories such as Ronald Knox's *Enthusiasm* and Norman Cohn's *The Pursuit of the Millennium*,[56] as well as the classic depiction of the absolute revolutionary provided by Dostoevsky in *The Demons*. Still he did want us to recognize the extent to which Dionysus had in fact returned as a powerful force in this culture and in our own hearts and minds. When he criticized the way untamed Dionysian energy was celebrated in *Equus* and in other creations of contemporary culture, he wanted us to acknowledge that such celebration met with rave reviews and audience enthusiasm precisely because it temporarily satisfied a deep hunger of our own hearts.[57]

Lynch himself turned to ancient theater for analogies and images to help us understand our present. For it is, he tells us, above all "the ancient Euripides with his great play, the *Bacchae*, in whom I place my final trust when looking for a master" to help us understand present outbursts of Dionysian passion.[58] The *Bacchae* provides perhaps the most terrifying and tragic image of the destructive fury of such passion—the image of a mother so transformed by pure Dionysian ecstasy that she tears her own son (the prince who had come to banish Dionysus) limb from limb and parades back to Thebes in triumph with his bloody head, only gradually awakening to the horror of what she had done. Yet more important than this climactic image is the way Euripides helps us to understand the escalating dynamic of hatred between Pentheus (the son) and Dionysus which had led to it. And more important still is the way Euripides simultaneously helps us discern

---

56. See, for example, IF, 91.

57. See above pp. 15–16.

58. Lynch, "What's Wrong," 421. The fuller analysis being summarized here also draws on Lynch's essay "Euripides' 'Bacchae.'"

an alternative that might have enabled Pentheus—and might enable us—to live less tragically and more fruitfully with the fearsome energies of this god.

For that, on Lynch's reading, is the central problem of the play. How do we imagine and live with Dionysus? How cope with the absolutizing energies which tend with such regularity to break into human lives and the life of the human city? Even more fundamentally, how respond to that ambiguous primal energy which must somehow find fruitful entry into our lives and into the life of the human city? How respond, especially when it again seems that the drums are rolling and apocalypse immanent?

One way, of course, is the reactionary path taken by Pentheus, strong man of Thebes, representative of reason and tradition, of law and order. His folly, Lynch says, "was that he rejects any and every form of the vision of Dionysus and in so doing rejects and imprisons half of himself, half of the drama of the mind."[59] He bans all celebration of Dionysus. More, "He not only rejects Dionysus; he insults him in every possible way, threatens him, and imprisons him."[60] In so doing he sets "extraordinarily severe limits to his image of reality, such limits as are bound to make reality finally strike back and assert itself."[61] He represents a total inability to imagine the fuller reality of Dionysus; or, what is much the same, his imagination is totally imprisoned by one fixed and absolutely threatening image of the god—and of that part of himself (and of ourselves) which is rightfully subject to Dionysus.

Thus dealt with, Dionysus responds by fulfilling Pentheus' worst fears. "His hatred is without limit, his vengeance without qualification . . . The true and great Dionysiac cult had not only let [ecstatic] forms of the imagination break out but had also given them healing. But this new Dionysus [of the *Bacchae* and of our own culture] does not cure; he escalates the mad images even more, so that nothing of the human is left in the human . . . There is no boundary for this Dionysus; he enters into the world, but makes the world disappear."[62] As Pentheus had allowed his image of Dionysus to narrow but escalate into *the* great threat, now Dionysus in turn, especially through the entranced person of his devotee Agave (the mother), absolutizes his own image of Pentheus (and of order and reason) as *the* great enemy of freedom and experience. And he destroys that enemy.

Lynch suggests that this is where we are (or risk being) in our national cultural wars, with narrowed and absolutized images of our enemies as

59. Lynch, "Euripides' 'Bacchae,'" 164.

60. Ibid.

61. Ibid.

62. Ibid., 171.

utterly treacherous and hateful, and of ourselves as utterly innocent, righteous, and beautiful. Thus when he reprinted his *Bacchae* essay in *New York Images*, he gave it the subtitle "An American Parallel."[63] "Waves of fantasy pour into the atmosphere. The two culture classes see each other as monsters, no less" (IF, 71).[64] We are no longer imagining the real, and no longer imagining with any irony but that of contempt.

Yet while the tragedy of magnificent hatreds is the dominant theme of the play, Euripides (unlike Peter Shaffer in *Equus*) also imagines Dionysus in alternative and more realistic ways. He helps us to see the fuller range of the god's presence and power in our lives—in wine and dance, in love and communal festivity. He, in other words, keeps his own imagination flexible and moving, even as he depicts the inflexible and narrowing imaginations of Pentheus and Agave/Dionysus. He thereby teaches us to imagine not only our own absolutizing images and tendencies, but also alternative and more human images of the power of Dionysus in our lives. Under such contrasting and ironic tutelage we come to understand how "the true and great Dionysiac cult" not only gave ecstasy a ritual place for expression, but also enabled more ordinary forms of Dionysian energy to find expression in daily life and community celebration. Euripides, then, provided for Athens, and does so for us as well, a finally healing image to guide the development of our passionate (Dionysian) hunger for purity and dreams and even excess. For that remains our great need, especially in these times of heightened contempt and apocalyptic expectations—to keep our imaginations free and flexible so that we might discern the always fuller range of the real; to keep ourselves free of those ironic sensibilities which fill us with fantasy and hatred; to be led by a different kind of irony, one that can welcome but also educate the deep Dionysian energy of faith, hope, and love.

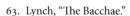

---

63. Lynch, "The Bacchae."

64. See the entire section in *Images of Faith* (66–73) where Lynch warns about the way our culture wars risk destroying that foundational faith without which no human society can exist. Lynch was arguably among the first to warn about this extreme in our present "culture wars." Perhaps even the first to suggest that term: "We are in the middle of a vast cultural crisis and division. The real war is at home. It takes the form not of the usual political divisions . . . but of a complete collapse of faith between the two cultural groups that constitute the nation . . . We are in the presence of the failure of belief (there is no belief left, the one class in the other); the lack of belief is intensified by a mutual contempt and fear such as has not often existed between two national groups in modern history. Our crisis over the Vietnam War was a trifle compared to this interior war and collapse of faith" (IF, 66).

Irony

So we come to the final part of this brief exploration of the dramatic journey of faith and hope, love and admiration, as they move into, give shape to, and are themselves educated and shaped by the stages and phases of our lives. We come, in other words, to Lynch's strong and perhaps initially surprising sense of the crucial role played by irony in enabling our Dionysian energies to enter and embrace the inescapably human reality of limitation. We will come in the end especially to the great poverties of illness, diminishment, and death through which faith and hope and love must move, but through which they can move humanly and "gracefully" only when they are tutored by an appropriately ironic sensibility.

For the energy of Dionysus must be educated as it enters the world so that it can enter and contribute to the real and human world. It is educated (and, as we have seen, also miseducated) by many things. Yet irony plays a special role because the primal force of desire must be met and finally "mastered"—not destroyed or repressed, but mentored and ruled—by an even greater force. Nor is that force just any irony, and especially not the easy ironies of contempt. Rather desire must undergo the more difficult therapy, indeed the difficult asceticism, of a far deeper form of dramatic irony which, though it has long been foundational to Western sensibility, has today too often been forgotten or brushed aside. And the "irony of Christ," Lynch further asserts, is utterly central to that deeper ironic tradition. Yet the irony of Christ "is Christ himself" (IF, 175).[65]

Images of Hope had already provided an extended discussion of how religion and psychiatry, each with its own resources, could provide therapies for healing the absolutizing instinct and thereby restoring and redirecting the energy of human wishing. At one point in that book Lynch wrote movingly about the suffering involved as we are purified of so many seductive but false absolutes—as we, in his words, "move through the fire into the valley of the human" (IH, 117). At the heart of this therapy is a reawakening,

---

65. Of course, such a bald assertion may be shocking not only to Christian sensibilities ("Is not faith in Christ the opposite of irony?"), but also to any sensibility bruised by religious absolutism and hungry for greater toleration. Yet, as we've seen throughout, Lynch's quite traditional theme is that Christ is the final source of the energy or grace that must and does befriend the great human energies of Dionysus and Apollo and Prometheus. For him this is simply a matter of belief for the Christian. Yet Lynch also asserts (at times quite explicitly, as we saw in his discussion of the dramatic arts) that the fundamental desires of the non-Christian must likewise undergo, albeit in ways specific to her situation and belief, education by the same irony that is embodied in the teachings and life of Christ, even if in her understanding that irony is named quite differently.

gradual or sudden, of our ability to imagine the world and ourselves realistically, in non-magnificent, non-absolutized terms.

Such reawakening is again central to the therapy or asceticism outlined
in *Images of Faith*, but now Lynch focuses more specifically on the "extraordinary human gift" of irony (x) and on our need for an ironic imagination
or sensibility as the fire that purges and the force that heals and educates.[66]
How, he asks, does faith—and now he means an already educated faith
and the power of such faith as it functions (both culturally and religiously)
through the person of parents and mentors and through that larger social
and cultural presence that he calls "the body of the sensibility of faith" (IF,
63)[67]—how does such faith imagine the world and work to educate the
primal energy of desire? Again, of course, in many ways, but above all by
means of irony.[68] For educated faith (as also mature hope and a developed
sense of admiration) constitutes a powerful form of ironic sensibility and
imagination. As such it works to purge and heal desire of its absolutizing
tendencies even as it leads desire toward embodiment in those habits and
practices of faith (and hope and love) which form both the life of the individual and the world through which she moves.

Yet the "logic" of such irony is not something neatly linear and open to
clear description. Irony does not work in the top of the head as some kind of
aesthetic puzzle or intellectual paradox. Rather irony works as a therapeutic
and dramatic force in the life of an individual as well as in the larger body
of a culture. It works through struggle and suffering—as we struggle again
and again through the stages of our lives to embrace the challenging reality
that great desires can be "realized" only by passage through the limitation
and poverty or "smallness" of actual human living. A full irony, in other
words, does not simply operate intellectually to "see through" Dionysian
pretensions; contempt is sufficient for that task. Rather it operates dramatically to help us "realize" (in life more than thought) that good taste of self
and world which is achieved as our great desires become embodied in finite

---

66. In the opening pages of *Images of Faith* Lynch clearly says: "I have chosen
irony, the ironic imagination, the irony of faith, the irony of Christ, as the real subject
of this book" (14). The second and the "more important" (77) half of his book focuses
entirely on irony, initially (in chapter 3, "The Structure of the Irony of Faith") by an
extended critical discussion of the many different forms of irony, and then (in chapter
4, "The Images of Faith and Human Time") by imagining the way irony operates in the
stages of faith's development. See also IF, 24–33 for a preliminary statement about the
ironic sensibility of an already educated faith.

67. The greater part of the second chapter of *Images of Faith* ("Reimagining Faith")
is devoted to this idea that faith (both human and religious faith) has a real "body" in
human culture and society. See IF, 53–74 and also 12–13.

68. See especially IF, 77.

but real wishes and achievements and perhaps especially in the sufferings of our lives.

One could, perhaps, imagine the dramatic power of irony as somewhat analogous to the life-transforming shock of a Zen *koan*, though it would be rare indeed for the transforming power of irony to be realized in a sudden moment (nor is it clear that Zen's realizations actually occur in such seemingly magical ways). Rather the right kinds of irony—those which once operated in "the true and great Dionysiac cult" and in the public ritual of Greek theater (in the *Bacchae*, for instance)—works in lived phases and stages to bring the soaring idealism and ecstatic expectations of Dionysian faith "down" or "back" into non-destructive and fruitful contact with ordinary life. It enlivens and enriches our lives with the great energy of desire even as it simultaneously purifies and transforms and thus "realizes" that primal force.

We may be thankful, then, that, despite pervasive ironies of contempt, such fuller or deeper irony is still to some degree operative in our world through that "body of sensibility" which comes to expression in great works like the *Bacchae* or Cervantes' *Don Quixote*, in the enduring thought of great teachers like Socrates and Pascal, but also in many more ordinary ethnic and religious and civic traditions and (perhaps most significantly) in the language and practices of parents and teachers and friends. This "body of sensibility . . . has taken several thousands of years to shape . . . [and is] a highly developed instrument" (IF, 63) carrying forward the forms of irony that can "meet and master" the emergence of primal faith into the world.

Take again, as does Lynch, the example of the fundamental situation of the infant and the child.[69] All childhood forms of faith are characterized by "decisive fantasy" (IF, 112). Initially "the faith of the child is absolute; that is its strength and its weakness" (IF, 111). Indeed, as we have said, the infant feels itself to be god, omnipotent in all its desires; and what it wishes (this breast, this warmth, this relief) is also absolute—the only thing, everything, god. It is a stage of pure Dionysian innocence and fantasy. The infant's faith is, in Freud's terms, pure illusion. Yet it is a necessary illusion; not an end but the very beginning. It wants god, receives the mother's breast, and knows no difference, not even the difference of self and other. Without such fantastic belief, sustained by the promise carved into the very nature of the womb and of maternal (and paternal) care, this primal force could not survive to begin its journey into life and development.[70]

69. See especially IF, 60–62 and more generally IF, 111–25 for Lynch's detailed discussion of the role of irony in early childhood development. See also IH, 58–62.

70. See IF, 58–60.

At a slightly later moment, when some differentiation has entered its world (or when, to speak more precisely, it first begins to have a world by recognizing elements of otherness), everything becomes divided simply and easily into absolute good and evil—the beautiful mother and the monstrous mother. Yet even among such infantile (and later childhood) absolutes, the work of irony has already begun—in the gentle irony of a mother's loving reassurance as she withdraws her breast; in the somewhat sterner ironies later embodied in the competitive presence of siblings; in the comic ironies of fables and fairy tales which begin to make fantastic sense of wonderful or frightening otherness. Fantasy still remains dominant in the infant and the child's desire, but it is slowly (and, one hopes, lovingly) moved by the experience of such ironies in the direction of reality. It is, in other words, the ironic sensibility embodied in the mother's loving disciplines, in early life rhythms, in songs and stories, and in many other personal experiences and cultural forms, that gradually leads primal desire from pure illusion into still fantastic but intermediate forms of a childhood world, and thence into the simpler and most immediate forms of reality.[71] And note again that such irony is not something merely intellectual. It is rather a real force, experienced in parental love and discipline, in sibling rivalry, in the often hard edges (but also the comic aspects) of events and relationships.

Thus does irony undertake the living and quite dramatic (even if quite ordinary) education of desire. Nor, for Lynch and those he cites, is this education simply an odyssey of disillusionment, a process which forces the child and eventually the adult to "get real!" in some stoic sense. For the dreams of faith's initial stages need to remain with us in two immensely important and related ways. First, Lynch reminds us, they really are prophetic since "we are told by a later [religious and Christian] faith that the cosmos itself will end on such a clear, heroic note, with the bright and the dark divided ..." (IF, 113).[72] Secondly, moreover, it is these dreams that must gradually be brought by the force of an appropriately ironic sensibility into fruitful contact with the temporal realities of our lives. Thus might the prophetic dream continually enliven and shape our good taste of self and world, even as such taste shapes and develops our ongoing appropriation of the dream.

For again, Lynch says, this "is the problem of every man at every stage of life," bringing together "his wishes and the real world, belief and reality" (IF, 118). The fundamental pattern by which the force of irony grows in our faith and allows our faith to grow into reality is already given in

71. See IF, 112–20.

72. See also Lynch's beautiful comments about his own love for "these [magnificent] images of the Apocalypse" (IF, 164–65).

childhood. Yet the pattern recurs in different ways throughout our lives as it faces challenges that are at once the same and different, until we must finally face the ultimate poverty and irony of our own inescapable death. Lynch traces those "same but different" recurrences in the final chapter of *Images of Faith.*[73] And I might well continue by discussing his analysis of these recurrent patterns. Better, though, that the reader take up that final (and admittedly quite difficult) chapter. Better that I here simply attempt a more schematic summary.

What, then, in more abstract terms, is the nature of "this extraordinary human gift" that we call irony? In his own chapter-long discussion of "The Structure of the Irony of Faith" (IF, 77–108), Lynch quite typically suggests that we not try "to define irony in one step." Rather, he says, we need to "grow into our definitions" (IF, 101) by appreciating the different forms and related kinds of irony that have developed in a long tradition of thought and sensibility, a tradition whose literary expression in the West stretches from Socrates and the Prophets to Thomas Mann and Samuel Beckett. It is a tradition exemplified by thinkers and writers as different as Cervantes and Pascal and Kierkegaard, and by "moments" as contrasting as Greek tragedy and the Babylonian Exile, the medieval Feast of Fools and our own popular forms (as in *Saturday Night Live* or *The Simpsons*) of mockery and unmasking.[74]

How does such irony function? At the risk of a somewhat arbitrary clarity, let me suggest three related functions that can be derived from Lynch's deliberately less simplified discussion. Yet let me again stress that for Lynch irony is no merely intellectual process. It is a matter of experience, of lived and dramatic passage.

In the first place, then, irony typically challenges us to see through or unmask appearances, especially magnificent and absolutized appearances, and so come to what is actually real. Thus the mother's chiding laughter (and her occasional irritation) enables the infant to move through both the

---

73. As noted, that final chapter ("The Images of Faith and Human Time") follows some of the most fundamental of the different forms or phases of this recurring pattern in our lives. As Lynch conceives them, these "phases" are less the typical chronological stages suggested by developmental psychology than differing forms of the ironic challenge which may occur and re-occur through various periods or stages in our lives. The names he gives (except the first and perhaps the last) to these phases in irony's education of faith clearly suggest their difference from standard "developmental stages." They are: 1. Childhood, 2. The Unexpected, 3. Building a Present Moment, 4. The Movement through Infinite Possibility, 5. The Passage through the Curse, 6. The Tragic, and 7. Death and Nothingness.

74. Lynch also calls attention to some of the many fine modern studies of irony. See IF, 82–83.

pseudo-omnipotence of its hunger and the absolute trauma of deprival, to begin to trust that food and warmth will return, and gradually to see that the mother is both real and other, but also really trustworthy. Analogously, the provocation of Socrates' (or any good teacher's) insistent questioning forces movement from the rigid security of cherished convictions to a humbler but wiser sense of both our actual ignorance and our limited but real intelligence. In the process we gradually realize that his doubting and ironic and even seemingly sacrilegious challenges are in fact a reliable doorway to reason, truth, and authentic piety. So, too, do Euripides' crushing ironies force us to see through the ecstatic magnificence of Dionysus and the pompous civility of Pentheus to the tragic reality of the man and the truer forms of the god. So too do the ironies of all good theater, cinema, and fiction work in our hearts and minds. As also the ironic passages, large or small, of our daily living.

In all such passages, the preliminary work of "seeing through appearances" also involves a second and more fundamental function. In Lynch's words, "*the usual quality of irony is the unexpected coexistence, to the point of identity, of certain contraries*" (IF, 84, emphasis in original). We have just noted some such contraries: otherness and trustworthiness, ignorance and wisdom, tragic suffering and the revelation of basic goodness. Lynch suggests that Pascal has perhaps best, and most ironically, limned the painful contraries that constitute the human condition:

> What sort of freak then is man! How novel, how monstrous, how chaotic, how paradoxical, how prodigious! Judge of all things, feeble earthworm, repository of truth, sink of doubt and error, glory and refuse of the universe.[75]

Of course, that list could be extended: weak but strong, dreamer of great dreams yet comically flawed, sinner but saved, mortal yet alive.

We have seen Lynch again and again warn of our tendency to absolutize and identify with one side of such contraries by excluding, mocking, and hating the other. Such is the well-trod path of the easy ironies of contempt. The challenge of a deeper irony is to see through *that* magnificent deception in order gradually to learn that these contraries not only can but *must* be integrated ("realized" or embodied) in one human life and in any decently humane culture.[76] Here are some of the ways Lynch expresses this deeper function of irony:

---

75. IF, 87 citing the Krailsheimer translation of the *Pensées*, 64.
76. This, of course, was the theme of *The Integrating Mind*. See Chapter 3 above.

It is necessary that there be a very close relationship and friendship between these two parts of man, so much so that it will be disastrous for either if it gets separated from the other. If we go about thinking only great thoughts in the name of faith, forgetting the human, we become mad dreamers, fanatical human beings, ruthless, absolutizers, destroying and not redeeming the human. (IF, 88)

The image of faith never separates out the good and the bad. It is very important that faith and incredulity in this body of faith be not separated out into two acts that have forgotten each other. (IF, 92–93)

It seems to be the teaching of Christ that good and bad must stay together until the final judgment. Imagine the horror of separating out the good in this life. (IF, 93)

I repeat that a frequent quality of the ironic situation is a fruitful relationship of what I have called the larger and the smaller line in the ironic situation. (IF, 95)

Mention of Christ and the idea of a "fruitful relationship" of the "larger and smaller lines" of human life brings us to the third function of irony, though it could just as readily be understood as the fuller meaning of what I have called the second function. For as Lynch makes very clear, it finally is not enough simply to say that irony enables us to remain sane and human by keeping "a very close relationship and friendship" between the contrary parts of ourselves. Deeper still is the challenge to understand the irony that it is precisely the weaker and smaller part of ourselves that is finally the only real and human way to the greater and larger part. Of course the real challenge here is not just to "understand" this irony in some merely notional way, but to imagine its reality and allow ourselves to be so moved by it that we risk embracing and actually living through "the smaller line." So that, for example, in really coming to recognize and thus suffering our ignorance we find the only path to deeper truth and wisdom. So that in suffering other forms of weakness and illness and mortality we begin to live as decent human beings.

It is, perhaps, easy enough to imagine some forms of irony: how the mother's gentle chiding can gradually transform the infant's sense of omnipotence; how certain rude awakenings shock youthful romance into healthier forms of realism; how the experience of our own ignorance and weakness can lead us to greater decency and truth. These are things most of us have at some point experienced, perhaps many times and to our deepening benefit.

Yet it typically becomes more difficult to actually follow this way of irony to its greater challenges, so that by embracing our own poverty we are able to embrace those others whom we call "the poor" and with them begin to inherit the earth; so that by actually losing our lives, we gain them; by dying, in both the many smaller deaths in our lives and the final death of our lives, we live.

The Irony of Christ

In saying these things, of course, we are repeating the teachings of Christ. Yet even more, we are describing the actual life of Jesus and the nature of *His* reality as savior: the poor man who is the Incarnation of God; the messiah born in a stable; the king who entered Jerusalem on a donkey; the teacher who embraced lepers, ate with sinners, and proclaimed freedom for prisoners; the imprisoned and executed one who was raised and exalted as Lord. It is *this* "unexpected co-existence, to the point of identity, of certain contraries," *this* particular passage through "the smaller line" of an actual life with all its limitation, its poverty, and its suffering and death, that allows Lynch to speak of "the irony of Christ," and to assert that "the irony of Christ is Christ himself." And to tell us that everything he'd ever written has called for "the concrete movement of faith and imagination . . . through the actual life of Christ" (IF, 81).[77]

Of course there have been and continue to be other models of the deepest irony which requires dramatic passage through "the small line" of suffering and dying as the way to "the larger line" of true greatness. Oedipus is one of our most celebrated examples, seeing truly only when finally blinded. Yet "there can be," Lynch argues, "no *a priori* and philosophical definition of the irony in the ironic image of faith" (IF, 95). There is only the particular story of Oedipus, as well as other particular stories and actual examples. Above all, for the Christian—and the Christian believes that it is for all humanity, however implicitly it might enter their lives—there is the story and example of Christ.

> [T]he irony of Christ . . . in all his particularity, *this* irony could not have been either predetermined or predefined. This irony is a special and (to put it mildly) imaginative intervention in the turbulent, pre-existing, sometimes mad history of the ironies of faith . . . [Indeed] Christ himself in his particularity is the final model for the successful relationship of the smaller and the greater line. (IF, 95)

77. See above p. 1 above.

The Incarnation, in other words, is God's definitive and most exemplary irony. For Jesus not only taught with irony ("Blessed are the poor . . ."), but embodied the irony he taught. This helpless infant, carpenter, itinerant preacher, and crucified criminal was (and is) Emmanuel, God with us. Even for the non-Christian, this life and story could embody a "final model for the successful relationship of the smaller and the greater line." The great Dionysus can be led by the force of this irony to inner identification with all that is small and common in our humanity, and thereby to realization of even his greatest dreams.

Yet this irony of Christ also takes many forms even within the Gospels, and certainly within that larger "body of sensibility" that has been developing now for more than three-thousand years. For it was the history of irony in the life and writings of the Hebrew people, perhaps most evidently in the experience first of exodus and later of exile, which set the terms and forms for the life of Jesus. One of Lynch's own favorite later expressions of this irony (aside, of course, from Ignatius' *Exercises*) is Cervantes' comic and ironic pairing of the "great man of La Mancha" with the lowly and very human Sancho Panza. "In the end," Lynch says, "the mad Don Quixote and the realistic servant Sancho Panza have moved much closer to each other than in the satiric beginnings of the story. The knight has grown down; the servant has grown up, [sic] they love each other, as the two parts in us should . . . It is a giant step beyond the murderous dialogue between Dionysus and Pentheus" (IF, 123–24).[78]

It is, moreover, crucial that we remain aware of the different forms of the irony of Christ, not reducing it to any one image (as, for instance, Hollywood typically does; as Mel Gibson did in his much ballyhooed film, *The Passion of the Christ*). Yet perhaps it will be permissible here, for the sake of brevity, simply to stress that the passage through death to life is in one way or another central to all these forms. Even the infant must "die" to its omnipotence, and precisely *this* dying *is* its passage to fuller life. Thus Lynch again and again says things like the following:

> It is ironic that [faith] feeds so strongly on nothingness and death. (IF, 90–91)

> The irony of Christ is unique. It involves mastery of the world, spiritual freedom . . . ; it works through death and weakness; it therefore dethrones every other pretentious idea and establishes the movement through the human condition, and the total

---

78. Yet it is a sad commentary on our present infatuation with the ecstatic Dionysus that Broadway's *Man of La Mancha* actually reverses Cervantes' healing irony by un-ironically glorifying those who "dream the impossible dream."

human condition (not the human condition of the beautiful people) as the way. Weakness becomes one of the great forms of power. Age, sickness, and death lose their power over man and take on another form of power. (IF, 101)

The culminating sections in *Images of Faith*'s analysis of the "phases" of desire's education by irony all deal directly with actual death, and with our culture's many ways of seeking to avoid its reality. The sections are titled: "The Passage through the Curse" (IF, 156–64), "The Tragic" (IF, 164–68), and "Death and Nothingness" (IF, 168–75), and each (to repeat one of my images) crosses the same field, the same reality, but from different angles.[79]

Death, then, is the final and most fundamental element of the "small line" through which we must pass to freedom and truth and salvation. Its many analogues in life replicate, each in its own way, that passage even as they prepare us for its final form. For death is both final stage and fundamental element in the education of desire by irony. It is, to say the least, deeply ironic that the great energy of desire must die in order to live and grow into a developed life of faith and hope, and in the end to be fulfilled as a resurrected life of love. That is the irony of Christ, and Christ himself is its exemplar, the first born of many who form the larger "body of Christ." Thus it now should come as no surprise that (to reiterate) Lynch says:

> [E]verything I have ever written asks for the concrete movement of faith through experience, through time, through the definite, through the human, *through the actual life of Christ*. (IF, 81, emphasis added)

An Option for the Poor

One repeated note in Lynch's discussion of irony can perhaps now serve both as a summary of this present chapter and as a bridge to the concerns of the next. In essence Lynch says that those whose desire has been educated by irony, and especially by the irony of Christ, will not only have learned to acknowledge and live with their own poverty, but their internalized sense of poverty will also turn outwards towards the poor of the world. Here are some of his words:

79. The concluding sections of *Images of Faith* provide a synthesis of Lynch's previous writing about death. See *Christ and Apollo*'s brilliant analysis (18–27) of Dostoyevsky's treatment of the death of the holy man Zossima in *The Brothers Karamazov*, as well as the entire chapter on "Tragedy" (65–90); the many comments in *Images of Hope* about our culture's inability to deal well with passivity and death (e.g., 39–42, 233–37, and 245–46); and the important essay "Death."

There should be a steady relationship, to the point of passion, between faith and the poor, between faith and Africa, Asia. But that will not happen unless there is first this interior and originating contrariety in which faith loves its own interior and poor humanity. (IF, 89)

On the one hand there are the superb and royal promises of faith. On the other they are related to and achieved in their opposites, in the human and in weakness. This is the central irony. The promises are especially made to the very poor, the weak, the suffering, the oppressed . . . It should be easier for those who . . . do not throw these weak, suffering parts of themselves into the exterior darkness of contempt and disgust but approach their own poverty and death with redemptive, affectionate images—it should be easier for them to . . . refuse, above all, to accept the terrible dichotomy between the rich and poor nations, and in the best sense to become completely "political" in their devotion to Asia, Africa, Latin America. In other words their ironic image of themselves should become politically productive. (IF, 160–61)

We could, of course, go further along this line of thought by stressing that it is those who indeed are poor who can and should be our foremost mentors in the education of desire. We can, in other words, perhaps best learn the central irony of faith not only from Christ, but from Francis and Clare, Mother Theresa and Dorothy Day, and also from our own experience with Sancho Panza and his many sisters and brothers in our contemporary world.[80]

Such ideas also point again to one of the key passages from Lynch raised up at the beginning of this book:[81]

[W]e are always faced with programmatic alternatives: We can decide to build a human city, a city of man, in which all men have citizenship, Greek, Jew, and Gentile, the black and the white, *the maimed, the halt, and the blind, the mentally well and the mentally ill* . . . Or we will decide to build various absolute and walled cities from which various pockets of our humanity will always be excluded. They will pose as ideal cities, and *will exclude . . . the Negro, the sick, the different.* (IH, 26, emphasis added)

It is to Lynch's more developed discussion of the building of the former city that we now turn.

---

80. See, for instance, Lynch's whimsical but serious "Final Image." See also his related comments in the "Introduction" to the subsequent issue of *New York Images*.

81. See p. 17 above.

6

Dionysus–Building the Human City

Having crisscrossed the rich field of Lynch's concerns from a number of angles, I return now (in this chapter and the next), as a final enlargement in my depiction of his thinking, to what was his grand and overarching concern from the start: the political, the *polis*, the human city, and explaining the foundational elements of a spirituality for public life.[1] "Enter into the city" Lynch had said in his inaugural editorial for *Thought*.[2] He repeated that exact phrase years later in the conclusion to *Christ and Prometheus* (127), the text we will take up in the next chapter. Here our primary text will continue to be *Images of Faith*, with Dionysus again as its guiding image. For one of the final goals of that book was to enable those whose life had been blessed with irony, especially "the irony of Christ," to become, in Lynch's words, "politically productive," even "completely 'political'" (IF, 161).

Lynch often cited the famous passage from *The Republic* where Plato suggests that we might see the human more clearly if we see it writ-large, so to speak, in the life of the city.[3] He followed Plato in this regard. For, as we saw especially in the preceding chapter, the individual's journey into a mature life of faith and hope and love depends from the first upon family and friends, society and culture. More generally, it is Lynch's constant refrain that the self is inseparable from its world. A good taste of self depends upon a good taste of the world, above all of the human world, the world of the human city. Thus, one of the great themes of *Images of Faith* is that the education of the primal human energy of faith, the education of Dionysian

1. It will soon be clear, moreover, if it is not already, that Lynch's talk about the political and the city returns to classical usage, as in Plato or Augustine, where "the city" encompasses politics and economics, culture and society, indeed all the theoretical and practical arts and sciences which contribute to the making (and sometimes the destroying) of human community.

2. See pp. 37–38 above.

3. *The Republic*, 2: 368–69. See, for example, IF, 55–56.

desire, requires above all the prior existence and continual development of an elaborated "body of faith" in this world. Yet that "body of faith" in its most elaborated form *is* the human city. Thus one of Lynch's most fundamental "images of faith," images of what real faith actually looks like in the everyday world, is the city itself. Central to *Images of Faith* is Lynch's dialogue with "the contemporary revolutionary" (especially those on the Left who were so outspoken when he wrote) about how *actually* (and not ideologically) to build a truly human city.

Building the trust, faith, and hope that constitutes the human city is, then, the theme of this chapter. It involves these central ideas from *Images of Faith*: 1) that politics is essentially and most fundamentally about human faith or unfaith; 2) that the body of faith that constitutes the human city, whether globally or nationally or locally, is seriously threatened today by various forms of unfaith, by pervasive ironies of contempt and images of exclusion, and by so many actual walls of separation and violence; and finally, 3) that we thus have immense need of sensibilities and imaginations shaped by appropriate forms of irony and by realistic forms of faith, hope, and love, by imaginations and sensibilities that might again and again "enter into the city" to work for its reconstruction—immense need, in other words, for the practices of a spirituality adequate to the challenges of contemporary public life.

The present chapter, then, can be understood as something of a reversal of the perspective of the previous, looking not at the journey of the individual into the world but at the world or the human city that supports (or hinders) that journey. Much has already been said in that previous chapter about those absolutizing forces and images which constitute in our city a "body of unfaith" rather than a "body of faith." Thus my goal here is less to explore again Lynch's discussion of the crisis of faith and trust that threatens the human city, though that will be necessary to some degree, than to hold up for thought and imagination aspects of his more positive call for us "to enter the city" and "build [again its] body of faith."

On Political Rhetoric and Images

I begin with two notes about political thinking and imagination, about the kind of thinking and imagining needed for such building. The first is a note of caution about political rhetoric and images. The second, which builds upon it (and is discussed in the next section of this chapter), is a note about the fundamental alternative between imagination and violence. Both are drawn from Lynch, the second much more directly.

Political rhetoric can easily just repeat the almost endless clichés and platitudes which flood the media and the mind when talk and thought turn to the *polis*. Some platitudes are undoubtedly very important and bear regular repetition; others are little more than trivial banalities which substitute momentary excitement or self-satisfaction for thought; still others are widespread and dangerous efforts to deliberately overload or oversimplify and manipulate our sense of reality. So it is as well with our many images of the political: of them and us, favorable or fearful, good and evil. Such images do not simply accompany, but are embedded in and actually undergird or ground the clichés and platitudes, giving them place in and thus actually shaping the realities of the city.

I ask the reader, as both an exercise and an example, to call to mind the images and clichés typically associated with "9/11": the repeated pictures of jets exploding into the twin towers, the darkened mug-shots of terrorists, the images of heroic police and firemen and of anguished onlookers. Then, as a final aspect of this exercise, I ask that one remember Mr. Bush's call, repeated constantly since by other voices with somewhat different words, for a "war on terrorism" to "rid the world of evil" and spread democracy around the globe.[4]

There clearly is much powerful reality and truth in these images and clichés. Yet there is also in them, especially because of endless repetition and their ritual or incantatory use, an almost irresistible force, or at least a very strong centripetal momentum, that reduces their meaning and truth into increasingly narrow, fixed and absolutized forms. They tend to become, whatever the intentions which lead to their repetition, essentially violent because they continually reduce the range of the real and the flexibility of response in thought, feeling, and imagination. This is true as much for noble images of heroism and freedom as for their polar opposites, our images of terror. They quite literally kill off, bit by bit or in sudden traumatic strokes, our fuller sense of the real, and thereby lead to many consequent forms of verbal and attitudinal violence, and often to many forms of actual killing.

One of our greatest needs, then, as we struggle for justice and peace in the human city, is for a continual renewal of attention to the actual in all its messy diversity. Such attention must deal with and work through the various clichés, platitudes, and images which play such a role in our city's "body of sensibility." Said differently, there is no cheap or easy way for us to attend to the full reality of the city and to work realistically in the arena of the political, broadly understood—though we are continually tempted by cheap and easy ways.

4. See pp. 21–22 above.

As I write, for instance, Jerusalem is still the hard and angry heart of war and occupation, and Damascus the center of terrible civil war. Terrorist bombs have shattered streets and lives around the world, in Mumbai and Madrid, London and Boston. Baghdad, one of the world's most ancient great cities, remains a site of continuing terror and commonplace violence, brother against brother, Dionysus and Pentheus again trapped in frenzied and fatal embrace.[5] Indeed, the aftershocks of "9/11" continue to cause the earth to tremble beneath cities and villages around the globe as violent decisions are taken by warring factions both great and small. And the poor are still with us, still "the vast majority,"[6] still suffering and oppressed, both at home and around the world.

Yet it is also true, perhaps even more true, despite the drumbeat of headlines, the clichés of pundits, and the hard reality of "9/11," that Lynch's beloved New York remains much blessed with regular decisions and acts of constructive imagination—both great and small, in public policy and personal practice, in politics and economics as much as in the arts and in daily life, all parts of that complex web of faith that maintains and, when needed (as it regularly is), rebuilds that great city. The same, thankfully, is the case in cities, towns and villages around the world—even in war-torn Damascus and amid the terror in occupied Palestine.

We must, then, examine our images and struggle to maintain imaginative flexibility if we are to continue to enter the real and human city. Thus Lynch would urge us to accompany his thought about the city with many forms of attention to the constructive as well as the violent, the local and small as well as the global and grand, down even to the immediacy of one's own neighborhood or residence. Without such attention and imagining, what he has to say may lead only to perhaps interesting but merely abstract theory. Yet the human city is not a body of faith or unfaith in some merely theoretical sense, but only because faith or unfaith is really present in actual human relationships, whether between nations and civilizations or in families and neighborhoods, whether in great corporations or in the small shops around the corner. For faith, as we have heard Lynch say, is "the primal and originating force in [all] (1) human politics, (2) relationship, and (3) thought" (IF, 35).[7]

---

5. See pp. 146–48 above.

6. See Michael Harrington's still very relevant 1977 study *The Vast Majority*.

7. See p. 127 above.

Violence or Imagination

One of Lynch's characteristic ways of developing such ideas takes us to the heart of the effort to build the city—and to the central issue in his dialogue with radicals and revolutionaries. He believed, as I have repeatedly noted, that "we are always faced with programmatic alternatives . . . to build a human city . . . or to build various absolute and walled cities . . . [The former] will always require an act of the imagination" while the latter will always involve violence (IH, 26–7).[8] Elsewhere, with specific reference to the revolutionary character of our times, Lynch again described this fundamental alternative between imagination and violence:

> The first part of the hypothesis I am proposing is that we deal with the whole of human life or death through the imagination or through violence. The second part of my hypothesis is that really, way deep down, violence is only an imitation, a cheap imitation, of the imagination . . . I hypothesize further that if we have entered upon a many sided period of serious revolution, then *the real quarrel for control will occur between the men of imagination and those we now call the revolutionaries, the men of violence* . . . The one group, the revolutionaries, whether of the right or the left, will attack and destroy. The second group, the men of imagination, will imagine; they will build and compose; where they destroy they will replace. They will not fall back on simple and loud thrusts of the will but on acts of the imagination.[9]

Recall for a moment those images and clichés about "9/11" evoked just above, and their centripetal tendency to reduce the range of the real and our flexibility of response. As I said there, that tendency can quite literally kill off our sense of the real and lead in consequence to many forms of violence. This is what Lynch means by calling violence "a cheap imitation of the imagination." It substitutes those easy and absolutized images which it requires for the wider and more flexible images achieved by the hard work of the realistic imagination. The latter's "greatest vocation . . . is to imagine reality" in all its complexity, "whether by finding or making it" (CP, 64). It always struggles to remain flexible and free and open to all that is real and human.

With that imagination, Lynch (or any woman or man not driven by narrowly fixed purpose and already held captive by rigid images) might

---

8. See p. 17 above.

9. "Death," 460 (emphasis added).

walk the streets of New York (even immediately after "9/11") and see, with "even the most superficial first look . . . that it has an endless number of stories of the human image to unfold, each altogether different. It's density of possibility is beyond compare. Its impossibilities of reduction to some single group, or thought, or language, or 'objective and measurable image' are equally without end." [10] Thus seen or imagined (since we only see through our images), the city cannot be reduced to walled camps which embody the violence of Pentheus and Dionysus. Nor can it, by an equal but less obvious and usually more pervasive form of violence, be reduced to "some fatuous terms of sweet normality" that refuses "admission to the look of the homeless, to the addict, to the vibrations of fear set up in us by the mentally ill, to our prisoners, or the birth of a blind foetus, or the enemy, or the very poor." [11]

Let me, even at the risk of hammering home the obvious, bring an end to this discussion of the fundamental alternative between violence and imagination by evoking the memory of one New York story that Lynch especially admired. [12] I refer to Leonard Bernstein's now classic *West Side Story*. For it, too, like the *Bacchae*, is a story about anger and violence, about enemies and hatreds, fear and death. Yet, also like the *Bacchae*, it is not the product of a rigid and violent sensibility. Like Euripides, Bernstein's imagination is not imprisoned by the violence he depicts. Perhaps even more than Euripides, perhaps because he tells his story on a smaller, less heroic scale, Bernstein's imagination more clearly moves through the violence to a tragic catharsis that restores faith. Indeed faith moves throughout his drama. It refuses to remain fixed on one or a few simple images of love or beauty, hatred or otherness. Rather it moves with music and dance, and also with the larger dramatic rhythms served by the music and dance, to reveal the complex and human faces of specific hatreds and loves, complexly human images of "us" and "them." It moves *through* this complexity, *through* this unfolding, not getting stuck or fixated at any point or by any cheap imitation of imagination. Thus we too move and are moved, by its imagining and by our own sympathetic participation, towards a more adequate and realistic image, a more real understanding of New York City and the wider human city.

In terms of the categories I have been using throughout this book, then, the fundamental alternative between violence and imagination helps us to distinguish between individuals and groups, as well as between episodes

10. Lynch, "Introduction," 3. In "Final Image," an earlier essay in *New York Images*, Lynch had followed a contemporary Sancho Panza into the streets of New York as this "ordinary man" sees the city with an imagination free of rigid absolutes.

11. Ibid.

12. See II, 52, 123.

and whole periods in a culture or a civilization, that are primarily shaped by a sensibility and spirituality rooted in will and violence, and those shaped primarily by that alternative sensibility and spirituality which will imagine and build a truly human city.[13] What our city needs, then, are women and men able to resist the appeal of the former sensibility, the seductive allure of essentially violent patterns of imagination and action, and able to take up the difficult asceticism of the latter, by imagining and building the actual and possible good of our city. We are though, most of us, caught between these fundamental alternatives, divided in our own sensibility between violence and imagination. It was towards healing such divided sensibilities that Lynch did all his writing—to articulate and call us to the kind of realistic and this-worldly spirituality and imagination that the task of building the human city requires.[14]

The Body of Faith

Let me return, as a next step in exploring Lynch's understanding of and call for such an appropriately "political spirituality," to his most fundamental idea that the city itself is best understood as a body of faith, and to the correlative idea that one of our most basic images of faith should be the worldly reality of the human city. Perhaps enough has already been said about these ideas; yet perhaps not since they run counter to prevailing ideas and images about both the city and faith. Thus a bit more elaboration and imagining will hopefully enable still greater understanding.

13. The fundamental conflict between spiritualities of imagination and violence is, of course, but another version of analogous and equally fundamental spiritual conflicts—totalizing vs. integrating, univocal vs. analogous, the magnificent vs. the messy—that Lynch explored throughout his work.

14. Because it is again such an important question among us, I wish to comment briefly on the relation of Lynch's fundamental rejection of violence to the ethical question about non-violence and justified violence. Lynch, to my knowledge, never addressed that question directly. I suspect he would not only have been continually critical of our too ready recourse to violence, but also suspicious of some romantic claims about non-violence. I am fairly certain, from occasional notes in his writings, that he would have accepted the ethics of justified violence (or the just-war tradition) as part of the typically difficult and messy, but very human effort to work towards real but of imperfect solutions to at least some of our actual conflicts. In the passage about the "men of imagination" and the "men of violence" which I have been using to frame this discussion of the political, he does clearly say, speaking about the "men of imagination," that they will not only "build and compose," but *where they destroy they will replace*" (see p. 164 just above). This is not to say, however, that he would have failed to appreciate and admire the importance of gospel non-violence and the often very effective role of non-violent resistance.

The city itself, the actual city (or town or village), is not simply a complex tangle or construction of objects and forces, people and institutions. Rather it is all of these precisely insofar as they embody human imagination and faith and sensibility. Nor is it primarily religious faith that they embody, though religion, and especially Christ, clearly can and should play a critical role. Rather the city embodies or actualizes those more basic forms of human faith and sensibility, forms of educated Dionysian energy, that enable us to live together with trust, hope, and admiration in various forms of citizenship and cooperation, in many shared inclinations and loyalties, in the forms of friendship that the ancients saw as so crucial to the life of the *polis*, and, ideally at least, in that inclusive option for the poor that is present when those many forms of Dionysian energy have been tutored, however indirectly, by Gospel ironies—or by related ironies rooted in different traditions of faith and culture. Alternatively, as we know all too well, the city can be or become a body of unfaith, a body and sensibility filled with contempt and exclusion, violence and destruction—a city of walled and well-armed camps. In actuality, of course, it is typically both; it embodies both faith and violence.

Lynch's own words from a succession of points in the argument of *Images of Faith* (punctuated by my emphases) may be most helpful here:

> [Faith exists, he says] not only in a vertical relationship with God and the unknowable, but also as horizontally alive, in the most imaginable way, in various forms of "embodiment"—individual, historical, social, political—to such an extent that it creates the very heart and core of human existence and human society . . . *Above all, it is so embodied in the political order that it is the very creating substance and life of the political order.* (IF, 12–13)

> [I]t is a mighty and originating torrent that gets into the guts and interstices of most if not all of human politics . . . (IF, 45)

> Can faith be embodied and thus imagined? I think it can. It can be . . . imagined if we conceive that it has not only a vertical life . . . but a horizontal life as well, directed toward creating and being the very essence of the life of man in society and politics . . . And so hard and deep is the relationship of faith to society that it is wrong for religious men to say that they apply or "relate" the principles of faith to society (make them relevant!). . . *Human society is faith itself.* And I do not mean thereby that religious belief, that is to say belief in God, makes society. *To say, rather, that belief in God has a body, and that this constitutes human*

society, comes much closer to what I mean. (IF, 56–57, latter emphasis in original)

Faith or the lack of it is in the veins of everything, constituting or destroying. It is the hard iron of everyday life. It is so present to us that it can bring us to the verge of a civil war of the emotions . . . Now it begins to be an understatement to state that faith has a body. *This body is the actuality or the death of the human community.* (IF, 67)

That last paragraph employs one of Lynch's regular strategies for thought and imagination: indicating the importance of something by highlighting its absence or its opposite. We've already noted that in *Images of Faith* he turns first to the figure of Medea to illustrate the power of faith by pointing to the terrible fury of its betrayal.[15] In a similar way Lynch urges us to imagine the centrality of faith to the very existence of the city by pointing to its loss in contemporary national life. He notes, somewhat sarcastically, that of course "powerful, evangelical, perfectionistic (and masochistic) instincts . . . invade the political order [of the U.S.] every six months" (IF, 46). Yet he thought, when he wrote *Images of Faith*, that we were actually approaching a far more extreme point of the actual death of faith in our national culture and politics. Again, in his words with my emphases:

As [faith's] presence is the very life of the political order, so its absence is its death . . . Now among us, for ten long years, our own country claimed the Vietnam War as our point of crisis. But I did not and do not believe this. I think that a far worse crisis was and is going on, *the true war, which is such a collapse of faith between the two major culture classes as has hardly ever occurred so sharply in our history.* (IF, 13)[16]

Is it immaterial to faith that *we are in the presence of vast waves of unfaith and distrust among men,* culture groups, social groups, nations? (IF, 65)

We are in the middle of a vast cultural crisis and division. *The real war is at home.* It takes the form *not of the usual political divisions—savage and enjoyable as these can be—but of a complete collapse of faith between the two cultural groups that constitute*

15. See p. 127 above and IF 35, 38–39.

16. He goes on to say that "These two groups are the middle class on the one hand and, on the other, the intellectual-academic culture" (IF, 13). I believe that in such usage, "the middle class" means not only the great popular "middle" of the American people, but especially the business and political groups which provide leadership for that class.

the nation . . . We are not only in the presence of the failure of belief (there is no belief left), the one class in the other: the lack of belief is intensified by a mutual contempt and fear such as has not often existed between two national groups in modern history. Our crisis over the Vietnam War was a trifle compared to this interior war and collapse of faith. (IF, 66)[17]

As evidence of the power of both faith and unfaith, Lynch then asks us to consider the role of language, for "language . . . belongs to the very marrow of the body of faith" (IF, 68). Thus a "deliberate politicization of language . . . [to] serve political and culture-class purpose is, despite its sophistication, a diseased attack on the body of faith" (IF, 68). "It was," he reminds us, "the collapse of mutual faith and of language that in great part led to the beginning of the collapse of civilization among the Greek city states at the close of the fifth century B.C." (IF, 69).[18] One might, of course, also note (as Lynch had previously done[19]) the more general vacuity and trivialization of language in advertising and popular media as a different kind evidence for the weakening of faith in our city.

Finally, in elaborating his belief that we were at risk of approaching the extreme point of the death of any real faith in our national culture and politics, Lynch returns to his central concern with the importance of imagination and images—and to the actual physical effects of the absence of faith in the current state of our cultural and political images. And I, in turn, urge the reader of the following passages to think simply about the "negative" advertising that has become the new normal during political campaigns.

> When the body of faith enters into a period of great crisis in a community the immediate visual faculties of human beings seem to enter into a remarkable state of near derangement . . . Above all this death of horizontal faith affects our very vision. I mean the literal thing we call vision: the seeing of things. Waves of fantasy pour into the atmosphere. The two culture classes see each other as monsters, no less. The consequences of the combination of linguistic and visual distortion are quite extraordinary.

17. See above pp. 67–70 and 147–48 for prior discussion of the separation of culture classes.

18. In support of this assertion Lynch provides a lengthy citation from Thucydides. See IF 69–71: "Society had become divided into two ideologically hostile camps . . . As for ending this state of affairs, no guarantee could be given that would be trusted, no oath sworn that people would fear to break . . . instead of being able to feel confident in others, they devoted their energies to providing against being injured themselves" *History of the Peloponnesian War*, Bk. 3, # 5).

19. See IH, 65–66 as well *The Image Industries* (passim).

> We can calculate that there must be an extraordinary negative life and set of drives here which require their own joy and satisfaction and which lead to a constant escalation in the images of a nation ... [And eventually to] an extreme "state of the images" which begins to lose touch with reality. (IF, 71–72)

> What becomes possible, and probable, are vast waves of fantasy or vast escalations of ordinary images. Under these conditions the "state of the images" is not anything in which one can place faith. (IF, 72)

> It is only when the categories, the differences between us, announce themselves as final and when the contempt of one category for another loses sight of [the ordinary] images made by faith, that the political order is in danger of real collapse. We cannot play with images the way we are doing without paying a great price. It is a game. It is the most volatile of games. And the vilest. (IF, 73)

It is vile and violent because, in the name of politics, it destroys the very possibility of politics by undermining that fundamental trust which is the ground and lifeblood of our city.

I would at this point only reiterate my own conviction that we are *essentially* still very much at the same place today, in the first decades of the new millennium—though some of the surface issues have shifted (to different wars, for instance, and to growing battles about gun control, health care, and the environment) and though thankfully there are today, as there were then, many counter-forces seeking to maintain and rebuild the city's body of faith and sensibility.

The Right Kinds of Irony

One such force, of course, is the power of irony. The city deteriorates and becomes a place of polarized violence and walled-off camps when Dionysian energies have not been educated and shaped by the right kinds of irony. Thus we turn, as next steps in this chapter's argument, to several concrete instances of the life of irony, both for worse and better, in Lynch's and in our own sense of the contemporary city. And I ask the reader to recall the various notes about irony made towards the end of the previous chapter: that it is an "extraordinary human gift" developed over millennia, in many different forms, and still developing; above all that it is not just some clever intellectual game but a powerful, dramatic experience, a form of therapy and asceticism; that it enables us to see through the appearances of pseudo-magnificent forces which would captivate our imaginations, and to hold together the many difficult contraries constitutive of human life; and that it can enable us to come, by suffering embrace of the many points of poverty and death in our lives, to the real participation that is possible for us in those glories promised by our ideals and dreams.[20]

A first "instance" of the life of irony in our city is one that continually preoccupied Lynch, so much so that it may have been his primary motivation for writing *Images of Faith*. It involves the kinds of ironies prevalent in the sensibilities and imaginations of our "artists and intellectuals."

It is obvious, of course, that any city needs the imaginative and constructive work of many different talents and institutions: good politicians and good police; good priests and pastors, rabbis and imams; schools and hospitals, supermarkets and small shops, parks and theaters; music and dance, cars and trains, roads, footpaths, and so many other places and patterns of movement and rest; good management, skilled crafts, and much hard labor. The list is almost endless and we regularly need to let our imaginations encompass that full body of talent and task, work and leisure, lest our own sense of the human city become narrowed and rigid because of the noisy passions of one or the other particular conflict or concern. It is, of course, also true (and this too must be included in our imagining) that the good city needs those many forms of noisy competition and conflict which are both inevitable and crucially important as elements of the co-operation of so many groups and individuals, so many vectors of interest and power, imagination and ignorance, success and failure.

Lynch's contribution to the building of the city always assumes and celebrates this diverse body of human roles and rhythms, harmonies and conflicts. His particular concern is always with the spirit of this body of talent and task, the spirit with which the work of the city is accomplished, and perhaps especially the spirit or sensibility which is operative in those many inevitable and necessary forms of competition and conflict. Do they remain expressions of some of the many different forms of educated faith and hope and love, expressions of realistic imagining, or have they become essentially violent expressions of Dionysian energy, uneducated by irony or fixated by ironies of contempt? Has conflict become so contemptuous, the images so escalated and polarized, that foundational faith is almost lost or at great risk?

As we have just seen, Lynch feared that our present culture wars involved not simply "the usual political divisions—savage and enjoyable as

---

20. See pp. 149–59 above.

these can be—but . . . a complete collapse of faith between the two cultural groups that constitute the nation" (IF, 66)—between "the middle class" and "the academic-cultural class." He was concerned with both these classes and with the need for appropriately ironic and self-critical forms of sensibility that would enable them to see through and de-escalate their fixated images and imaginations. Yet he was particularly concerned, as we have already seen,[21] with those he typically referred to as "the artists and writers" or, especially in *Images of Faith*, as "the intellectuals."[22] It was above all to and for them that he did virtually all of his writing. It was their habits of mind, spirit and imagination, their sensibility and spirituality, which he sought both to challenge and assist by means of the fundamental Socratic-Ignatian therapy he articulated.

They—the critics and commentators, dramatists and poets, priests and public philosophers—play an especially crucial role in the human city. "[F]or there is between [persons] of intelligence and society a mutual give and take that nourishes the mind and being of each . . . The whole vocation of the former is to give light to the people; but [they] will seldom find light in any other source" (IM, 117–18). It is, then, the special role of "writers or thinkers or artists or poets to form images of the major points of life and death, and thereby to help the world cope with them."[23]

Where else should the people (and the city) better turn for adequate understanding of emerging realities in Shanghai and San Francisco, or continuing tensions between Teheran and Washington; for critical appreciation of literary and dramatic arts, and for dealing with fears about the economy and the environment; or about the role of biological science and genetic technology in the origin and reproduction of life? Where else should the people be able to turn, especially today with an increasing loss of traditional forms of community and education, to find the right ironies for dealing with major issues and conflicts, to develop an integrating and ironic sensibility which might enable them to resist prevalent temptations towards either violent ideologies or disgusted withdrawal?

Lynch continually recalled how Aeschylus and his fellow dramatists had developed that public theater in Athens which by its many ironies, both comic and tragic, subtle and shocking, educated the body of faith that was Greek civilization at its best. He also regularly pointed with gratitude to the similar efforts in our times by Dostoevsky and Dickens, Bernstein and Beckett, and many others. He did not even hesitate at one point to claim that

21. See pp. 67–70 above and all of Chapter 4 above.
22. See, for instance, IF, 46–48, 107–8.
23. "Death," 459. See also IH, 212.

"artists and intellectuals" constituted "a kind of natural priesthood of light, communicating light and guidance to the people, leading the people and not [themselves] to the heights of freedom and truth" (IM, 47).

Yet Lynch did not have a simplistic or romantic image of this culture class. What he prized above all was their actual or potential freedom and independence of thought and imagination, free not only from pressures external to their expertise and purpose, but above all from the kinds of internal pressures that can and regularly do reduce their priesthood to little more than the squabbles of partisans entrenched within fortified walls. Thus he lamented their growing conformity, their tendency to group into polarized camps, to think as what he sarcastically called "culture gangs" hawking "package deals" (CP, 45)—fixed and absolutized positions on a whole range of major but in fact significantly different issues. For the sad and very dangerous reality to which Lynch returned again and again—in his critique of film and literature and theater in both *The Image Industries* and *Christ and Apollo*, in the essays of *The Integrating Mind*, and perhaps especially in *Images of Faith*—is that the forms of imagination and irony most prevalent among today's intellectuals are those of contempt for "this filthy, rotten system" and for those with "real" power who run it.

> Never [Lynch wrote in the early 1960s] has there been such an abysmal gap between the many and those who by vocation should be its creative and imaginative leaders . . . There is now a tradition of alienation, of criticism . . . among the writers and intellectuals (IM, 46).

> [T]here is [he wrote a decade later] a vast difference between the superb competence of our academic culture in the area of its specializations and the mediocrity of its role as world of political opinion and political culture . . . It is in fact very dubious that a nation can prosper if the academic community refuses its support; but it is even worse off if that community gives its support to an inward conformity and hysteria, a primal faith of its own (IF, 47–48).

> This is indeed what has happened and what is happening . . . The intellectuals are becoming a social class preoccupied with themselves, living in the minds of one another . . . [They] begin to be increasingly turned in on themselves (no longer the teachers of society) and . . . they react with increasing uniformity, predictability, and rigidity to every issue . . . (IF, 107–8).

> In such circumstances the intelligence [of artists and writers and academics] does not emerge as one of the educators of primal

faith; rather it conspires with the negative stages of primal faith.
Above all it conspires in the production of exaggerated images
according to whose terms "Ordinary politics are the kingdom
of darkness, ideological politics are the struggle of light against
darkness." (IF, 47)[24]

Of course the "artists and intellectuals" are not alone, nor even primarily responsible for this situation of cultural warfare that rends the body of faith that is the human city. Lynch never says it quite this way, and I may betray my own class bias in so putting it, but immensely powerful economic and technical forces are the more fundamental causes of this cultural warfare.[25] Yet this is, so to speak, their nature, the nature of Dionysian and Promethean power unless checked and countered and educated. For Lynch (standing in the tradition that, at least in the West, begins with the Prophets and with Aeschylus and Socrates) such checking and countering should be the role (the prophetic and priestly vocation!) of the "artists and intellectuals." They must protest and must lead very real and really imaginative revolutions, both great and small. It is their ironies which are needed today to for healing and restoring the faith of the city. Yet (again) literally everything depends on the spirit of their ironies.

Lynch clearly wrote *Images of Faith* in part to criticize the artists and intellectuals, mentors of the radicals and revolutionaries, for having allowed facile and contemptuous ironies to dominate their consciousness and their work. He tried to call them, first among all, to the difficult asceticism, indeed the difficult conversion, involved in the transformation of their ironies. To call them, first of all, to become deeply ironic about themselves. Their forceful criticism and prophecy are today much needed, even desperately needed. Yet only if they again speak and write with ironies and imaginations that also bring healing to their opponents, to the managers of power, and to all the inhabitants of the human city.

Sex, Gender, and Family Life

As a second "instance" or illustration of the need for such ironic healing in the life of the city, I turn to that cluster of continuing and often fiercely controversial issues suggested by general terms like "gender" and "sex,"

24. Lynch is here citing Shils, *The* Intellectuals, 28.

25. As we shall see in the next chapter, Lynch's analysis in *Christ and Prometheus* of modern technical and bureaucratic systems is clearly supportive of this judgment. As was his critique of "the commercial mentality" in both *The Image Industries* and *The Integrating Mind*.

"marriage" and "family." Lynch took up such issues only somewhat indirectly in discussions of dramas like *Medea*, the *Bacchae*, and the *Oresteia*—all stories of faith and betrayal, revenge and tragedy in the lives of families.[26] As we have seen in the previous chapter, he clearly understood the role of Dionysian passion and the need for healing irony in this deeply personal arena of human life. He may not have taken up issues of "sexual politics" more directly simply because of a sense of limited personal experience and expertise. I nonetheless raise up this area for greater discussion because it is clearly foundational to the life of the human city. It may well be a cliché, but is true nonetheless, that the family is the fundamental building block of human society—the city in microcosm and ground for the larger life of the "human family." Thus the politics of family life, which today involve so many divisive issues, are crucial for the life of our city. Yet they also imperil the body of faith since divisions so frequently escalate into polarized positions, into many walled camps filled with so much contempt—both in the actual lives of too many families, and even more in the wars dividing culture classes and involving, for better and worse, the passions and talents of our "artists and writers." Here as much as anyplace, then, there is need for many healing therapies, much hard and realistic imagination, and the right kinds of irony.

What might such irony look like? The general answer is as easy to say as it is hard to realize in practice. It would, by criticism and imagination, by stories both comic and tragic, by analyses both gently persuasive and even on occasion fiercely mocking, lead the warring parties to de-escalate their image of enemies and, perhaps even more important, of themselves. It would help them to keep their much-needed struggles human, to find common ground where possible, and to struggle without the absolutizing which so often rends the bonds of trust and hope in our city. It could lead them to acknowledge limits to their convictions and positions, to be open to possible truth in other positions, to begin to imagine realistic and thus truly human developments in current efforts to re-embody gender and re-understand sexuality and reproduction. It would enable all of us to move with imaginative sensitivity *through* the great and complex desires as well as the painful frailness and vulnerability of relations between women and men, parents and children, men within themselves and women within themselves, in the effort to imagine a truly human future for gender and sexuality and family life in the global city. It would gradually force us—for, again, dramatic or experienced irony is a powerful force—to come to honest terms with

26. I have previously referenced his discussions of the first two. He also returned often in his writing to the *Oresteia*, but his most extensive discussion is found in CP, 77–94.

our own poverty of spirit and imagination, to come down from visionary mountain tops and enter real struggle "in the valley of the human." It would, in other words, introduce an element of humility (of humanity and down-to-earthness) into the dramatic struggles of our families and of the human family. For what are the many forms of healthy irony but forceful invitations to real humility; just as the many ironies of contempt are little more than terrible expressions of pride.

Perhaps one or the other more concrete example will help here. In the preceding chapter I have already indicated the central role of irony in the development of the child and the adolescent, bringing the absolute dreams of those stages of life into gradual and fruitful contact and interaction with simpler, often harder, but finally more rewarding realities.[27] How much needed are such ironies in the subsequent sexual and romantic *journey into partnership and marriage* as it is today played out at home and across the globe. It is no exaggeration to say that we are in desperate need of the kinds of realistic (and thus ironic) teaching and story-telling and counseling that will help the young (and not so young) both to see through the silly but pervasive images of sex and romance which cloud minds and mislead imaginations, and to see and embrace realities both deeper and richer.[28] Ideally such critical ironies will "see through" seductive images more by appropriate forms of laughter and gentle mockery than by condemnations which typically only deepen division in hearts and imaginations. Yes, there undoubtedly are occasions for prophetic denunciation, but everything depends on tone and context, on whether criticism further polarizes, within and between ourselves, or enables us to move towards more realistic imagining and acting, both for our own lives and for the life of our city.

Yet if the need for such irony is true for the journey into partnership and marriage, how much more for the far longer and finally far more crucial *journey of marriage* which today is so often shadowed by discouragement and fear, by anger and division and divorce. Here, it seems to me, our cultural struggles are less fundamentally about sex than about gender, about roles and responsibilities in childbearing and work, reproduction and production. These struggles, involving as they do both heavily sacralized and increasingly secularized values and images, will not end soon, nor will their resolution be easy. For they are part of the modern "promethean moment" (which is the focus of the next chapter), part of the struggle to renegotiate sacred and secular understandings in the gender and sexual liberations

27. See pp. 151–52 above.

28. It is, of course, arguable that the greater contemporary problem is no longer exaggerated images of sexuality and romantic love, but a pervasive trivialization of sex and a correlative debunking of love.

which we simultaneously seek and fear. It is a struggle which must be played out in the public square, yet borne and lived through by ordinary men and women with all their strengths and vulnerabilities, and by families both functional and dysfunctional (as all our real families inevitably are). How much need, then, for public sermons and stories that de-escalate passions and images by developing more healing ironies. Such speaking and writing (it bears repeating) is above all the responsibility of the artists and intellectuals, the poets and the priests, just as they also bear much responsibility for today's fevered imaginations, angry images, and violent polarizations.

Nor should we allow ourselves to haughtily minimize the importance of such "sexual politics" because of "far more important" concern with economic justice and war and peace—what the fevered imaginations of too many still see as the ultimate "politics of light against darkness." For it is, again, no simplistic truism to say that the state of gender relations and families is utterly crucial to the health of the human city around the globe. Families (whatever their forms) remain one our most fundamental schools of sensibility, of virtue and vice, one of the places where we all learn or fail to learn (not just in our heads, but in hearts and spirit and imagination) those forms of educated faith and hope and love which make for the sanity and humanity not only of our individual lives, but of the life of our city. Indeed it is no exaggeration to say that the family is the first great school of irony where we, for good or ill, first form the basic images that enable us to then understand the ironies taught in human stories, both great and small. Even more fundamentally, it is through the long journey of family life, in daily realities as well as traumas and transitions, that we experience the ironies that can bring the energies of sexuality and romance into fruitful (or failed) embodiment in both personal and political life.

It should be clear, moreover, that what I have just indicated in general about the central role of irony in both the journey into marriage and the journey of marriage and family life can be said equally about many more specific contemporary struggles: about homosexuality; about abortion and the control of birth and death; about work and adequate income and benefits; about health care and child care and schooling and all other public supports for and extensions of family life. None of these struggles is easy and we are continually tempted by totalized images of right and wrong, us and them, light and darkness. Here too Lynch's thought alerts us to both the danger of easy ironies of contempt and the necessity of more difficult forms of irony. These struggles will and must go on for the good of the city. Yet (again) everything depends on sensibility and imagination, on the right kinds of irony. Such irony need not mean compromise, though there is always much more room for that than we are typically willing to imagine. It certainly does not mean giving up convictions, for these struggles often do involve matters of good and evil, though they typically also involve many related (but less clearly moral) convictions about better and worse, sound or foolish.[29] But such irony does mean a real and sustained effort (a difficult asceticism) to achieve the right tone, style, and rhythm—the right sensibility—for the spirit which governs us and our city. The alternative, as always, is between realistic imagination and violence.

The City's Poor

If matters of sex and gender have troubled the human city throughout its history, that is certainly true as well for matters of wealth and poverty, for issues of economic and social justice.[30] These, then, are my third "instance" of the significance of Lynch's thought about faith and irony for politics.

Yet I have already discussed Lynch's understanding of the relationship between irony and the poor at the end of the preceding chapter.[31] At this point in the present chapter, moreover, I hope that Lynch's sense of the need for the right kinds of irony in building our human city is clear enough that its relevance to conflicts about economic justice can be readily imagined. Thus I shall here simply review several of Lynch's pointed comments, some deliberately repeated.

It remains true, despite the tremendous gains in human and economic rights achieved both by economic growth and by struggle and revolution during the past several centuries, that we still face, both nationally and globally, great and growing poverty and inequality—what Lynch once called "the haunting, daunting, tragic possibility [of] very likely . . . growing polarization into a world of only very rich and very poor."[32] The at times agitated presence of the poor, at home and globally, is one of the most central realities tearing into the human body of faith, and thus one of the central

29. "It seems to be the teaching of Christ," Lynch says at one point "that good and bad must stay together until the final judgment." He then mockingly adds, "Imagine the horror of separating out the good in this life" (IF, 93). Yet are we not continually tempted to do just that, to play god in our righteous crusades?

30. Since concerns about racism are, as I write, once again being raised with great and deserved passion in this country, I need to stress that I intend, as Lynch clearly did, to include racial justice within the larger categories of economic and social justice. In doing this I am simply following Lynch's lead even though I know, as presumably he did, that there is very serious debate about the complex relationship of race and class, racism and poverty.

31. See pp. 158–59.

32. Lynch, "Final Image," 30.

challenges we all face in rebuilding that body as Pope Francis continues to remind us.

In the by now oft-cited passage about "The City of Man" at the start of *Images of Hope* (26)—about always facing "programmatic alternatives" between violence and imagination—Lynch contrasts the city "in which all men have citizenship," which "will always require an act of the imagination which will extend the idea of the human," with the exclusionary city of walled and armed camps. Twenty-one years later, in one of his last published writings, he lamented that we typically have failed to make that inclusive act of imagination:

> [I]t is we ourselves who, for our own purposes, severely delimit our image of the human and refuse admission to the look of the homeless, to the addict, to . . . the very poor . . . It is we ourselves, for our own narrow purposes, who delimit the glorious and open image of the human into a narrow ideology or some fatuous terms of sweet and perfect normality.[33]

Lynch's point in these and related remarks is not simply to exhort us to an evangelical concern for the poor. Rather his *particular* point is given with the idea of fundamental alternatives, and with the assertion that thus far we, for the most part, have chosen to "severely delimit our image of the human and refuse admission to . . . the very poor." His point, in other words, is not simply that there must be many forms of political action: aid and charity; movement politics and political campaigns; and, yes, protests and strikes and even class warfare when that may prove inevitable and morally justified. Rather his basic point is that there must be a fundamental and "political" conversion in our common sensibility and our shared body of images: *from* one that "refuses admission" to the poor *to* an image that *really* includes not only the poor but all of our own poverties. Such conversion is, of course, fundamentally a matter of the sensibility and spirituality that operates in the social-political arena.

Without such fundamental conversion of heart and sensibility, all of our political movements and our endless debates about poverty and inequality remain either so much pious but empty rhetoric or just another occasion for expressions of contempt for the "others" who disagree with "our" policies and programs. The final result will, sadly, be that lamented sarcastically in the play "*Marat/Sade*": "The revolution came and went, unrest was replaced by discontent."[34]

33. Lynch, "Introduction," 3.

34. Peter Weiss, *Persecution*.

Without fundamental conversion of our hearts and imaginations, all of us will continue, whatever our pieties and charities and politics, to delimit our image of the human "into a narrow ideology or some fatuous terms of sweet and perfect normality." We may have been led into such delimitation by forces in our politics and media which serve powerful interests by their endlessly fatuous images of "sweet and perfect" *and affluent* middle class "normality." Or we, perhaps especially our artists and intellectuals and radicals, will in our own way also delimit our image of the human by a narrowly accusatory focus on those interests and by imagining ourselves (we and the poor) as passionately engaged in a war of pure light against utter darkness.

Given the seductive force of such simplistic images, whether of middle class normalcy or of righteous contempt—and it is important to note that many of us live with divided sensibilities, captivated simultaneously by both sets of images—what might make possible the conversion of heart and transformation of imagination that Lynch rightly calls us to? The answer, of course, is that there is no simple answer to that question, no one way to such transformation.

Yet for Lynch, whatever the particularities of each individual and political situation, the force of irony, and especially "the irony of Christ," will be fundamental to the process of conversion. For, to reiterate, it takes the force of experienced irony (whether subtle or mocking or even shocking in style) 1) first to break through the seductive appearances of our images of normalcy and righteousness, 2) then to help us realize that, if we are to become more fully human, we must hold together the beautiful ideals of peace and justice expressed even in such simplistic images with the actual and very human realities of poverty and weakness, especially our own poverty and weakness, and 3) finally to enable us to suffer those experiences where, by embracing (or moving through) such poverty, we come into such justice and peace as are actually possible in this world.

Here, again, are Lynch's words for such transformation of sensibility and for the kinds of politics that it could and should entail:

> There should be a steady relationship, to the point of passion, between faith and the poor, between faith and Africa, Asia. But that will not happen unless there is first this interior and originating contrariety in which faith loves its own interior and poor humanity. (IF, 89)

> On the one hand there are the superb and royal promises of faith. On the other they are related to and achieved in their opposites, in the human and in weakness. This is the central irony. The promises are especially made to the very poor, the weak, the

suffering, the oppressed . . . It should be easier for those who . . . do not throw these weak, suffering parts of themselves into the exterior darkness of contempt and disgust but approach their own poverty and death with redemptive, affectionate images—it should be easier for them to . . . refuse, above all, to accept the terrible dichotomy between the rich and poor nations, and in the best sense to become completely "political" in their devotion to Asia, Africa, Latin America. In other words their ironic image of themselves should become politically productive. (IF, 160–61)

I would here add only a repeated and quite straightforward clarification from Lynch. There are many ways in which we may come to love the weak and suffering parts of our own humanity—by our own experience, for instance, of illness and ignorance, of loss and of death. Yet quite often it is precisely by actual and sustained contact with the poor among us that we are led to such embracing love of our own poverty. The poor can often be our best teachers, as Sancho was for the Don.[35]

Irony, Time, and Political Action

My final "instance" of Lynch's discussion of irony as an appropriately political virtue does not involve a specific political class (like intellectuals and artists) or a specific political issue (like poverty or gender), but concerns the significance of his thought about time for political action of all kinds. For reflection on time was, as we have seen, a constant in Lynch's writings—especially in *Christ and Apollo, The Integrating Mind*, but also in shorter writings like his reminiscence about the East River.[36] It was also central to *Christ and Prometheus*, our next chapter's central text. Thus discussion of time's ironies and political action will also serve as a something of a transition to that next chapter.

While my guiding text here is the concluding fourth chapter of *Images of Faith*, "The Images of Faith and Human Time" (109–75), I will not attempt even the briefest summary of that quite dense writing. Rather I will simply evoke its theme with little concern for specifics or citation.

35. One very important recent call for such "coming together," specifically focused on racial division in this country, is the theologically infused and realistically imagined book by Christopher Pramuk, *Hope Sings*. See also the publisher's website for the book (www.hopesingssobeautiful.com) which provides online space for such coming together.

36. See above, pp. 24–25 for the East River essay and chapters 3 (for *The Integrating Mind*) and 4 (for *Christ and Apollo*).

One succinct way, using the language of *Images of Faith*, to articulate
the overall point of Lynch's thought about time and human action is to note
that time is perhaps the greatest and most powerful force of irony in political life as well as individual life. It is, one could even say, God's great irony—
a comic irony since time can be and often is essentially hopeful, though we
know that it can also be deeply tragic.[37] For the dramatic movement of both
comedy and tragedy, on the stage as in life, not only takes time and involves a
sequence of "acts," but also involves time's hard, even cruel, but also creative
ironies.[38] Is it not, for instance, fundamentally both ironic and comic that
we dreamers of great dreams and planners of important, even magnificent
projects—we children of Apollo and Dionysus and Prometheus—can and
must actually live only in the step by step smallness of actual human time.
Whatever the glorious dreams of last night, or the great plans for tomorrow,
even the greatest political and military leaders must still put one foot and
then another on the floor each morning, still speak or write only one word
at a time in order to complete a sentence, much less a grand oration or an
entire book. Human time is inescapably momentary and we are essentially
time-limited, indeed time-*bound* creatures.

Yet human time is not simply momentary. It is also sequential and di-
rectional—a matter of stages and phases intended (by God and ourselves) to
get someplace. Thus it can and should be comic (in the word's most fundamental sense) as a source of realistic hope. Yet we pursue that directionality
and achieve realistic hope only by moving in time and growing through life's
stories and stages—only as Dionysian (and Promethean and Apollonian)
energies are continually tutored by irony and thus brought "down" into reality by such passage and suffering.

We may well curse the reality of time, and perhaps often do—when
we are tired or bored and can't wait to end some drudgery, or when, by contrast, we are excited and can't wait for an anticipated goal, whether returning
home or departing on an adventure, initiating some plan or attaining some
victory. For political leaders like Macbeth, as well as for ordinary folk, the
"petty pace" of "tomorrow and tomorrow and tomorrow" often seems God's
curse rather than any blessing.

37. One thinks, for instance, of the tragically ironic contrast between glorious, initial expectations for quick success and the hard lessons of reality in most wars—in "the
Great War" as again in both Viet Nam and Iraq.

38. Tolstoy's *War and Peace*, to take one classic example, depicts history's cruel
mockery of both Napoleon's grand delusions and the pseudo-magnificence of the Russian nobility. Yet it also depicts a gentler, more comic and creative irony in the way the
romantic dreams of its protagonists are "tutored" by time and eventually realized in
marriage.

Yet blessing it fundamentally is, according to Lynch, however difficult or tedious or ordinary the actual passage. How so? Because time is God's great instrument for saving us from the many false absolutes and mad visions, the towers of Babel which continually tempt us and our leaders to leap from the small but firm path of the human. Yet that path is always temporal and time always leads or forces us back to it. Or, perhaps better and more fundamentally stated, time itself *is* that inescapably human path. For time is not just the relentless ticking of some great cosmic mechanism. Rather, whatever the physics of cosmic time, human time is for us (even for the great theoreticians of such physics) essentially rhythmic and dramatic, not some external thing but a force interior to the moments and directions of our lives and of our city. In Lynch's oft repeated phrase, human time is the "stages and phases" of actual lives, the rhythms and drama of real life in contrast to revolutionary fantasies of great leaps forward or Gnostic dreams of escape to a timeless utopia. Human time is, in other words, an interior structure of stages and phases which are going someplace, moving into the real realization (if I may be forgiven such a phrase) of the great desires we have felt, the great plans we have made, and the great promises we have been given—perhaps especially those desires and plans, promises and prayers, for justice and peace "on earth as it is in heaven."

That human time is going someplace, or striving to go someplace, is the constant teaching of experience: of the child coming to its self, the adolescent learning to realize dreams, the conflicted struggles and always partial resolutions of human politics, and even the experience of the elderly (and the rest of us) in learning how to die. It is also the essential teaching of Christian faith about the meaning of Creation and the coming of God's Kingdom.[39] For God not only created time as a great good, but in Christ entered and fully lived through human time—lived into and died because of the actual politics of his city—and in so living has led and continually leads us to the realization of what has been promised.[40]

It is, of course, at times immensely difficult to believe what we are taught by such experience and by faith. Perhaps today especially, in this particular Promethean moment, it is very difficult to believe in the significance of the very small dimensions of human time which can seem quite literally

---

39. Such is also true, with many obvious differences, for Judaism and Islam. I cannot take up here what seem to be radically different understandings of time in Eastern religions, especially Buddhism. Yet it may be important to remember, and not just a silly truism, that the Buddha himself attained nirvana through the stages of a very human journey, and that Buddhist political struggles today, in places like Sri Lanka, Thailand, and Myanmar, remain subject to historical stages and ironies.

40. Such is the central theme of the chapter on "Time" in *Christ and Apollo* (31–64).

nothing at all by comparison with modern awareness of the vast stretches of cosmic space and time. Lynch, at least, was very aware of this "Pascalian" dilemma.[41] For the seeming indifference of the "infinite universe," with its billions of years and millions of galaxies, to our infinitesimally small earthly existence does often strike modern sensibility as a particularly cruel (even absurd) irony.[42]

Nor need we look only to the silence of the stars to feel such irony about the relative insignificance of human life. For our Promethean moment entails other great temptations, often in direct rebellion against this modern sense of cosmic indifference. I refer again to the continual temptation of the "American Adam" to forget and even deliberately flee the past, to imagine the fantasy that *totally* new beginnings are actually possible in this new promised land.[43] Then to the more specific or historic temptations that especially concerned Lynch in *Images of Faith* and, as we shall soon see, in *Christ and Prometheus*—temptations to absolutized dreams, both Dionysian and Promethean, about the human city and, far worse, the temptations of those actual and terrible political movements (both reactionary and revolutionary, at home and abroad) that have sought the violent realization of such fantasies. For who today dares easily to proclaim the meaningfulness of human time and history—that the "stages and phases" of human time really are "going someplace"—in face of Holocaust and genocide and the failed gods of revolution and counter-revolution.[44] Before such political realities, in such times, do not Macbeth's powerful words seem to speak the more fundamental truth that "the petty pace of tomorrow and tomorrow and tomorrow" is "a tale told by an idiot, full of sound and fury, signifying nothing."

Neither faith nor experience has any easy "answer" to these cruel ironies of recent history and contemporary times. The interwoven sections of Lynch's final chapter in *Images of Faith* take up, one after another, different but central aspects of time's difficult ironies, building towards a final section on "Death and Nothingness." The writing is dense and difficult because of the difficulty of those ironies, and the difficulty that both faith and experience

41. See especially IF, 24–31, 144–56.

42. The phrase "infinite universe" comes from Alexander Koyre's book, *From the Closed World*, which Lynch references in *Images of Faith* (30).

43. See pages pp. 65–67 above and IM, 18–37 for "The American Adam".

44. Lynch explicitly takes up Jewish and Christian struggle with the reality of the Holocaust (how believe what has been promised in the face of such evil?) in the final chapter of *Images of Faith*. See IF, 127–29, 136–37, 143–44. See also his extended reflection (IF, 147–52) on Ivan Karamazov's rejection, because of such evil, of any promise of eventual harmony.

have in struggling to realize their meaning. Lynch certainly provides no easy answers. Rather he continually says, throughout this concluding series of reflections, that faith and experience can only find meaning and hope—can only come both to know and to believe that life's stages and phases are going someplace—by the difficult passage through these ironies, by undergoing (or suffering) time's continual pull "down" into the small lines of human life wherein alone the great hopes and promises, both personal and political, are actually (and ironically) realized. Put differently, even the times when we curse time or when time seems to curse us, indeed perhaps especially those times, cannot be somehow cast off into some outer darkness or in some other way "transcended." (That particularly modern idea of transcending is pure fantasy.) Rather they must be lived through, and it is in the passage of time, in these stages and phases of life, that irony works its greatest transformations. That, again, is the promise of both experience and faith. That is finally what Lynch calls the irony of Christ. And it happens only in time and only because of time's hard edges and passages. In the words of his East River reminiscence: "Always two steps forward and one back" to the realization of life's "*muddy fleshed-out* dreams."[45]

What, in summary then, does the irony of time have to do with politics, with building the human city and with a spirituality for public life? It must suffice here simply to say that there will be no quick and easy road to dealing with the widening divide between rich and poor, or the distrust between intellectuals and managers, or the war between family values and feminism. No quick path, as we are about to see, to renegotiating the fierce contemporary tensions and oppositions between secular and sacred. No great leaps forward or great escapes or apocalyptic climax.[46] Such temptations are always forms of violence. The real way ahead for our city is a human one, however often we may be misled by promised fixes or escapes. The way ahead for the *human* city will be governed by time's ironies and by the dramatic rhythms of action and suffering which embody and teach those ironies. That is what we were taught by Aeschylus during a previous Promethean moment, and what we are again being taught by today's politics if we but have the imagination and sensibility to understand and live through them rather than seek some impossible transcending.

---

45. See p. 25 above.

46. Lynch tells us how much he loves the promise of "a new heaven and a new earth" in *Revelations* 21. See IF, 164–65. Yet he references that promise in his discussion of irony precisely to emphasize that our human way to such beauty is, once again, *through* the inescapable temporal realities of tragedy and death.

7

Prometheus–The Secular City

Having seen how Lynch called us to forms of irony which help us to struggle humanly and imaginatively with some of our most difficult political problems, we now turn to what is perhaps the most fundamental or foundational political struggle of our era. I refer to the many-shaped and truly agonic conflict between the growing power of secularity and the residual force of the sacred, the ancient struggle of Prometheus and Zeus as it plays out again during this third "Promethean moment" of history. And if, perchance, one is tempted to regard theological debate about "the secular city" as just an episode in "the 60s," I suggest they think of recent discussion about "the clash of civilizations" between "the West and the rest,"[1] of the ongoing bloodshed and terror which exemplify that clash, and of increasing concern about persecution and religious freedom both in this country and globally.

Lynch wrote about this foundational political struggle in *Christ and Prometheus* (1970), a book which, whenever I return to it, I am tempted to regard as his greatest (or at very least his most historically significant and imaginative).[2] My overriding interpretative category in this chapter, then, as it was his in that book, will not so much be "irony" as "drama"—or, perhaps better, the very dramatic ironies involved in contemporary struggles caused by the global process of secularization. As we have seen throughout this book, Lynch continually called for forms of sensibility and spirituality strong enough for fruitful passage through this inescapable drama. Thus here again he turns both to Aeschylus and to Ignatius, and above all to Christ, for the imaginative strength needed as we encounter the powerful,

1 See, as examples of a large literature on the topic, Samuel Huntington's seminal 1993 *Foreign Affairs* essay "The Clash of Civilizations?" and Roger Scruton's 2002 book on *The West and the Rest*.

2. Unless otherwise noted, page references in the text and in footnotes of this chapter are to *Christ and Prometheus*.

crucial, and yet immensely disturbing emergence of modern Promethean secularity.

We know that from time immemorial the human city has been built on sacred foundations and has functioned under a sacred canopy.[3] Not only have places like Jerusalem or Mecca or Benares been holy cities, but all cities have, in a more fundamental sense, been sacred for their inhabitants—dedicated to and protected by gods or sacred powers. Think of Athens and Athena, of pre-Christian Rome's divine emperors, or of the linking of papacy with empire in Christian Rome. In *Christ and Prometheus* Lynch references Fustel de Coulanges' classic study *The Ancient City* to explain that "Greek and Roman civilizations," while clearly quite secular and not "holy civilizations," nonetheless "tended towards a total formalization of life under formally religious images" (10–11). He then briefly reviews the history of Byzantine and Roman Christianity, the thought of Augustine and the poetry of Dante, and finally the character of medieval Christendom and its extension thru the Reformation to illustrate the predominance of this sacral sense of the human city in all the pre-modern periods of Western civilization (11–13).

Always previously in the West, then, and still today in many non-Western civilizations—think, perhaps most obviously, of many forms of Islam—all the human (or secular) energies involved in the social, economic, cultural and political dimensions of the human city functioned within or under a prevailing system of sacred ideas and ideals, rituals and images. To be sure, as far back as we know there has always also been what Lynch calls "the secular project" whose "great symbol . . . was Prometheus." In his words:

> By secularity and the secular project I mean the march of mankind, in the autonomous light of its own resources, toward the mastery and humanization of the world, in the objective terms of all the arts and sciences as these have taken shape and are still taking shape in history. The great symbol of this project was Prometheus, who first gave man fire, then the alphabet, then every other resource by which we have been struggling out of darkness. (7)

Yet until relatively recently this secular project "could [only] be *seen as an occasional thrust outside a basically religious image of the world*" (7).

---

3. The reference, of course, is to Peter Berger's now classic text on the sociology of religion, *The Sacred Canopy* (1967).

In the West, though, beginning with the Renaissance—Lynch thus recounts the oft-told story of our modernity[4]—and taking firm hold with the various revolutions of the Enlightenment, there has been an immense dramatic thrust of this perennial secular project away from a "religious image of the world" (or at least independent of sacred tutelage and restraint) and into its own autonomous identity. This thrust is evident in the modern development of all the human sciences and arts, the technologies, professions and practices which are today so fundamentally constitutive of the human city. Thus for the first time in human history it really makes sense to speak of "the secular city."

Lynch takes this modern emergence of an independent secularity as simply given and quite obvious—even if descriptions of and, perhaps especially, reactions to it vary widely. Thus in the opening section of *Christ and Prometheus*[5] he speaks of the "march of mankind, in the autonomous light of its own resources, towards mastery and humanization of the world," the march symbolized by Prometheus which *today* constitutes "an overwhelming presence," "a major new explosion of energy and ideas." It is "so vast a secularity that it *is* qualitatively new and overwhelming." It is characterized by an "explosion into new hypotheses" (new ideas, new possibilities, new discoveries and continual exploration) in "the objective terms of all the arts and sciences as these have taken shape and are still taking shape in history." It is the dominant historical reality of our time and, as we now recognize, it is global in its reach and penetration. This vast presence finds us fascinated by and typically quite given over to "energy and power" which, Lynch does not in the least hesitate to say, are such "magnificent things." Yet it also, as we shall see, typically finds us just as deeply troubled and afraid. Prometheus, for both better and worse, has become a symbol for the dominant force transforming our world.

Still, to repeat, what is most new about this secular march is not only its magnitude, though that (again) is "so vast that it *is* something qualitatively new," but the fact that it is no longer simply "an occasional thrust outside a basically religious image of the world . . . [N]ow it is an overwhelming presence within which the religious imagination must learn to exist" (7). In saying this Lynch was clearly distancing himself from the now largely discredited "secularization hypothesis," the view long assumed in many "enlightened" tellings of the story of modernity, that "man come of age" would eventually have no need for religion, that the victory of Prometheus over

4. His full recounting of this story involves the entire lengthy "Prologue" (1–36) to *Christ and Prometheus*. See especially 13–21.

5. Subsequent citations in this paragraph move both backwards and forwards from Lynch's just cited preliminary definition of secularity on p. 7.

Zeus would at last be complete and final. Indeed, as we will see, Lynch in the 1960s clearly anticipated more recent scholarship about the persistence and current resurgence of the sacred. Even more significantly, he clearly anticipated the widespread violence that has accompanied this resurgence in many parts of our global city. He anticipated and articulated, in other words, crucial aspects of what can now be seen as one kind of "post-modern" reaction to modern secularity.

Lynch wrote *Christ and Prometheus* as his contribution to "the secular city debate" that developed in theological circles in the late 1960s. His book is a clear and strong affirmation of the reality and good of the modern process of secularization. Indeed he goes so far as to see it as a necessary aspect of the Christian understanding of salvation.[6] Yet in so affirming secularization he simultaneously and emphatically affirms the foundational truth of religious and Christian belief about human life and the world. For one of his book's fundamental arguments is that all genuine secularization (as opposed to many false forms) is humanization and thus central to God's purpose in both creation and salvation. Thus he did not welcome some of the "secularization theology" that was then receiving much attention. Indeed, a key part of his contribution to the 1960s debate was his strong criticism of what he regarded as simplistic images of "man come of age" and "religion-less" or "demythologized" Christianity. He reserves praise, for instance, only for "the descriptions of this [secularizing] process in the opening chapters of Harvey Cox's *The Secular City*," not for its subsequent theologizing (30).[7] The title of his own book clearly emphasizes Lynch's sense of the continuing need for a strong religious presence, above all the presence of Christ, if the modern emergence of Prometheus is to achieve even part of its great promise and not be reduced (as it already too often has been) to fantastic but terribly destructive forms of "prometheanism." In order to remain true to itself, in other words, and thus a genuine form of humanization (and salvation), the secularization process needs the full and critical strength of the sacred forces of the religious imagination lest it be reduced to an absolutized and dehumanizing secular*ism*.

Enlarging Perspectives

Another aspect of Lynch's contribution to that 1960s debate (and to present thinking about secularity and sacral resurgence) is his quite typical effort to

6. See 42–43.

7. See 8 for Lynch's brief evocation of the 1960s secularization debate and 11 on Cox.

enlarge our perspective on this fierce and very real conflict, lest imaginations become fixated and violent like those of Pentheus and Dionysus[8]—as
so many imaginations were when he wrote and have been since. He worked
for such enlargement in at least two major ways, each drawn directly from
his mentor Aeschylus. For, as Lynch says in the very first sentence of *Christ
and Prometheus*, "the genius of Aeschylus is able to direct our thoughts to
the constant dramatic process by which human civilization moves through
pain towards higher moments of achievement . . . " (3). It is, moreover,
the Prometheus of Aeschylus' imagining who is "the legendary initiator of
human culture and sufferer because of it" (3). *This* Prometheus "is finally
reconciled with Zeus, in such a reconciliation with himself and the world as
we ourselves, more than we think, still long for" (3).[9]

Lynch's first enlargement of perspective has been discussed previously.[10] He reminds us that contemporary secularization is simply the latest
stage in a world-historical human project. "The great symbol of this project
was [and remains] Prometheus, who first gave man fire, then the alphabet,
then every other resource by which we have been struggling out of darkness" (7). There have been, moreover, three truly epochal "moments" in the
march of Prometheus through history. The first was that hardly imaginable
moment, "about a million years ago," which first saw the emergence of human beings. It is, Lynch says, "the moment where . . . Prometheus descended
with fire to give the very first elements of human resource to our race" (101).
"Something like this," Lynch does not hesitate to say, "is what actually must
have happened, had to happen . . . " (62). "The second great revolution was
the emergence of man (principally in three locations, the valley of the Tigris
and the Euphrates, the valley of the Nile, and the valley of the Indus) into
the forms of civilized society . . . " (102). The third "supremely important
moment" is our own present, "the enormous thing called 'modernization'"
(104).

For Lynch, to repeat, Prometheus symbolizes "the march of mankind,
in the autonomous light of its own resources, toward the mastery and humanization of the world" (7). It has been a march of many moments in
different places and cultures, a march continually moved forward by new
gifts and discoveries of "fire and alphabet," of knowledge and technique, of
imagination and realization—an historical march marked both by crucial
continuities and continual change. Yet so dramatic and significant has been

---

8. See pp. 146–48 above.

9. See also 56–57 and 63 where Lynch contrasts Aeschylus' imagining of Prometheus with other far less adequate imaginings, both more ancient (Hesiod) and quite
modern (Goethe, Shelly, and Byron).

10. See pp. 16–17 above.

the secular emergence and the consequent transformations and sufferings of our era that it is best understood as only the third truly epochal phase of this continuous march. It was, of course, during the second "moment," during the rise of ancient Greek civilization, that Aeschylus wrote his plays in order to help his city deal with the challenges to its sacred foundations posed by the new experience of secular power given with civic development. Thus it is not surprising that Lynch turns to Aeschylus for guidance today. For ours is also such an epoch: a "major new explosion of energy and frontiers in the . . . secular project," a time of immense "forward and autonomous movement of human action and history through the arts and sciences, through economics and politics and the whole social reality, towards great but autonomous human goals . . . " (7).

Yet from its beginning, and this is Lynch's second and more fundamentally "Aeschylean" way of enlarging our perspective, "the march of mankind towards the mastery and humanization of the world" has never been a straightforward story of progress. It has always involved a dramatic rhythm of action and suffering, change and reaction, effort and guilt, liberation and punishment.[11] With many others, Lynch finds examples of this pattern of dramatic action and reaction at various points in Western history.

> The beautiful energies of the Athenians move into a position of guilt, cruelty, exploitation of the surrounding world . . . The Renaissance explodes into a miracle of human energy and achievement; the Reformation, in great part a radical and guilty criticism of the new leap forward, follows close on its heels. (13)

Nor is this simply a typical pattern of ordinary political or religious conflict. From the first it has involved a far more foundational struggle between sacred and secular powers and sensibilities, both *within* each of us and *among* us in the human city—a struggle that not only divides sacred and secular imaginations, but divides the sacred imagination within itself (as it struggles to understand itself in the midst of secular developments) as well as the secular imagination within itself (as it struggles for direction, for boundaries, and for absolution from a deep sense of guilt). Prometheus, we must remember, *steals* fire *from the gods* as a gift for human beings, and suffers the wrath and punishment of Zeus. His (secular) rebellion against the (sacred) order of the world seems, in other words, to place human emergence and development in fundamental opposition to the sacred. This was the challenge faced by the Athenians: how to reconcile their new and growing sense of human power and civilization with their traditional sense of the

---

11. See, for example, 3–4, 13–14, 39–40.

sacred? It was to imagine, to dramatize, this challenge and thereby enable his people to better struggle with it that Aeschylus wrote about Prometheus and Zeus,[12] as he had previously in the *Oresteia* written about the founding of Athens.[13] Today it again seems that efforts to appropriate the modern gifts of Prometheus also, almost inevitably, involve an intense and dramatic battle with "Zeus"—with a traditional, at times residual yet still deep and recently again resurgent sense of the sacred.

Thus the movement of human history, the slow and often tortured struggle for humanization and autonomy, has *always* been characterized by a dramatic cultural and political struggle between secular and sacred sensibilities within us and in our city. It has always involved a many-sided sense both of real progress and terrible transgression, of righteousness and guilt, of liberation and wrath. The *dramatic* character of this human struggle has been most evident during periods of great change. It is the drama in which we are again engaged and which we must imagine rightly and realistically as we seek hope and direction in again rebuilding the foundations of our city.

Deep and Painful Divisions

I turn, then, to Lynch's actual and "Aeschylean" imagining of the Promethean struggles of our time. His organization of *Christ and Prometheus*, not into conventional chapters, but into a Prologue, three Acts, and an Epilogue, is intended, he tells us, to suggest the dramatic "rhythm of a Greek play" (6). By this he means that there will be no straightforward progression in the struggle between Prometheus and Zeus that leads to some climactic reconciliation in Christ. Rather, the movement of Lynch's imagining is typically far more complex and realistic: weaving and reweaving, circling back again and again as each "act" suggests different aspects of the action-reaction pattern of great drama and of contemporary history. We are thereby challenged not only to resist reducing the story to some neat form, but even more to

12. See 58–62 where Lynch reminds us that the *Prometheus Bound*, which we have, was the first of at least two (*Prometheus Unbound*) and perhaps three plays wherein Aeschylus, continuing the pattern evident in his other plays, would have understood the struggle between Zeus and Prometheus *dramatically*, as an historic process involving great hostility and polarization and only gradually, *through* that suffering and *through* many acts and stages, achieving an imagined reconciliation on new and more adequate terms.

13. As we will see below, while he took Prometheus as the primary symbol for the secular project, Lynch actually makes the more complete text of the *Oresteia* (where we have all three plays leading towards the foundation of Athens) the primary model for his own understanding of the struggles which today engage us. See 77–80, 83–86, 89–95.

take up as our own the difficult task of imagining this fundamental struggle of our time in more realistic ways.

Yet here, once again, I can offer only a summary sketch while still hoping to evoke some sense and taste for the fuller movement of Lynch's thought. Thus, after some preliminary reminders about Lynch's understanding of images and imagination, I will, in this section and the next, provide further detail about Lynch's view of our most foundational political problem: the painful divisions and hostilities we experience both between and within the sacred and secular imaginations of our time. Then, in subsequent sections, I will suggest a number of contemporary instances of such division and struggle. Finally, I will take up Lynch's portrayal of the difficult journey we must travel, and the challenging spirituality we shall require, in healing such divisions for the good of our city.

Lynch thought it necessary to begin *Christ and Prometheus* with some notes on his use of the terms "image" and "imagination."[14] For we generally tend, I suspect, to think of images as fairly superficial things, perhaps because we are constantly bombarded by so many superficial images. We may also still think of "the imagination" as some particular creative or artistic faculty. Yet Lynch thought that images were more fundamental than any one faculty, indeed far more fundamental than ideas. Ideas, of course, are immensely important. We are now, as was he, using ideas to talk about images and imagination, about secularity and the sacred, history and drama, and so on. Yet Lynch was quite right to focus continually not just on a "battle of ideas" but on the divided and conflicted state of contemporary imaginations. For, again, images can be, and typically are in the case of our more important images, far deeper and more powerful than ideas. In Lynch's way of speaking,[15] *images are our most basic way and finally our whole way of dealing with the actual world.* Images are the way the world comes to us (through the individual and cultural images that are constitutive of our imaginations) and thus also the way we move into the world and actually maintain and develop our world through the use, adequate or inadequate, realistic or narrow and violent, of our imaginations. There are, in other words, no "pure facts" or "pure objects" or even "pure ideas." Everything that we meet, and that meets us, including our very selves, is framed within some larger context of imagining. Thus our more fundamental images are both very powerful and quite complex, built over time and through experience. They embody not only facts and ideas, but feelings, and not just any feelings but some of our

14. See pp. 23–27. For previous discussion of Lynch's understanding of imagination see pp. 100–102 above.

15. I summarize here from pp. 23–25, 41 n.2, 71, 76–77.

deepest passions and ideals, hopes and fears—about freedom and meaning, secularity and sacrality. Thus they are as central to our individual lives as they are constitutive of the body of faith and sensibility that is our city.

If, once again, such claims about images and imagination still seem odd or exaggerated, I ask the reader first to consider the cumulative effect of the media's endless repetition of superficial images (whether of sex and gender, immigrant and citizen, terrorist and patriot, or poet and priest); to consider the effect of continually superficial images on both our individual and our communal sense of the world, on our good or bad "taste" of both self and world. Then I ask the reader to consider (for Lynch is about to ask us to undertake such an effort) the difficulty of any struggle, whether personal or communal, to transform deeply rooted images (even if they be superficial), to break through habitual ways of seeing the world, to move beyond precious or comforting or threatening images, to find a way through polarized hostilities (especially when we really feel the hostility and are invested in the polarization). As individuals we know the difficulty of such transformation in our own lives. We also continually witness, in the various cultural and political struggles of our times, the still greater challenge involved in the social and structural transformation of shared images and imagination. Such difficulty, often immense, is clear testimony to the power of images and to the challenge of new imagining, as also to the need for a powerful spirituality if we are to achieve a needed transformation of our images.

Since its beginnings, then, the process of modernization (in the many dimensions of the human city: political and economic, social and cultural; in all the sciences and arts, both theoretical and practical) has always been accompanied by pervasive imaginative action. It has been sustained by images of progress, enlightenment, and liberation, even as it has continually provoked images of fear and reaction, especially (but not only) from those sectors of ourselves and our city embodying the traditional and sacred order of things. Thus our images of both sacred and secular, or, better put, our own sacral and secular imaginations have, to put it mildly, been deeply disturbed by modern secularization. No longer are the many "secular" aspects of our city given their ultimate shape and deeper meaning by a prevailing or overarching sacred imagination. For these realities have developed autonomously, which is to say outside of and at times in opposition to, even in revolt against, that traditional canopy of sacred images. Their meanings are now given almost entirely by the secular imagination itself, by the many ways in which the secular project, independent of sacred tutelage, imagines itself, and by the adequacy or inadequacy of its own images.

If this description sounds abstract and perhaps extreme, then contrast the typical architectural skyline of the modern city with that of the ancient and medieval city. Now skyscrapers dominate, not cathedrals and palaces. Or if this seems too simple a way to imagine modern secularity, think of our universities (for I shall return to them below). I remember once holding in my hands the large compilation of course offerings for just one semester at one of our country's premier state universities. It ran, if memory serves, to well over one-hundred large pages of small print. I flipped through to find courses in the humanities since they were my primary interest, courses in philosophy and religion, as well as literature and history and the various fine arts. This university had well-respected departments in all these disciplines. Nonetheless, even when taken together, the course offerings from all these disciplines constituted no more than ten or so pages. The type was small so there was a good range of interesting courses in those pages. Yet the overwhelming number of course offerings in that large booklet were in various technical fields, in the endless subdivisions of the sciences and practical arts which were the main business of the appropriately named "secular" university. Traditional humanistic offerings were simply dwarfed by the newer secular fields of study. Theology was clearly no longer queen. In fact it could not even be found, since all the humanistic studies, including the study of religion, were also appropriately "secular" in methodology and intellectual commitment.

Of course for many, even most citizens of the modern city, perhaps especially in the U.S., sacred forms and presences remain precious and at times vitally necessary. Yet, to repeat Lynch's words, the secular has nonetheless become "an overwhelming presence in which the religious imagination must learn to exist" (7). Some elements of the religious imagination (call them more "liberal" if you wish) have sought to welcome new secular realities, to accommodate to them and support them. Others (call them more "conservative") have reacted defensively, fearing that accommodation is little more than a slippery-slope to capitulation and a eventual loss of sacred identity and truth. This, of course, is a fairly typical way of telling the story of 19th and 20th Century Theology, as also of both ecclesial and political history.

Invariably, then, our imagining and thus our actual experience of the relationship between sacred and secular has shifted dramatically. The old center does not hold. Tension and even tormented opposition at times now seems more characteristic of this changed relationship, perhaps these days especially from the side of the sacred imagination. Nearer the beginnings of modernity, during the French Revolution for instance, the greater furies often came from the secular side. Yet the sacred imagination of today remains still largely oriented by its past or "sacramental" way of encompassing the human city. It still, in other words, feels called and compelled by its "long-term vocation . . . to bring total unity to the universe under God" (7). Yet it now typically finds itself marginalized and excluded (or made irrelevant) by the massive presence of an independent and functionally indifferent (though at certain times and places still actively hostile) secular project. It feels threatened, moreover, not only by such indifference and occasional hostility, but also because its own images of secular developments are often images of a wasteland, a world of superficial getting and spending, without depth of meaning and purpose; or, even more darkly, they are images of fateful decline.[16] Finally, then, and most fundamentally, the religious spirit and imagination feels itself marginalized and threatened because it as yet has "no acceptable image of secularity, no image of 'the world' within which it can live and breathe" (6), no adequate way of imagining and thus relating to and engaging with this now separate and vast secular presence. "That it must do so and cannot yet do so is almost a definition of [its] present crisis" (7).

The sacred imagination, then, lives in a divided state. That is to say, *we* live divided, with secular and sacred dimensions of ourselves separated, with too few points of fruitful contact, and too little deeper integration. The religious imagination often reacts by adopting a newly defensive and at times absolutized image of itself and of its relationship to secularity, either by implicit or deliberate withdrawal into its own sacral enclave (and thus even greater internal separation from the larger "secular wasteland" within which it must nonetheless continue to live) or by more active and at times fierce opposition to a demonically-imagined secularity which must either be converted or conquered. In either case, *this* new image (of its relationship to secularity) is not its traditional image of "bringing all to unity under God," nor is it an image and thus a taste of the world "within which it can live and breathe." For *this* new image is essentially oppositional and often violent.

Similar dynamics are, of course, also at work in the secular imagination's understanding of sacrality, in the images of relationship to the sacred which are operative in the secular parts of ourselves and of our city. For, as noted, much of the *modern* secular project's proud history first involved rebellion against various forms of sacral restraint and then evolved into a sense of its own coming of age and "no longer having need of that [religious] hypothesis." Today, of course, in the face of some forms of religious

16. Lynch (31–34) points to Graham Greene and T. S. Eliot, and to a series of French writers from Bloy and Bernanos to Mauriac and Julien Green, as Catholic sources for "the whole tradition among us of . . . the world as wasteland." And to dialectical theology, "from Kierkegaard to Barth," as Protestant sources that have also given "theological status to the degenerative image of secularity."

resurgence, the secular project (both in the city and within each of us) must on occasion again defend its truth and its autonomy from what it experiences as the attacks of religious reactionaries. Thus it is tempted once again to imagine itself as the pure force of light standing firm against the powers of darkness.[17] And we again find ourselves divided, often not even knowing where the light and where the darkness.

Yet the more significant problem for the contemporary secular imagination, at least in the West, is not this sense of the need for renewed resistance to sacral forces, but a far deeper division within itself, within its own troubled and even tormented images of its own project. "At one pole" in Lynch's description of this division, "there is [our] love and admiration of energy, power, greatness, genius, and all the forms these splendid things can produce." Yet this is countered by "the opposite pole [of] deep distrust of this energy and genius—a fear, almost a hatred of the great world they are always creating" (17). Indeed, Lynch says, it is not in the least "melodramatic" to say that the contemporary secular imagination finds itself trapped between "enormous energy and enormous contempt" (20).

Of course our (secular) imagination has many different images of the secular project and thus of its own secularity. Many are affirmative and comforting, as when we generally embrace the advances of medical science and practice. But others are exaggerated and burdened with magnificence and fantasy, as if we might actually expect a final cure for all disease, or at very least uninterrupted "progress" in the continual improvement of health care. Still others, partly in response to such exaggeration, but even more in our general response to the "overwhelming presence" of secular development, are fear-filled images of gigantic technical systems or of one homogenous and universal "technological society" that dwarfs and alienates us.[18] We are left, for example, with a growing fear of physical health without human wholeness, of the loss of any grounding (or "organic") connection to nature, of exclusion from or manipulation by rigid new systems of care—generally, then, with fear of the monstrous birth of some new Frankenstein in our medical systems![19] And similar examples of both "enormous energy and

17. So might we understand the bluster of Christopher Hitchins' and Richard Dawkins' "new atheism." For a delightful skewering of their typically absolutized pretensions see Eagleton, *Reason*.

18. See, for instance, Lynch's use of Jacques Ellul's *The Technological Society* to discuss the idea totalized technical systems (34). More generally, all of "Act I" of *Christ and Prometheus* provides an exploration of dehumanized forms of the secular project that need to be criticized and transformed.

19. Something like this is probably contributes to the intensity of continuing reaction to "Obamacare."

enormous contempt" can readily be found for any sector of the contemporary secular project.[20]

For "the tradition among us of the world as wasteland" is hardly limited to religious intellectuals and religious sensibility. If anything, it is even greater among secular artists and writers, and more furious still among "the new revolutionaries . . . whose mockery is, by ambition, without limit" (21).[21] For today it is primarily secular voices that create an atmosphere of contempt in our cities. It is (to repeat some of Lynch's images) the "culture gangs" both right and left (recently of Tea Party and Occupy) that establish "armed camps" and sell "package deals" of political righteousness. They, far more than sacral voices, escalate "the war at home" between our culture classes, the at times furious distrust and even hatred between Dionysian artists and intellectuals and Penthean managers of our Promethean project.[22]

A Time of Reaction and Contempt

Before turning to several contemporary examples of these divisions which tear at our city's body of faith, I want first to add two further notes about Lynch's analysis. The first simply reiterates a regular, but central theme in his writings about our tendency to totalize our imagining of issues and oppositions. The second is a note expressed with particular clarity in *Christ and Prometheus* about what today is often called our "postmodern" present.

In the previous pages I have not hesitated to suggest the presence of violent and absolutized images in the divisions within and between the secular and sacred parts of ourselves and our city. Yet it is also important for our own thinking and imagining to distinguish between real divisions and absolutized images of those divisions. It is, of course, at times quite difficult to make that distinction in practice. Still, a clear idea of the difference may be of real help in the practical struggle of such discernment.

There is, to put this matter differently, a real and honest, a disturbed, perplexed, and very painful division within the religious imagination and between it and the secular project. This is the basic fact and problem that we must understand and imagine in its complexity if we are to move to

20. Lynch introduces this idea about deep division *within* our secular images and imaginations in his "Prologue" to *Christ and Prometheus*. Yet the scope of *this* division and the need for its healing runs throughout the book, perhaps especially in Acts II and III.

21. See 17–21 where he mentions, among other artists and intellectuals, Sartre and Brecht, Pinter and Miller. See also 16–17 for his critique of Herbert Marcuse.

22. See, again, pp. 146–48 above.

heal it. Yet such real division and our images of it are, inevitably it seems, accompanied and shadowed by unreal or fantastic images. There is, in other words, real reason for the religious imagination to fear the secular project, to fear the loss of its own religious identity and role, and to fear the very real excesses and errors and violence of the secular project. Evidence to support such fears can be found almost everywhere. Yet not all our fears are so real. The very importance of the real fears is itself one of the many causes of exaggerated fears and fantastic images of fear. The same can, of course, be said about other elements of the religious imagination: its sense of the rightness of its cause, of anger at dehumanization and violence, of beauty loved and truth affirmed. There is in each case, and many others, something very real and important in the religious reaction to secularization. There is also a tendency, at times seemingly inescapable, to move into an exaggeration of images, an absolutizing of righteousness and anger, beauty and truth, and thus to an extreme polarizing of real divisions.

Of course, all of these things can and need to be said about the secular imagination with its inner divisions and its troubling images, both of itself and of the sacred. There is almost always, layered onto or woven within such divisions, with their affirmations and hopes as well as their legitimate fears and angers, the burden of many shadow and fantasy forms that contribute so greatly to polarizations and violence. We very much need the analyses of our secular intelligence, the articulation of real fears and hopes both by the managers and by the artists and intellectuals. Yet we also need to fear the totalizing tendencies on both sides of this secular intelligence, to discern the package deals and culture gangs and violence that regularly invade and escalate their images of the secular project and of sacral resistance to it.

Thus when we join Lynch and others in the effort to transform our images of sacred and secular, to heal the divisions in the body of sensibility that is our city, we face something of a double task. Not only seeking new ways for sacred and secular imaginations to overcome their divisions and find forms of cooperation in a renewed mutuality of influence, but also, almost as a precondition of that task, struggling to exorcize the fantastic but very powerful and destructive demons that escalate images and polarize divisions, and thus overburden efforts to heal them. In practice, of course, these two therapeutic tasks are typically interwoven and inseparable, which is perhaps why Lynch does not make this distinction quite as neatly as I have.

Secondly, then, this same double challenge has always been there for those, like Aeschylus, who have sought reconciliation between Zeus and Prometheus. Yet it may be especially great for us today because we stand *now* (in the 1960s when Lynch wrote and still today) at a particularly dramatic and painful stage or turning point in the more than two-hundred year history of the modern project. Lynch did not himself use the term (though he clearly understood the reality), but ours is a time that others have since called "post-modern": a time of increased questioning, growing disillusionment, and mounting criticism of the entire Enlightenment thrust of modern secularity, and thus a time of even greater deepening in the divisions and polarizations within secular and sacred imaginations as much as between them.

Those divisions and polarizations have, as noted, been there from the beginnings of modern secularization. Remember again the French Revolution's violent rejection of sacral forms. Yet remember as well, to give two quite different but equally classic examples of the secular imagination's critique of its own "progress," both Mary Shelly's *Frankenstein*[23] and Karl Marx's analysis of deep alienation caused by the spread of capitalism. One could also point to cultural revulsion at the "Great War" as a major instance of escalation in the secular imagination's self-doubt and self-hatred.[24] Lynch clearly knew these many ways in which "writers and critics" had turned against the secular project during the 19th Century and again during the 1920s and through the Great Depression. As he also knew firsthand how the 1950s saw elite revulsion against the superficiality of affluence ("the organization man") and almost total disenchantment with communism ("the god that failed").

We have, then, long been inundated with intellectual and artistic expressions of contempt for our modern (secular) "wasteland." Yet such contempt, Lynch thought, may well have reached an apogee of sorts during "the 60s," a period when, both here and abroad, "the new revolutionaries" among the young, led on by "artists and intellectuals," turned with such fury against so many aspects of the modern project. That contempt continues still. Think, for instance, of some (though certainly not all) of the fearful images accompanying growing concern about environmental devastation. Or of the endless successors to the sensibility of *The Godfather* and *Apocalypse Now* which are increasingly featured on the global screen.

Lynch, as I've said, wrote before the word "postmodern" had come into common usage, yet it is fair to say that he quite clearly saw us living through a thoroughly post-modern experience, at least in the sense that the secular imagination is filled with very important, yet also dangerously escalated

---

23. The book's original subtitle was "The Modern Prometheus."

24. I have already referred (p. 144 n. 51 above) to Paul Fussell's *The Great War* for its account of the effect of the First World War on British letters: a radical escalation in ironies of contempt to the point where they became and have largely remained almost the norm for sophisticated sensibility.

levels of skepticism about the achievements of the Enlightenment.[25] Religious contempt for those achievements may well again be on the rise and receiving much attention, but he thought it dwarfed by the doubt and reaction still on the rise within the secular imagination itself. For many feel, in disturbingly deep ways, that the "hypothesis of the Enlightenment" no longer works. We are continually reassured by political and managerial leadership that it does work, and we repeat this to ourselves "crying out like children: It works! It works! It works!" (6). Yet many no longer fully believe what we hear and repeat, though neither do they imagine and embrace any clear and realistic alternatives. Minds and imaginations, then, are often dominated by negative insight and the secular project often feels like "a hopeless trap" since we are "not yet in touch with the new" (81), with some believable way forward. In this we are much like Aeschylus' Orestes whose imagination was trapped in a cycle of revenge that no longer worked, but who could not imagine an alternative. Indeed Lynch thought that our times could well be called "the age of Orestes" (5). At the center of *Christ and Prometheus* (77–87), he developed a detailed analysis of the *Oresteia* in order to urge that Aeschylus' dramatic imagining of such entrapment might help us to understand ourselves better.

Lynch believed, as I've noted, that *this* inner division and contempt—this point of feeling trapped, with no way forward or back—is what today most endangers the life of our city. It embodies the second act of "the Aeschylean rhythm" of our time: the largely necessary stage of reaction and purification and suffering that inevitably follows the forward movements of human history. It is "postmodern" above all by being "anti-modern" and yet in largely hopeless and thus deeply contemptuous ways. It is, moreover, burdened by the extremism of its critical doubts. In Lynch's own words:

> The crisis today is partly a wish to correct some of the inhuman
> qualities of the movement forward; as such it is altogether nec-
> essary. But it is also in part a reaction of fear and puritanism in
> the face of the human project; as such it is purely reactionary. (4)

Lynch wrote *Christ and Prometheus* to help with much-needed criticism and correction of the secular project. Yet he especially wrote to call attention to the reactionary extremism which is so prevalent in this postmodern moment, in the secular project itself and in religious reaction to it.

Unfortunately, in *Christ and Prometheus* Lynch himself only occasionally (and only in a passing way) gives very specific examples of the divisions

---

25. See, for example, 4, 30, 46, and especially 89–91 (Act II, Scene II, "The Passage") and the entirety of Act Three, "The Search for Innocence" (101–20).

and entrapments that concern him.[26] He more typically gives concreteness to his ideas by reference to the "good imaginers around us" (88)—he mentions Sartre, Brecht, Beckett, Kafka, Ionesco and Camus—who have helped us to understand our sense of being trapped by and within the secular project. Yet even for those of us familiar with the work of these good imaginers, our present distance may make their images of our present as abstract as Lynch's ideas. Thus, in order to "flesh out" his thought, to make it more immediate for us, I turn here to four current instances or examples of the foundational problem that so concerned him. And since I am concerned here only to evoke such examples, I will in what follows be sketching with very broad strokes.

Sexuality and Gender Once Again

As a first example, I return to matters of sexuality and gender and the "cluster of continuing and often fiercely controversial issues" noted in the preceding chapter.[27] There I emphasized how the politics around such issues "imperil the health of the human body of faith [the human city] since they so frequently escalate into polarized and absolutized positions." What needs adding here, though it is quite obvious, is the extent to which the politics around these issues become ideological precisely because they are a battleground between and among the forces of sacrality and secularity.

It is almost a cliché to note that virtually all societies have understood and ritualized matters of gender, sexuality, and family life in predominantly sacral terms. That remains, I believe, generally true today. I would even venture the speculation that the obsessive sexualization of so many aspects of contemporary life, including the massive growth of pornography, at least in part involves a deep hunger for the sacred, albeit in secular and often anti-sacral guise. For Dionysus remains a deeply sacral force even when his energy is no longer tutored by religious ritual and restraint. Sexual images and experiences almost always retain a residual connection with the sacred. Thus even their supposedly most liberated or secularized forms represent, I am suggesting, a "return of the repressed"—now less of repressed sexuality than repressed sacrality!

Yet it is also true that there are few areas of modern life where the forces of rationality and secularity have so continually sought liberation from sacral tutelage and restraint. Are not, for instance, the many stages of modern feminism precisely a battle against the old patriarchal gods (even

26. See, for instance, 81 or 96–97.
27. See pp. 174–78 above.

if they at times seek to recover feminine forms of sacrality)? Have we not employed an immense effort in the physical and social sciences to better understand matters of sexuality and gender and family relations? Has there not been a consequent and equally massive development of new technologies, new industries, new professions (from birth control and fertility enhancement to personal counseling and divorce law) so that we can better control and more freely manipulate these once so sacred matters?

Today this massive secularizing effort continues full force, even as we also search, at times desperately, for deeper and perhaps sacred meaning in sexual experience and family life. Thus the politics of our times, in both advanced industrial and newly developing countries, and in virtually every religion, give continual evidence of the divided and conflicted state of both sacred and secular imaginations with regard to matters of gender, sexuality, and family. Nor is this conflict limited to the obvious warring camps that regularly grab headlines. For perhaps nowhere are the inner divisions of our own imaginations and our own confusions about the way forward (or back) so painfully evident once we have the courage to face them.

The Modern University

Families are invariably connected with schooling. Thus it is not in the least surprising that today the education of the young provides a second example of the struggle between secularity and the sacred—from matters of prayer and the teaching of evolutionary science in public schools to recent forms of revolt against all public (or secular) schooling. I should like, however, as my second example, to focus on analogous struggles and the sense of entrapment that one finds today in *higher education*. Above I noted the dominance of technical and value-free studies at a major secular university. My concern here is broader, with the *modern* university as such, whether large or small, secular or religiously-affiliated. For there are few more explicit embodiments of the Enlightenment project than the university as it has developed in the modern world.

We know, of course, that universities began in a medieval and sacral context (whether in Christendom or in the House of Islam). We also know that a predominantly sacral context was still prevalent in the beginnings of higher learning in this country. Finally, we know the often-told tale about the gradual secularization of higher learning as, in this country, the (Protestant) seminary model was gradually but relentlessly replaced, especially since the latter part of the 19th Century, by the "new" model of the research university.[28] Seminaries and divinity schools, where they survived, simply became one special and typically quite small school alongside the many newer schools and departments which had become central to the identity of the modern university. Scientific and technical rationality, in its many forms and applications, had replaced Theology as the ruling "Queen" of university life and thus as the prevailing paradigm for rationality and intelligence.

Yet today a growing number of critics decry the "soul-less" state of the modern university which, they argue, no longer represents the opening or liberation of human intelligence, but a narrowing and closing of mind and spirit. For some the university has lost any unifying sense of purpose; it can no longer honestly claim to be a "*university*" for its center does not hold. Rather it has become a "multiversity," a vast marketplace of "specialists without spirit" serving the highest bidder—typically the deep pockets of global corporations or various branches of government. In the process the young are pretty much left to their own choices and devices in this supermarket of ideas and expertise.[29]

Of course the research university nonetheless remains the epitome of the Enlightenment project to advance knowledge (and thereby freedom) by the intensive application of rationality unconfined by sacral limits and directives. Its achievements continue to be embraced and funded as absolutely necessary for modern life. Yet protests and calls for reform have multiplied since they again came to the fore during the student and faculty movements of the 1960s. They represent, to use Lynch's language, both the painfully divided present state of the secular imagination with regard to its own project, as well a continuing reaction of the sacred imagination against the separation of modern intelligence from the integrating power of sacral foundations and purposes.

Yet such divisions and the sense of entrapment to which they lead, the sense of not knowing the way forward (or back), are perhaps even better illustrated by the current situation of religiously affiliated colleges and universities. For it had long seemed to their supporters that such schools had largely escaped the separation between faith and intelligence, between sacred and secular imagination, that is typical of their secular counterparts. Today, however, they may actually provide a clearer indication of the fundamental tension between sacred and secular that is characteristic of the *modern* university in any of its forms. For increasingly the character of their

---

28. See, for example, Marsden *Soul*.

29. See especially the powerful critical essays by George Grant: "The University Curriculum" and "Faith and the Multiversity."

religious affiliation has become a matter of concern and debate.[30] Critics argue that religiously-affiliated schools (all but perhaps the most conservative) have in fact slowly followed the secularizing pattern of larger universities, especially as these schools have grown and expanded their range of programs. Typically such expansion has come *both* in response to a religiously pluralistic and also to a religiously indifferent market demand (at times, ironically, a demand for "value-centered" but not denominationally-controlled or faith-based education), *and* also to compensate for seriously diminished personnel and financial support from religious sponsors. As a result, such schools, according to their critics, are "religious" in name only, or only because of the window dressing provided by some institutional traditions and by some student services.

Partly in response to such criticism (but only partly), most religiously-affiliated schools are today engaged in serious self-examination and institutional renewal in order to reaffirm their religious identities and to integrate newly expanded programs into their religious mission. Yet the central problem that they face in all such efforts is the problem that has been at the heart of the modern university since its beginnings. That, of course, is the problem (at least for religious faith and the sacred imagination) presented by the autonomous development of human rationality (of knowledge and disciplines, practical professions and technical expertise) apart from any reference to sacred beliefs, practices and imagination. Whatever the quite serious intentions of religiously-affiliated institutions to bring academic programs within the sacred canopy of their religious purposes, the reality typically is that the various disciplines and programs of modern knowledge and expertise know (at best) only an *external* relationship to such religious purposes.[31] Their own *inner* purposes and dynamics have long been established by the secular understandings of science and technique that find their clearest practical expression in professional organizations, in licensing and accrediting agencies, and in the larger (secular) graduate programs which train the younger and often better academically qualified members of faculties and administration.

The march of secularity, then, continues in the remarkably successful development of the forms of knowledge and expertise that are embodied in the modern university, in both its secular and its religiously-affiliated forms.

30. In Catholic schools this concern was, in part, precipitated by John Paul II's 1990 encyclical *Ex Corde Ecclesiae*. Analogous forces have been operative in many Protestant schools.

31. At worst, of course, there are relationships of often latent, but nonetheless deep hostility between various forms of modern rationality and the university's religious purposes.

Yet the internal self-criticism, the inner divisions and turmoil, along with external criticism aimed at the universities, again illustrate what Lynch saw as the dominant character of the present stage of our Promethean era. It is a time of critical reaction, sometimes of immense hostility, directed towards the secular project, a time of painful division both within secular and sacred imaginations and between them, a time with too little clear sense of a way forward. [32]

The Modern Nation's Emergence

My third example is so global and complex that I can here make only very general comments. Yet it is so crucial for the future of the human city that I dare not omit it. I refer to the typically conflicted *development of the modern nation* or nation-state, and thus also to recent international developments which both threaten national identity and provoke extreme, reactionary forms of nationalism.[33]

What was said above about the sacred foundations of the traditional city is, of course, true for the nation, the city writ-large, whatever the many evolving forms of national life over the span of human history. Yet the rise of the *modern* nation, while now largely taken for granted in the West, is in fact one of the most significant forms of the march of secularity. If the university provides a particularly focused embodiment of Enlightenment intentions, the modern state represents the most powerful and important expression of those intentions. It was quite often born in revolution against the older al-lied sacral powers of church and monarchy. Thus the French and American revolutions are rightly taken as paradigmatic for the emergence of this new form of nation state. Typically, then, the modern nation has involved at least a clear separation of the state from the church, and often it has embodied different forms of opposition to the political power of organized religion and the social force of sacred purposes and limits.

---

32. The modern development of the arts provides a further example that closely parallels that of the universities, both in the predominantly secular character of today's artistic mainstream and in its divided sensibility with regard to the secular project. As Lynch argued at length in *Christ and Apollo*, much of this secular mainstream of contemporary art has turned, at times with extreme gnostic contempt, against modern society (against, in other words, the broader march of modern secularity).

33. By "nation" I mean quite simply what our common sense and both our his-torians and newspapers understand as nations. I will also be using the terms "nation" and "state" interchangeably. Nations so understood remain today the most significant form of modern political life despite the growing force of international and globalizing systems and the continuing reality of neo-imperial or neo-colonial power.

Yet despite such separation, we in the U.S. seem to have experienced throughout our history an almost endless pattern of both sacral-secular co-operation and conflict. Various forces in our national life have continually sought to assert sacral influence in politics and culture (some to the point of claiming that the U.S. is, or must again become, "a Christian nation"), just as other forces have fiercely resisted and sought to limit such influence. Such conflict has often simply represented a necessary modern struggle to renegotiate the relationship of secular and sacred. At other times, however, it has involved extreme polarizations that have threatened to tear apart the nation's fundamental body of faith. The present period in national life has often, for instance, seen especially painful instances of such hostility in part because of the resurgence of often fundamentalist forms of sacrality (which parallel even more extreme resurgences around the globe).

European nations, though they came to the political separation of church and state in different ways, nonetheless are today, by most accounts, even more thoroughly secularized. That would seem to have been the view of Pope Benedict XVI (2005–2013) who made a rhetorical crusade against "secularism" and "the tyranny of relativism" in Europe one of the hallmarks of his papacy. Ironically, though, the nations of Western Europe today also experience a particular and at times fiercely acute form of secular-sacred polarization because of the increasing presence of mainly Muslim immigrants from the global South.[34] Perhaps this is simply a short-term phenomenon, but it is also possible that this new form of sacral-secular tension will be a long-term affair for the entire West since it is clearly influenced by the violent emergence of religious "fundamentalism"[35] in the Middle East and in much of Africa, and by the flood of refugees from that violence.

In the post-colonial Middle East and Africa and Asia (and to some extent in Latin America) the struggles within and between the forces of secularity and sacrality are typically more recent. In some nations the "modern" separation of secular and sacred has not yet occurred or seems simply an externally-imposed and superficial residue of colonial control. Some argue and hope that it will never happen, that the whole dynamic of modern secularization is a Western problem, and that modernization can and should happen elsewhere without secularization. Others find this view simplistic, a

---

34. See, for example, Philip Jenkins' nuanced social analysis in *God's Continent*, and Nicholas Boyle's important philosophical study of European identity *Who Are We Now?*

35. I use the term "fundamentalism" for the sake of brevity, fully aware of the on-going debate about its accuracy when applied to non-Christian religions. I do, however, find support for my use in Malise Ruthven's argument that the term may be used for different religious movements (Muslim and Hindu, for instance, as well as Christian) because of the "family resemblances" among them. See his *Fundamentalism*.

nationalist form of nostalgia which ignores the continuing global penetration of the Promethean project.

At very least, the particularly acute form of tension between sacral and sacred forces that we have recently come to associate with the term "fundamentalism" has clearly served to focus attention around the globe on the foundational issue that concerned Lynch. On the one hand, successive waves of post-colonial nation building in Africa, the Middle East, Southern Asia, and even Latin America seem to represent the latest phase of this political dimension of the march of secularization. Yet resurgent religious forces have in a variety of ways challenged the secular character of emerging nations and the globalizing forces they typically embody. The resulting inner turmoil in many post-colonial states (perhaps especially now in the Muslim world, but certainly not only there[36]) represents a major contemporary instance (perhaps *the* major instance) of the continuing struggle between sacral and secular forces in the modern nation state.

What should be clear, then, even from this very brief evocation of the history and forms of modern nationalism, is that Lynch is fundamentally quite right. Central to the politics of the human city throughout our new Promethean era has been an ongoing battle within and between the forces of Prometheus and those of Zeus.

Environmental Crisis

My fourth and final example of the anguish of secular and sacred divisions in contemporary experience is even more global than the emergence of modern nations, yet it is less easily described. I refer to what is increasingly understood as our environmental or ecological crisis; what is spoken about in terms of water and air pollution, global warming and carbon footprints, desertification and the loss of biodiversity. The sense of crisis has led to political movements and reactions on many fronts and to conflicts about a series of interrelated issues. Yet such conflict about an environmental crisis is less easily framed within the secular and sacred terms I have been using in previous examples.[37]

36. Hindu and Sikh forces, for example, have challenged the secular character of the nation in India; Buddhist and Hindu in Sri Lanka; evangelical and perhaps fundamentalist forms of Protestant Christianity are on the rise throughout Latin America; and the situation in Africa, while diverse and fluid, clearly involves widespread charismatic (Christian as well as Muslim) agitation.

37. Clearly Pope Francis' important 2015 encyclical *Laudato Si'* represents a major religious intervention in contemporary environmental debate. Yet while a good part of that document gives clear expression to Christian faith, Francis deliberately addresses

Most would agree that issues about our environment arise as a result of the vast Promethean developments of our era. Yet concern about the destructive effects of such developments has arisen primarily among our (largely secular) scientists and artists and intellectuals. Religious thinkers and institutions have generally come late to these issues and concerns, even though some early writing from the environmental movement blamed our Western religious heritage for an historic lack of care for the earth.[38] Thus at present the major forms of division and conflict about our environment occur primarily *within* the secular imagination. They are, once again, primarily conflicts between the Penthean managers of modern developments and growing Dionysian outrage at their blithe disregard for the despoliation caused by such developments.

Yet, as noted above, Dionysus is always a powerfully sacral force. Thus such outrage does seem to involve a clearly sacral dimension or powerful undercurrent, even if traditional religion has generally not, until recently, been its immediate source. How else explain the correlation, loose though it be, between environmental awareness and renewed interest in Native or Indigenous religions, in the more contemplative aspects of Asian religions (even as, ironically, Asian countries race for leadership in promethean technologies and economies), and even in aspects of Celtic Christianity? Or the now growing theological concern, on many fronts, to bridge the separation between religion and science that characterized the modern era and to envision new forms of integration between faith and the cosmos?[39]

Whatever the complex and as yet (at least for this writer) unclear interweaving of secular and sacred sensibilities in the growing sense of environmental crisis, it seems nonetheless true and quite important that today's awareness of environmental crisis is a major part of the "postmodern" pathos which Lynch saw as an inevitable purification for the march of modern secularity.

As a conclusion to this short discussion of examples of contemporary secular-sacral conflict, it seems important to remember Lynch's fundamental teaching that all these struggles will be fought either with the polarizing force of will and violence or with the civilizing forces of imagination.

---

all humanity, especially the secular centers of scientific-technical and economic development as well as political and cultural leadership around the globe. Thus his argument is also framed in rational and ethical terms.

38. The critique focused on terms like "dominion over" in older translations of Gen 1:28 and argued that such biblical texts set the pattern for a misplaced emphasis on human domination of nature. Today this critique of religion is generally regarded as far too simple.

39. I again note especially David Toolan's *At Home in the Cosmos*.

Everything, then, continues to depend on which spirit or spirituality sets the tone for and guides the contemporary struggle between Prometheus and Zeus. Or, put more concretely, it depends on whether the next stages in the history of religion, as well as the next stages in the development of the Promethean project, are determined by the rigid imaginations of fundamentalists (whether religious or secular, left or right), or by those with more flexible and more realistic imaginations seeking to chart an authentically human course for the our global future.

Lynch's Contribution

We come, then, to the particular contribution which Lynch makes in *Christ and Prometheus* towards charting that future by analyzing present divisions between Zeus and Prometheus and helping us move through many present forms of fear and reaction, entrapment and anguish. Since the elements of his contribution have already been suggested in preceding sections of this chapter, I will here simply resort to enumeration (without much citation) as a way to recapitulate his sense of the way forward for our secular city.

1. Lynch's basic response to the divisions and violence of our present situation is quite straightforward and, at least in the saying, quite simple. It is the constant theme we have seen in all his writings. We must *move through* present oppositions between Zeus and Prometheus by *courageous and difficult imagining,* or, perhaps better said, by *imaginative action,* and this on many fronts. Family life and the university, nation and the environment are but four of a great number of arenas where such imaginative action is needed. We suffer and hopefully we learn from the inevitable conflicts of such imagining movement, and we suffer because of "easy" but typically totalized images which continually tempt us. For an ideological tendency is present not only in the world, but within each of us. Thus Lynch calls us to transform our images, to strip them of such escalation and violence, to enlarge their sense of the truly human and thereby to undertake more realistic ways forward. He continually reminds us that there is no magic in the politics of the human city, any more than in the journey of our own lives. All proclamations of one way, of a shining path or a great leap forward (or, for that matter, of certain doom) are dangerous fantasy. They embody a sensibility that does violence to the complexity of the world and to any truly human ways of moving into the future.

2. Given the divisions and hostilities of our present, we need, Lynch says at the beginning of his book, *many different efforts at such imagining, from many sides and from around the globe*—from religious and secular

leaders, from managers and technicians as well as from "artists and intellectuals," and from "ordinary" folk everywhere—to help us move towards a more human future for our global secular city. We need, in Lynch's words, "many images by many people" (9), and the imagining that Lynch proposes in *Christ and Prometheus* "should be only one of many such images by many people" (7). We need many efforts because, again, *there really is no one way forward.* That technological fantasy (just as its religious counterpart) is one of the great dangers threatening a truly human secularity.[40]

Nations and peoples, just as individuals and families, must be allowed to emerge in their own fuller and diverse identities. More fundamentally, of course, there is no one way because the human future really is open and we are free to realize that future or, better put, those futures. In Christian theological terms, Lynch grounds this affirmation of the real openness of the future on the doctrine of creation, especially the creation of human freedom.[41] Yet our better secular thinkers, chastened by the failure of modern ideologies, also base their hope on similar convictions about freedom and diversity.

3. It should, then, be evident that such imaginative action is *necessarily dramatic* in several related senses. Emphasis on the dramatic character of the way forward is the overriding thought of *Christ and Prometheus* and perhaps the book's most general contribution. We must know and imagine that any realistic way forward will happen in human time and be limited by time's partialities, fallibilities, and ironies. Thus our image of action for the good of the city must include a strong, indeed a governing sense of the inescapable Aeschylean rhythm of action and suffering and learning, effort and check and renewal, liberation and guilt and reconciliation. Said differently, the imaginative action we must undertake is dramatic because it involves the succession of struggles we call history. Imagining realistically human ways forward is itself a continual form of doing, perhaps the most fundamental form of political action. It frames and directs our movement into the world, *and* it suffers and learns through that movement. Thus it must be a continual process of re-imagining, of purifying and transforming our images as we act and suffer and learn, again and then again. This is the dramatic action to which we are called in the politics of our city. Its difficulty, its

40. See, for instance, pp. 53–54.

41. Thus Lynch continually challenges not only the homogenizing vision of technical rationality, but also the traditional religious image of "God's plan" insofar as that image negates the real freedom of human beings and the consequent real openness of the human and secular future. That is the argument of the "Epilogue" to *Christ and Prometheus* which will be taken up in this book's next and final chapter. See also pp. 49, 55, 71 as well as discussion above (pp. 70–78) about "The Problem of Freedom."

continual temporality and partiality and suffering, helps to explain both the constant temptation towards fantasy and the need for a strong and sustaining spirituality.

4. Lynch believed that our biggest need is for "*a new image of the secular*" (his book's subtitle). Both religious and secular imaginations need a transformed and more human (and thus dramatic) image of the modern secular project. The religious imagination so that it can live and function within this immense new presence, not driven by fear and reaction. And the secular imagination so that it might be liberated from the burdens and illusions of many original and continuing images it has of itself. The religious imagination, of course, also needs a new image of secularity so that it can then find authentically sacred ways of actually meeting and engaging, criticizing and helping *our* great Prometheus in its own process of self-criticism and transformation. Such ongoing and thus dramatic imagining by both sacred and secular forces is today, to repeat, our most fundamental form of action for the good of the city. It involves really "working at" and "working out," over time and in stages, a renewed and constructive interaction of the sacral and secular forces which will continue to be constitutive or foundational for any truly human city.

5. For Lynch, the most basic element in the religious imagination's new image of secularity must be what has been the true center of the modern secular project since its beginning—*the idea and goal of independence or autonomy and what Lynch also calls "unconditionality."*[42] The religious imagination must, in Lynch's terms, take "the risk of secularity" and really allow the secular realities of the world, above all of the human world, to emerge on their own terms, free from prior conditions set by sacred (or sacramental) direction or restraint. Here are his words:

> Emergence is another good word for what I am after, particularly if emergence means the emergence of the identity of things. Secularity stands for a universal principle of emergence, of everything moving into its own and into self-possession. It wishes to communicate life to things, to people, to peoples (at this moment to Asia, Africa, Latin America), to fields of study and disciplines (biology, physics, chemistry, astronomy, medicine, music). (42)

The secular imagination, of course, has long taken this "risk," though often has seen it not as risk but as some inevitable march of progress and liberation. For the religious imagination, full acceptance of the autonomous emergence of things and people, science and culture, involves a major, even a radical

42. See especially 39–42.

break with its own past and its own prior sense of purpose and meaning.[43] Yet Lynch also stresses that, whatever the sense of loss experienced by the sacred imagination, the process whereby secular realities emerge into their own fuller and independent realization is *both* the essential meaning of the secular project *and* a meaning which the religious imagination, at least the Christian imagination, should not only accept, but encourage and support.

> There is no reason why this . . . image of secularity, based on inward life . . . cannot be describing a universal principle of redemption and salvation, as wide as the world in its interest, and covering the wide range of history and society in a more complete image of redemption than we have been accustomed to imagine. (42)

Yet, and this is crucial for Lynch's entire effort to provide a new image of secularity, such acceptance must be neither naïve nor static. Many of our images of emergence and autonomy are filled with fantasy and falsehood. Imagining and realizing authentic autonomy—the emergence of things and people into truly life-giving identity—is a dramatic process, filled with half and false starts, with conflict and suffering, with learning and much purification. As Lynch suggests and as we see daily, the post-colonial emergence of Africa and Asia and Latin America into their own independent life has long involved and continues to involve immense struggle and all too much violence. So too, and perhaps most fundamentally, the emergence of the human person into her full identity and autonomy. Lynch does not hesitate to say that "Autonomy is not a defiance but grace" (140). Yet realized and authentic autonomy—whether for Africa or the individual person—involves the continual drama of movement towards greater interiority and self-possession, towards "a good taste of self" (134) and thus also the correlative need for a good taste of the secular realities of city and world. It clearly is not an exaggeration to say that now, several centuries into the Enlightenment project, we are still struggling for adequate images of autonomy that will bring such "good taste" of both self and world. Indeed we are perhaps struggling now even more than in the past, at least that is Lynch's sense of our present (post-modern) stage of doubt and hesitation, paralysis and reaction.

6. As Lynch sees it, the primary struggle for the religious imagination involves *the necessary relinquishment of its sacred images of the world, but not a "demythologizing" of its own sacred truth.*[44] Its struggle will continue

43. See 10–12 and 27–28.

44. See 25–31, 46–47. The distinction between "demythologizing" religious realities and "desymbolizing" worldly realities is crucial for Lynch and the reason he opposed some theological approaches to secularity. They would, on his understanding, reduce

to require "vast stripping and de-symbolizing processes" (26) by which the realities of the world emerge from under a sacred canopy into the light of their own identity and autonomous meaning. This struggle will often be so difficult that Lynch does not hesitate to say that the "risk of secularity" will feel like a "descent into hell" for the religious imagination (26).

If this seems exaggerated, think, as but one example of such "stripping," of the immense difficulties the Catholic Church had in accepting the modern separation of church and state. It involved giving up a millennial sense of its proper role in political life as the divinely appointed and politically established religious ruler of Christendom. It took very real conflict, often violence, and the sufferings of many centuries (of Reformation, Enlightenment, and Modern eras) before Catholicism could, at Vatican II, fully accept (and benefit from) such a relinquishment of its traditional images of political order. Nor is this simply a Catholic problem as recent neo-Christendom movements in the U.S. attest, and as even more serious Muslim and Hindu and Buddhist struggles indicate.

Think also, as another example of this feeling of "descent into hell," of the ways in which contemporary struggles around gender and about family life also involve, for the traditional religious imagination, a pervasive sense of sacred realities and roles threatened or already lost. Some would even suggest that gender and sexual issues today are, around the globe, the traditional religious imagination's "last stand" (or great revolt) against secularizing processes.

Yet, as already noted, for Lynch the Christian imagination can and must finally (though not naively) accept the unconditional autonomy of secularity, albeit almost always with accompanying feelings of loss and guilt, because it can understand the emergence of things and persons into their own identities as the fuller purpose of both creation and salvation—as "a more complete image of redemption than we have been accustomed to imagine" (42). It can, then, and must find a renewed sense of sacred purpose precisely in its role as servant and critic to the deeper needs of the secular project. Is this not, for instance, the fundamental meaning of *Gaudium et Spes*, Vatican II's "Pastoral Constitution on the Church in the Modern World"? Yet this is precisely why the religious imagination cannot allow its truth to be "demythologized" or diminished. It can only play its crucial role in the new secular order if it retains a full sense of its own truth and power.

---

or "demythologize" the truth of religion to make it relevant to "desymbolized" secularity, but the result would mean "a confrontation between a pigmy and a giant" (125). The secular project needs no such demythologized religious pigmy; it needs the full strength and assistance of religious truth if it is to continue its own challenging task of purification and transformation.

(I will return in the next chapter to these ideas which Lynch himself develops most fully in the "Epilogue" to *Christ and Prometheus*.)

6.1. Given the importance, in recent U.S. Catholic discussion, of the idea of a "sacramental imagination" as one of the distinguishing characteristics and important contributions of Catholicism to contemporary culture,[45] it may be helpful at this point to relate that discussion to Lynch's ideas about the need to "desymbolize" and relinquish sacred images of the world.

Lynch notes that much of the modern religious imagination has tended, as a primary strategy for dealing with secularity, to continue the path taken during the Renaissance when "we moved along with the new forms of the secular and the human but we tried to keep them deeply fused with the forms of Christian symbolism and history" (136). He also notes that "The Catholic imagination [it is one of the few times he uses the term] has not been happy [with] unconditionality and tends much more to seek the final sacramental view" (49). Yet despite these acknowledgements, he also says: "I am clearly proposing that the Catholic image must pass through severe changes" (50) and "I want to get to [a] nonsacramental and unconditional goal" (50–51). He also cites approvingly the idea that "a religious, sacramentalist view of nature seems to do justice neither to the nature of God, nor to the nature of the world" (50).[46] Finally, and quite early in his text, he stresses that "If the religious imagination stays with its older images of symbolic, referential, and transcendent meaning [for the world] it will be forced to accept . . . defeat. I do not mean," he adds, "the defeat of Christ . . . I mean the pure and flat defeat called real inconsequence" (15).

All of this would seem to mean that Lynch's thinking must run counter to recent claims about the importance of and need for the Catholic sacramental imagination. It seems to suggest, moreover, that Lynch is rejecting his own Jesuit tradition of "finding God in all things" and thus the famous and beautiful words of his brother Jesuit Gerard Manley Hopkins that "the world is charged with the grandeur of God."

Of course everything depends upon what is meant by a "sacramental imagination" and what Lynch means by stripping and moving away from "older images of symbolic, referential, and transcendent meaning." It is at least very clear that Lynch is saying that the forms of sensibility and imagination which functioned for Christian consciousness of the world through the Renaissance (and continue today in many forms and places) need to

45. I am thinking above all about many writings by Andrew Greeley, but also of important contributions from Michael Himes and others. David Tracy's more theoretical discussions of "the analogical imagination" seem to me to have a somewhat different character and point.

46. The citation is from Fennell, "Theology," 29–30.

be replaced by a sense of the world that honors and affirms autonomous secular meanings—that is to say, meanings and images which come forth with a removal of "the sacred canopy" and thus express the emergence of people and things into their own inner or immanent meanings.

Yet Lynch also clearly affirms that this "unconditional" emergence of autonomous meaning not only can, but should be understood as central to the broader meaning of the doctrines of Creation and Redemption. Does this, then, somehow mean that "finding God in all things" and the "Catholic sacramental imagination" remain valid ideals on Lynch's terms? Lynch himself, of course, never addressed this more recent question. My sense of his meaning is that we may perhaps be said to "find God in all things" precisely by discovering or liberating their own, inner and autonomous meanings—which is exactly what the modern scientist should be doing, as also the artist and politician as well as technicians like the business manager and the engineer, and even perhaps the theologian.[47] When things and persons are enabled (by our "secular" rationality and imagination and technical capacity) to come to a fuller and freer development of their earthy and temporal identities—to a "good taste" of both self and world—then they are freely and more fully realizing God's creative and redemptive purposes. Is this a sacramental way of understanding? It all, again, depends on what one means.

Finally, then, if by the "Catholic sacramental imagination," one simply means that Catholic religious or liturgical experience, with its emphasis on the physical and the senses (on "smells and bells," sacraments and sacramentals, saints and stained glass), predisposes one for increased sensitivity to the autonomous and "desymbolized" truth and goodness of the physical universe and of earthy (or secular) human realities, then I think Lynch would strongly agree. His opposition to "demythologized" religion was fierce precisely because he saw how much the full power of the religious or sacral imagination is needed to help with healing the immense division and pain within the contemporary secular imagination.

7. For if the struggle for new forms of sensibility and a new image of the secular is difficult (even "a descent into hell") for the religious imagination,

---

47. It seems to me that the growing literature about religion and science is involved in just this project—accepting the newer meanings discovered by science and then asking what implications they have for our understanding of God and faith; *not* the somewhat "reverse" procedure of assuming traditional religious meaning and using it to name the deeper or transcendent meaning of the scientific understanding of the world. Another way in which theology is responding to the new sense of secularity is exemplified by Elizabeth Johnson's *Truly Our Sister*. It is an effort to recover for our times and for contemporary women the full secular reality and experience of the mother of Jesus. Of course the entire "historical Jesus" quest and debate is, for better and worse, a similar theological response to the secularizing imperative of modernity.

that same struggle already is and will continue to be far greater for the secular imagination, if only because of the immensity and dominance of the Promethean presence in our world. Yet just that (secular) struggle to purify and transform our many deeply-conflicted (secular) images of the secular project and *in that way* to find a new, more authentic image of the secular is the goal towards which Lynch moves throughout *Christ and Prometheus*.

What enables him to avoid naiveté when he speaks of secular emergence as an aspect of Christian salvation is his awareness of the difficulty and the constant dramatic struggle involved in the movement of secular reality into authentic autonomy. That secularity could and would move progressively and straightforwardly into such autonomy remains perhaps the central illusion of the Enlightenment. For the modern secular project, as all earlier Promethean moments, has been filled with real failure and real evil. It has also, as we have seen, continually been accompanied by distorting images of itself, by fantasies of magnificent progress and fears of a total wasteland. Such distorting images, we must remember, are very real and powerful forms of human action which invariably add to the failures and evils in the secular project. Lynch at times calls these "counter-images" because they "counter" or misdirect the march of authentic secularity, and he suggests that their name is legion.

Thus the task of discernment and transformation—the task of understanding and resisting the real evils to which secular emergence (like all things human) tends, and also of distinguishing counter-images from authentic secular emergence—is both continual and continually difficult. It is an active and a dramatic task, no mere arm-chair "imagining" but the kind of realistic imaginative action that can and should be at work in our cultural and political struggles to build our human city.

Since it remains so central in these struggles for transformation of the secular imagination, let me return again to Lynch's analysis of the deep polarizations in our nonetheless inescapable and much-needed culture wars.[48] Both our artists and intellectuals, on the one hand, and our politicians and "middle class" managers, on the other, have not only allowed their own images of the secular project to become deeply infected with escalation and fantasy, but have fomented the spread of such polarization throughout the culture so that our city's foundational body of faith is threatened.

The politicians and managers are more typically seduced by various "prometheanisms" (Lynch's term for secularism's ersatz forms and fantasies)[49]. Yes, by "older" and still operative Enlightenment promethean-

48. See pp. 168–70 above.

49. See especially 57–72.

isms that dream of constant progress and total victory. But also by "newer" technical prometheanisms that construct massive bureaucratic systems for endless production and consumption sustained by endless getting and spending.[50] The danger of all such prometheanisms is that they represent will and imagination that has lost touch with the human and resists effort to recover the "smaller line" of real human need and wishing. Here are some of Lynch's words for this problem:

> It is here, in these areas of life that have become self-enclosed and independent of the human, that true secularity is meeting its worst contemporary crisis . . . [T]he most notorious independent form is *technique* . . . It is an endless process if it does not confront itself with the human . . . (54)

> I am concerned with the fundamental endlessness of secularity cut off from the broad totality of human sensibility. This counter-image comes out more clearly when we turn to the world of objects . . . [We experience] an endless proliferation of objects . . . an independent world with no relation to the human . . . There are too many things, too many people, too many sensations . . . It seems impossible to stop the proliferation, the escalation, the endlessness . . . [T]here is no space left; it has been taken away by objects; nobody knows how to turn the process off; there is the beginning of an altogether new kind of cosmological insecurity in the air; there is a subterranean panic [that] hides itself under the form of violence, as insecurity always does. (88)

Finally, of course, it is the politicians and managers and technical experts themselves who must struggle and suffer through a purification of their imaginations so that their projects and systems might give expression to a far fuller vision of human emergence than that presently embodied in images of economic and technical "progress." Ideally they will be helped by the critical imaginations of our artists and intellectuals. Yet, as we have seen again and again, the imaginations of this latter class have too often been seduced by various forms of gnostic contempt for the promethean wasteland and for the class enemies who manage it. They are seduced, in other words, by such a bad taste of the world that they flee into fantastic forms of interiority which they (incorrectly) see as the only possible way to regain some good taste of self. Again, in Lynch's words:

50. One of the strengths of Pope Francis' discussion of our environmental crisis in *Laudato Si'* is his clear and forceful description of the "dominant technocratic-paradigm" (see Chapter 3, # 101–36) which has played such a great role in causing the crisis and is presently such an obstacle to needed change.

There are vast waves of feeling among us that do not hesitate to characterize every version of the outside and of otherness as enemy . . . The outside is often enemy to interiority. The world is enemy. There is a warfare going on between me and the world. (56)

Now imagine, and this was the constant goal of Lynch's efforts throughout his career, that these polarized culture classes might actually collaborate in seeking a many sided and humanizing transformation in our imagining of the secular project. NOT that there would be no culture wars, but that such wars, however impassioned, would not be seduced by the continual temptation to escalate and polarize images of self and other. They would, rather, finally be part of a common struggle for the human and for the humanization of our city.

As a way of summarizing Lynch's contribution to such collaborative effort, let me recall the dramatic structure of *Christ and Prometheus*. Each of the book's three "Acts" is an effort to imagine the substance of such action to transform our images of the secular. They are analogous passages through three crucial dimensions of that effort. The first ("The Search for Man") begins with the fundamental secular ideas of unconditionality and autonomy and then challenges us to move beyond abstract and ahistorical ideas into authentically human understandings of unconditionality and autonomy. The second ("The Search for Light") begins with our post-modern sense of entrapment and seeks to imagine the passage, the movement and the suffering, of working towards more authentic and less polarized images of the modern project. The third ("The Search for Innocence") imagines passage through the evils of that project, both very real evils and a vastly exaggerated sense of evil, and also through the accompanying furies of blame and guilt, towards some shared sense of innocence, some good and human taste of life in our secular city.

I have attempted in all the preceding sections of this chapter to give an initial sense of the substance of these "Acts," yet I again recommend that the reader take up Lynch's own far richer discussion. And Lynch himself would then remind us that his effort to analyze the struggle for transformed images of secularity must not stand alone. It needs the collaboration of many others in such imaginative action for the good of our city.

8. It should also be clear, Lynch says at one point, *"how difficult a spirituality is necessary"* if we are to have a civilization based on unconditionality" (45, emphasis added). And on the very last page of his book Lynch returns to that necessity:

> It will take every resource of the religious imagination to help men to say no to every form of hysteria, to every ideological group, to every package-deal way of interpreting reality. That the mind should stay free and think its own thoughts within this hysteria is no mean task . . . To live without hysteria will need a *very powerful spirituality.* (142, emphasis added)

The temptations continually proffered by a spirituality and sensibility of violence can be resisted and the courage for continued realistic imagining can be sustained only by such spirituality, and that means by a strong body of sensibility that will support and guide us. The resources and habits of this spirituality can and, thankfully, do come from Prometheus himself (as also from Dionysus and Apollo)—from natural passion and virtue and the strengths (still or newly) present in our secular lives and professions. Yet, as Lynch has just said, "It will also take every resource of the religious imagination." It will, as he puts it in his title, involve *both* Christ *and* Prometheus. Thus it is crucial that the sacral imagination of Christianity, in the West and now globally, struggle towards a transformed image of the secular which will empower it to befriend and critically support the secular project during this "post-modern" time of its own darkness and division. We turn then, in the next and final chapter, to direct consideration of the Christian resources for this much needed spirituality.

And while it may be premature and too simple, I cannot resist suggesting that the person and actions of Pope Francis might provide a good concluding image for this chapter as well as an introductory image for the next. For his "image" (in the fuller, embodied sense Lynch gives to that word) has become popular in both religious and secular quarters since, or so I believe, it brings a healing *touch* to painful divisions discussed in this chapter and throughout this book. It does so, if we are to take the man at his words, because it expresses the healing presence of Christ in the streets of our secular city, streets into which Francis especially calls his fellow Christians in a mission of witness and accompaniment.

8

Christ and the Valley of the Human

While Lynch never gave the title "Christ and Dionysus" to one of his books (as a parallel to *Christ and Apollo* and *Christ and Prometheus*), it is nonetheless clear that the constant intention of all of his writing was to bring the befriending spirit and power of Christ to the great human powers symbolized as much by Dionysus as by Apollo and Prometheus. As he said in the passage with which I began this book, "*everything I have ever written asks for the concrete movement of faith and the imagination through experience, through time, through the definite, through the human, through the actual life of Christ*" (IF 81, emphasis added). We have seen such "concrete movement through experience . . . time . . . the definite . . . the human . . . the life of Christ" analyzed throughout this book, at each stage in its unfolding of the sensibility and spirituality which Lynch called us to.

The theological center and foundation of that sensibility and spirituality clearly is Christ. Yet it is not "the Byzantine Christ, the Pantocrator: the ruler and dominator of all things" (CP, 26). That image and understanding of Christ reigning "over the whole world" and giving from above "his own form" to it (CP, 26) remains even today one of compelling power and great beauty. It gave meaning and shape to the human city, and thus to the powers of Dionysus, Apollo, and Prometheus, throughout the Christian centuries of western civilization. It is, however, a different image and understanding of Christ that Lynch has in mind for our times and our challenges, one that began to emerge with fuller clarity during the Renaissance, especially in the thought of Ignatius. It is "a creative Christ who lets secularity come into its own form and life" (CP, 26), who moves *with* and *within* the power of Dionysus and Prometheus and Apollo as they move us, both as individuals and as a civilization. It is a prophetic and servant Christ who befriends, tutors, mentors, and, yes, also criticizes and "ironizes" our deepest passions in order to bring them to real and not fantasized fruition. It is, then, as we have seen previously and will emphasize again here, "the actual life of Christ"—his living in and through real time—through which Lynch would have us move and by which we must be tutored, corrected, and befriended.

Thus the sources of "the very powerful spirituality" that we need today are *both* Prometheus *and* Christ, Dionysus *and* Christ, Apollo *and* Christ. In more traditional theological terms, the sources are both nature and grace, both Creation and Incarnation-Redemption. Yet Lynch himself rarely takes up for explicit discussion such traditional categories and beliefs. He was not, as I've said, "doing theology" in any typical sense: not focusing on the standard issues and categories of most ecclesial or academic theology. He was, rather, writing as a Christian philosopher and a public intellectual, speaking above all to the "artists and writers," that is, to other public intellectuals, whether they were Christians, persons of other faiths, or secular humanists.[1] He was concerned to indicate the challenging meaning of Christ for the issues which arise today from the energies of Dionysus, Prometheus, and Apollo—above all to suggest ways that Christ works with and within these energies, in the stages and rhythms of human time, as they struggle (that is, as *we* struggle) for ever more human forms of life in our city.

Said differently, while he was certainly aware of developments in contemporary theology, Lynch himself only occasionally discusses the theological ideas (about Creation and Redemption) which he uses in his writings. Most typically he simply assumes their meaning—and his understanding of their meaning is quite traditional, though often developed or employed in remarkably creative ways. Yet in this final chapter, as a way of recapitulating ideas implied throughout this book, I want to turn to several places where he does explicitly discuss his Christian faith and theology. My goal is to move fairly quickly and perhaps somewhat superficially through these texts, in several quite straightforward steps, in order to recall and highlight the theological foundations of the spirituality that was everywhere his concern. And since my goal is recapitulation, I will at times be citing Lynch's words at greater length so that, at the end of this book about his writings, the reader may savor and perhaps struggle with their insights.

---

1. As I have had occasion to note previously, Lynch did not assume that the many non-Christians in his intended audience would accept his own believer's understanding of Christ. Rather he thought that Christ could (and should) serve, even for the unbeliever, as a model—as a cultural icon or a philosophical ideal or pattern—of the character of human life and the necessity of passage through "experience . . . time . . . the definite . . . the human."

A "New Theological Age"

Let me begin by returning to the essay Lynch wrote in 1956, near the end of his tenure as editor of *Thought*, for the 400th Anniversary of the death of St. Ignatius.[2] Titled "St. Ignatius and the 'New Theological Age,'" it was explicitly written as "a double plea . . . To thoughtful Christian men and women, and especially to the theologians and writers among them . . . But . . . also . . . to the modern non-Christian thinker and writer . . ."[3] The plea was essentially the same to each audience: that they pay great and sympathetic attention to contemporary movements of spiritual awakening which were developing among "ordinary" people, and that in addition they "consider whether [Ignatius' *Spiritual Exercises*] might not have some shocking relevancy" to these movements.[4] His essay was, then, a sensitive analysis of both important "signs of the times" in this "new theological age" and, in its second part, of the significance of Ignatius' Christology as a model for response to the spiritual awakenings evident in these times.

Lynch's claim that various forms of spiritual and religious awakening characterized the post-World War II period was hardly unique. Many shared that observation. What was particular to Lynch was his analysis of the character of this "new theological age" and the "great spiritual crisis [that] has begun to invade our whole culture."[5] He spoke of a "crisis" because, as he saw it, the two predominant forms of spiritual awakening he identified—an awakening to spiritual depths *within* the self and a search for God or divinity *beyond* the self—were (1) typically and tragically separated from each other, the latter often emerging as a reaction to the pain and frustration of the former; and (2) both were also quite separated from, even reactions to, the mainstream of contemporary life. Thus, however important the need expressed in these awakenings, they nonetheless involved "a kind of theology, a kind of faith, a kind of leaping, which leaves the human situation untouched and in terms of which God is only being used as an escape."[6] The secular mind, then, is rightly skeptical of these awakenings. As the Christian should also be somewhat skeptical. For the central task of Christian theology and life has always been to relate or connect God, self, and world, not to separate them.

2. See above pp. 32–37.
3. Lynch, "St. Ignatius," 206.
4. Ibid., 207.
5. Ibid., 192.
6. Ibid., 202.

Of course we have seen this "same" critical analysis in almost all of Lynch's subsequent writing: in the dialectic of disgust and dreams he found in literary culture, in the walls of separation and contempt characteristic of political life, and in many other forms of retreating or leaping "which leave the human situation untouched." Yet in this early essay Lynch was explicitly concerned less with a literary or a political problem than with a fundamental spiritual and pastoral challenge. How, in other words, might "thoughtful Christian men and women, especially the theologians and writers among them," engage the spiritual developments of our times in such a way that they will not get lost in the dead ends of either a purely private spirituality, alienated from the world, or a purely transcendental religiousness that "turns God into a form of escape from reality"? And how might secular intelligence also respond, on its own terms, with corresponding critical sympathy to these new developments? In his essay, Lynch answers these questions with "the Ignatian plea that we direct our search for God [or for beauty and good] *through* time and reality and the self."[7] For the basic pattern of Ignatian thought, indeed the basic pattern of all Christian theology—the pattern exemplified above all by "the actual life of Christ"—is that one can come to an authentic sense of self and to real encounter with God only by movement through experience and time, through the stages and phases of life in this world, and thus only by engagement with the realities of our human city. Not by flight from the actual self and the real world.

Much, of course, has changed, perhaps especially in the Catholic world, since Lynch wrote his "New Theological Age" essay. The "new theology" which anticipated Vatican II and the theology which flowed from the Council has typically been shaped by a very strong sense of the need for engagement with the world, with contemporary human experience and the concerns of the human city. The same, of course, can be said of much Protestant theology, and of many of the concerns expressed in our secular arts and sciences. For there is, as Lynch had again stressed in *Christ and Prometheus*, a pervasive hunger in our world for more authentic and inclusive forms of living.

For all such developments we must be thankful. Yet I believe Lynch would still say (and I do not hesitate to say) that the problematic "disconnects" analyzed in the "New Theological Age" essay remains very much with us. The review of Lynch's writings in all the previous sections of this book— his analyses of our arts and politics, our therapies and technologies—at very least suggests that much still remains to be done to develop the body of faith

---

7. Ibid., 214.

and sensibility needed to sustain a real and fruitful connection between self and world, and thus between self, world, and God.

So I turn now to three subsequent texts where Lynch explains in greater detail the theological grounding for such development. And if discussion of these texts has an explicitly Trinitarian character, then I am only slightly more responsible for that than Lynch himself.

God and Creation

At one point in *Christ and Prometheus* Lynch makes the following suggestion about Christian belief in "incarnation." It is a good example of his creative use of traditional belief:

> Let us imagine that there has been a double incarnation, one at the creation and the other at the birth of Christ . . . Let us suppose that twice God put on our mind with which to think. The first time He did it He made the world. He made it according to all the things that have parallelism and resonance for the body and spirit of man: its density to touch, its light and colors to see, its sounds to hear; it is only when the two come together, man and the world, that the world becomes what it is. (CP, 71)

Clearly a contemporary biologist would rightly explain this "parallelism and resonance" between the world and the "body and spirit of man" in appropriately evolutionary terms. Yet a scientific understanding of the correspondence between humanity and its world does not negate what Lynch says about the doctrine of Creation and theology's way of explaining the connection between self and world and the Creative Source of both.

Later, in the extended "Epilogue" to *Christ and Prometheus* (121–42)—the text I want to take up more fully here—Lynch returns to a traditional aspect of the doctrine of Creation: to the idea of *imago dei*, that the world itself, but especially the human, is created "in the image and likeness of God." He is not, however, content simply to reiterate that beautiful belief as a way of explaining the connection (close to one form of identification) between God and the self and the world. Rather he seeks to penetrate to the foundation of that "image and likeness," to the idea that God simply *Is*, that God is Existence, what Paul Tillich called "The Power of Being" and Scripture names the great "I AM." For the truly ultimate source of existence or "inner life [is] the absolute self-possession and self-identity of God" (130). By the originating and sustaining act of Creation, God gives existence as "self-possession and self-identity" to the world, though clearly always in

finite and analogous forms. Said differently, it is precisely by the evolutionary and historic emergence of the world and the self into their own (secular)
autonomy and self-possession that world and self fully express their reality
as beings created and sustained by God and thus as "images" of God. For
they receive their autonomous identity and independent existence from the
pure or absolute autonomy and identity of the self-existent God.[8]

In this "Epilogue" Lynch further tells us that, as theological ground
for his "new image" of secularity, he is seeking "a common logic" (129) that
binds secular and sacred even as it differentiates them. Finding a legitimate
religious or sacral way to imagine and affirm the clear and growing emergence of the secular into its own autonomous existence had been the basic
goal of *Christ and Prometheus* from the first. Yet he had also continually told
us that he did not want this affirmation of the autonomy of the secular to
be achieved by any demythologizing or diminishment of the sacred. Indeed
(as we saw in the preceding chapter) he argued that the full emergence of
the secular world (and thus of the self) into real and not fantasized forms of
autonomy requires the full power and critical support of Christ. Here in the
book's "Epilogue" he provides the philosophical and theological explanation
for that secular emergence and for the sacred as its sustaining ground. For
(to use traditional language) the "prime analog," the first, formal, and final
cause of the independent and fully secular reality of the world is the Creator
God who is existence. Here are some of Lynch's words explaining this "common logic":

> The central history of the whole of the Old Testament is a sepa-
> rating out of God from all other gods and from all idols. The
> idea and location of the sacred as divine self-possession . . . be-
> comes absolutely clear. God tells the Jewish people who He is:
> "I am that I am." "Thus shalt thou say to the children of Israel, I
> AM hath sent me unto you." . . . Everything else that is specifi-
> cally sacred is sacred in a secondary sense, and in relationship

---

8. In saying this, Lynch clearly knows that it contradicts a prevailing image and
understanding of autonomy as purely self-grounded. Yet he is not simply making a
theological assertion about Christian belief in Creation. Rather he argues in a variety
of places that this prevalent image of autonomy is itself one of the major errors of contemporary thought and imagination. It reflects, as he says at one point in the "Epilogue,"
the "image of the outside as enemy" which has a "long, tenacious" history and "is still
a powerful force among us" (CP, 138). *Images of Hope* (and the argument of Chapter 5
above) provides his clearest argument against this dangerously absolutized image of autonomy and interiority, as well as a strong counter argument about the necessity of the
"outside" or the "other" (of help and receptivity) for any true development of interior
autonomy. This was also the central argument of Lynch's essay "The Problem of Freedom" (IM, 63–96). Indeed it was the central argument of *The Integrating Mind*—that
contraries need and interpenetrate each other. See Chapter 3 above, esp. pp. 70–78.

to *this* marvelous identity of God: the Law, the sacred vessels, the temple . . . the priesthood, the sacrifice, the ark . . . This secondary order of the sacred had as its first purpose the formal declaration and honoring of the divine identity. (CP, 130)

But this does not preclude such a God from being infinitely outgoing, full of love, responsive, historical . . . He is what He is, an absolute principle of identity, the God of complete inner life, and father of every other specificity in the universe. (CP, 130–31)

We can be especially aware of what this means if we bring these images of identity and emergence to the human world. What human beings seem to hunger for at all costs is a sense of self-possession that is the same thing as the good taste of self. Nor is this a selfish phrase, for it also includes the good taste of other-ness. (CP, 134)

We must not only remember that the secular project of man lives within the same logic and image as the sacred. It is also precisely this logic which preserves the identity of, and the abso-lute difference between, the sacred and the secular. The two have their *separate* identities. (CP, 135)

For, finally, the autonomy of the secular, the autonomy of the world, comes from the outside we call God. It is . . . a creation of the secular by the sacred. So much is this the case that if there were no secular world the sacred would have to create it. "I have come that you may have life and have it more abundantly." Au-tonomy is not a defiance but a grace. (CP, 140)

This extended meditation on the doctrine of Creation is, then, the first way in which Lynch (with Christianity) understands and explains both the necessary connection and the real difference between God, self, and world. Yet as noted Lynch also stressed that "there has been a double incarnation . . . [T]wice God put on our mind with which to think" (CP, 71). At the end of the "Epilogue" Lynch develops this thought by turning to that doctrine explicitly named the Incarnation. He first reminds us that many false and pseudo-forms of secular autonomy need to be purified and transformed, and recalls the great difficulty and challenge of such transformation. The entire dramatic structure and development of *Christ and Prometheus* is, as we have seen in the preceding chapter, his way of emphasizing the agonic character of this struggle. That is why the full power of the sacred is needed "as a principle of assertion of all that is most essential to the idea of seculari-ty" (CP, 141). Yet precisely because of the immense difficulty of the struggle,

Lynch ends the "Epilogue" noting that something more than a common logic *of ideas* is needed to sustain the emergence of authentic secularity.

> [I]t is completely naïve to think that the assertion of itself [by the sacred] should come as assertion of a pure Idea and not an embodied, an institutional Idea. For the counterforces it has to deal with in the secular order, the forces of evil or of passivity that run counter to a truly human order, are too powerful to be dealt with by a pure Idea. They require the Son of God himself as opponent; they still require to be met by a distinct and recognizable embodiment of the sacred; Christ is the prime paradigm of all redemptions. (CP, 142)

We return, then, to Ignatius and to Christ: to the actual embodiment or Incarnation of the principle of inward life within the struggles of human history, and to the stages and phases of life in time which constitute both "the actual life of Christ" and the actual human journey towards such autonomy and inwardness.

The Actual Life of Christ

It was above all in the pages of *Christ and Apollo* that Lynch most fully articulated his Ignatian understanding of Christ as the second and most central theological ground for understanding the foundational connection between self and world and God. In fact, so deep is this "connection" as it is embodied in Christ that Lynch in this text frequently speaks of "penetration."[9] We may remember that he uses this term first to argue that it is only by "penetration" into and moving through the finite and limited actualities of life that we, whether in life or in literature, come to the fuller meaning which is the goal of all of our striving. The second part of the book's argument stresses that Christ is at very least (i.e., for the non-Christian) our foremost civilizational "model and source" (xii) for such penetration. Of course for Lynch himself and for Christianity, Christ is far more than simply a civilizational icon. He is God's actual Incarnation, God's fullest penetration into and union with human life in time and history—so much so that Christ's life not only models but empowers and shapes the basic structure of human movement through time and history. Indeed, as we shall see in the next section of this

---

9. See, for instance, CA, xiii, 14, 15, 16, 51 and the entirety of Chapter 7, "The Theological Imagination" (161–85) which provides a sustained critique of the contemporary loss of a sense of *"inter-penetrating"* levels of being and the resultant "flattening" of sensibility in much modern and even Christian literature.

chapter, Christ, the new Adam, is the basic form or the ontological (that is, the real and foundational) structure of a new Creation.

Here, to begin, are a series of citations from *Christ and Apollo* which provide Lynch's words: *first* as a reminder of the argument (detailed above in Chapters 4 and 5) that to get anywhere in literature or in life we must move through the finite actualities of this world, especially through the limiting reality of time; and *then* for the subsequent argument (which is the important point here) that Christ is our primary model, source, and activating form or pattern for that movement.

First, then, Lynch's words about the definite:

> [This books "principle point" is] that the literary process is a highly cognitive passage through the finite and definite realities of man and the world . . . that literary insight comes from the penetration of the finite and the definite concrete in all its interior dimensions and according to all its real lines . . . (CA, xi)

> My own attitude towards these images of limitation . . . is that the images are in themselves the path to whatever the self is seeking: to insight, or beauty, or, for that matter, to God. This path is both narrow and direct; it leads . . . straight through our human realities, through our labor, our disappointments, our friends, our game legs, our harvests, our subjection to time. We must go *through* the finite, the limited, the definite, omitting none of it . . . The finite is not itself a generality, to be encompassed in one fell swoop. Rather, it contains many shapes and byways and clevernesses and powers and diversities and persons, and we must not go too fast from the many to the one. We waste our time if we try to go around or above or under the definite; we must literally go through it. (CA, 7)

> True understanding is gained only through entering the contours of reality, for such understanding is an illumination that comes out of a passage through *experience*, this illumination leading to another experience, and this to further illumination, and so on, even unto death. (CA, 33)

Now Lynch's words on Christ as model and source for such penetration into the realities of life in this world:

> I mean Christ to stand for the completely definite, for the Man who, in taking on our human nature (as the artist must) took on every inch of it (save sin) in all its density and Who so obviously did not march too quickly or too glibly to beauty, the infinite, the dream. I take Him, secondly, as the model and source of that

energy and courage we again need to enter the finite as the only creative and generative source of beauty. Finally, but only at the end of this book and in a provisional chapter, I raise certain ontological questions about Christ as the creator and the actuality behind a new imagination and a new creation. (CA, xii)

The attitude I am proposing as a model . . . is exemplified in Christology . . . [W]e too need to go no further than the earthly, concrete, limited Christ and descend with Him for the grasping of everything. Whether we believe in Him or not, He represents an ideal point at which the imagination can relax in the strain of its double aspirations [for both concrete experience and fuller meaning and beauty]; if He is there, then at that point at least we can keep penetrating more and more deeply into the detail of him, who is penetrating the detail of life as a way to life, and let the other side of the picture—the dream, the divine, the unlimited, the beauty—take care of itself. (CA, 15)

Finally, Lynch's words about Ignatius' emphasis on "the actual life of Christ":

Christian belief is in its essence belief in a Man who, having "created" time, could not possibly be hostile to it; who . . . entered it and grew into it with such subtlety and power that He is not the enemy of but the model for the imagination and the intelligence. He is the enemy only of the romantic imagination and the pure intelligence as ways of life. (CA, 50)

The phases of the life of Christ are the mysteries of Christ. But it is the time of man which He re-explored. . . [His life] is the perfect sign and accomplishment of the mysteries or stages of human life, that they are, on a level much more intense than ever before, an intrinsic path to the infinite. (CA, 176)

Perhaps there is little need to say more. Yet I suspect that the contrast which Lynch himself makes in *Christ and Apollo* between several prevalent ways of misunderstanding Christianity and the thought of Ignatius may provide further clarification of the fact that "the actual life of Christ" is the central theological foundation for the spirituality he calls us to.

As a first kind of misunderstanding, Lynch notes the sad reality that for some Christians "Church-going is on a level . . . with going to a romantic movie in the evening after having worked hard all day" (CA, 47). Having immersed themselves in the demands of real time all week, they are allowed to escape from the burdens of time at Church. For them, in other words, Christianity and the story of the life of Christ has too little to do with the actuality of their lives and serves instead as a way of transcending or leaping out of temporal reality.

Then Lynch turns to more formidable foes, at least in terms of theological and intellectual misunderstandings. First, to "many of the most intelligent men of our day [who] have attempted to reduce the idea of Christianity to a set of non-temporal 'doctrines'—to purely intellectual statements, in the Cartesian sense . . . that have, they maintain, no relation to modern experience and the human condition" (CA, 47). In context this remark is focused on those critics of Christianity (think of Marx and Freud) who reject religious faith and doctrine because they quite legitimately want beliefs and commitments to be related to experience and the actual human condition. Elsewhere, however, Lynch notes that a similar misunderstanding of Christian doctrine prevails among "some Catholics" who wish to defend the purity of doctrine from pollution by the messiness and changing character of experience and time.[10] Lynch agrees that we surely must "fight for the purity of dogmatic truth," but pleads that we not be "guilty of that dichotomy which would make dogma reside in the pure mind and give it no relation to human reality, to sensibility, or to all the mighty energies of the imagination's bloodstream" (CA, 139). Such an idea of "pure" Christian truth would, in effect, contribute (and has contributed) to the kind of rootless, reactionary search for a God separated from the world which Lynch in his "New Theological Age" essay had seen as one of the problematic spiritual tendencies of our time. It would, Lynch concludes, give us "half a Christ" and leave all the actualities of human life and sensibility to the flattening distortions and distractions of "the culture engineers" (CA, 139).[11]

Against all these misunderstandings of Christ and Christian doctrine—the implicit intentions of many Church-goers, the anti-Christian critique of contemporary atheism, and the effort of some Catholics to preserve "doctrinal purity"—Lynch stresses with Ignatius that "Catholic doctrine is the very reverse of [their magical ideas] . . . [I]t is a divine command of the mind and the will to enter, on the divine and human planes, into an historical, actual and *eventful* set of facts which penetrate reality to the hilt" (CA, 58).[12]

10. Such Catholics "believe that 'ideas' and some strange version of dogma they have themselves concocted is [sic] the one and only thing that matters. These Catholics believe [in] the saving of souls . . . but by the saving of souls they mean . . . the saving of the top of the head, and they are in danger . . . of themselves concocting a new doctrine of ideas without sensibility, even one of salvation without works" (CA, 139).

11. We have seen (in Chapter 4 above) that *The Image Industries* provided Lynch's most explicit critique of such "culture engineers."

12. As "evidence" for this understanding of doctrine Lynch points to the Liturgy,

Finally Lynch turns to a yet more formidable source of misunderstanding, to the great Protestant theologian Karl Barth and especially to his "magnificent commentary on the Epistle to the Romans" (CA, 16).[13] For Barth, he notes, "would seem, at first glance, to be insisting in his Christology on the definiteness and particularity of Christ" (CA, 16), and thus on the actual historicity of Christ which is such a scandal for both the "cultured despisers" and the "escapist believers" noted just above. And in one sense that is an accurate understanding of Barth's Christology. Yet it misses the crucial point that Lynch wants to make about "the actual life of Christ." For Barth's emphasis on the unique "historicity" of Christ focuses on "the great historic Christic moment [which is] meant to cancel all history" (17), and thus seems to exclude not only the phases and stages of the life of Christ, but also the stages and phases of human life and history. Christ, for Barth's commentary on *Romans*, is the great exception, God's great act of grace which saves us "nevertheless" or despite human life in sinful time. Christ is the *sola gratia* of the Reformation who by the *event* of his intersection with time redeems without works, even (it would seem) without the temporal sequence of Jesus' life and works. History is thereby reduced to "historicity," to an idea of once-for-all penetration into time. Yet such an existentialist understanding of historicity actually represents a typically modern escape from time—a momentary touch that rebounds "immediately" (I use the word both temporally and theologically) from actual time into God's eternity.[14] Said somewhat differently, in terms of Lynch's later discussion (CA, 169–77) of T. S. Eliot's understanding of Christ and time in the *Four Quartets*, both Eliot and Barth understand Christ and salvation in terms of a basic image of a saving "intersection" with time rather than the kind of "penetration" that means "movement *through*" time.

---

which annually reviews the real events of the life of Christ, and to the Creed which starts and ends with eternity, but in between is all about "that time through which Christ passes and that time through which doctrine implicitly commands us to pass" (CA, 58–9).

13. It should be clear, from recent page references in my text, that Lynch's discussions of misunderstandings that contrast with Ignatius are spread throughout *Christ and Apollo* and not ordered in the sequence that I have given them.

14. Whether Lynch's interpretation of Barth's great commentary is accurate (which I suspect it is) and whether his critique is accurate for the whole of Barth's theology (which I suspect it is not) is for present purposes beside the point. Lynch's concern is to construct a contrast between prevalent ways of "misunderstanding Christ and Christian doctrine" and Ignatius's Christology. In his new preface for the 1975 Notre Dame Press edition of *Christ and Apollo*, Lynch notes that there are a few things "I would change," among them "a few places [where] my pen was not as ecumenical as my heart was" (CA, vii). Yet he does not explicitly mention his critique of Barth.

In contrast to all of these misunderstandings of Christ's relationship to time, "the Ignatian plea [is] that we direct our search for God through time, reality and the self" (CA, 61). Lynch further explains this "Ignatian plea" by stressing that there is a two-fold method in Ignatius' *Spiritual Exercises*, each part leading to greater emphasis on the *actual life* of Christ, on Christ's movement through time as recounted in the Gospels.[15] First, Ignatius would have us move "*proportionally* through the life of Christ," that is, "step by step" (CA, 54) through the sequence of particular events in the life of Christ, resisting all temptations to jump forward to some favorite event or some premature conclusion. The so-called "weeks" of the *Exercises* are a design to guide this proportional or sequential movement. Secondly, at each stage of this sequential movement Ignatius asks us to be "altogether concrete" in considering the particular scene or event. This command to imaginative concreteness, to enter the particular event or scene with the use of our senses and imagination in order to see the setting and the people, feel the emotions, hear words, smell and taste the concrete and limited actuality, is typically referred to in discussions of the *Exercises* as "the composition of place." It demands that we enter as deeply as possible into the Gospel narrative, and to stay with it in prayer, allowing God's Spirit thereby to illuminate both our understanding of the text and its significance for the present stage of our own life.

The *final* goal, then, of such spiritual exercise or practice is to allow the grace and love of God to enter the time and actuality of our lives in order to elevate them into contemplative love for God—such love as "soars far beyond all the loves and ecstatic, timeless leaps of the new escape theology" (CA, 55). But the *way* to such soaring love of God is, so to speak, not vertical leaping but horizontal penetration.

Here are Lynch's words explaining this relationship of goal and method in the *Exercises*:

> Thus . . . we have an extraordinary and at times disconcerting document which combines, in unified and sharp strokes, time, detail, definiteness, actuality and glory. But Ignatius is not coursing through man and the human self, with all the reality that goes with it, as a purely secular fact. Rather in his prayer he is coursing through the *mysteries of the life of Christ* as the latter advances through the full human scheme. For him, then, there is no separation between our advance through Christ and our advance through man and time, even unto death, even unto the death of the cross. Therefore, it is impossible to find in his

---

15. See CA, 54–60 and also my previous discussion of the method of the *Exercises* pp. 34–37 above.

thinking any form of "pure theology," that is, pure angelism, or pure secularism. His Christology and his humanism are one and the same thing. He was remarkably strong in his sense of fact, history and the present moment, but he took these strong perceptions from the study of theology and the life of Christ. (CA, 55–56)

It should be unnecessary to go any further with this analysis of the Ignatian plea that we direct our search for God through time, reality and the self. Perhaps it is evidence enough for us to call him the full secularist and the full theologian in one breath and one moment. (CA, 61)

Thus the Ignatian understanding of Christ penetrating time to get to glory should challenge even the secular humanist to continually bring the soaring passions of Apollo, Dionysus, and Prometheus "down" into realistic connection with and penetration into the ever limited actualities of our lives and of our city. Even as a still prevalent cultural model, the actual life of Christ can so inform or shape these passions that they achieve human form and thus move us towards real (not fantastic) truth and good and beauty.

Yet for the Christian, the life of Christ is more than a cultural model. It is the actual (ontological) form or the graced inner cause of all our striving in time—always proportioned to the actual and historic particularity of our lives. Thus Paul can say, in the words Lynch quotes on the final page (197) of *Christ and Apollo*: "I live, yet not I, but Christ in me."[16] Or, in a formulation of this truth composed some 1800 years later by Lynch's fellow Jesuit, Gerard Manley Hopkins: "[The just man] Acts in God's eye what in God's eye he is—/ Christ—for Christ plays in ten thousand places, / Lovely in limbs, and lovely in eyes not his / To the Father through the features of men's faces."[17]

Finally, as a brief "addendum" to this discussion of Lynch's Christology, I here raise a question about the relationship between his thought and developments in contemporary Christology. I am thinking especially about interest among biblical scholars and theologians in a renewed quest for "the historical Jesus." I am also thinking about the related development in some systematic theologies of a "Christology from below."[18] Lynch himself, while

16. Gal. 2: 20.

17. Hopkins, "As kingfishers catch fire," *Poems*, 51.

18. The term has been used to describe the effort of some quite orthodox theologians (Karl Rahner, for example) to invert the fundamental categories of Christology given us by Nicaea and Chalcedon (fully human and fully divine in one person) by starting with the human Jesus who is the focus of "historical Jesus" research—i.e., starting "from below" in contrast to the method of traditional Christology which started

probably aware of such developments, never comments on them. His Christology, as we have just seen, is a traditional "Christology from above" with its emphasis on the descent (or incarnation) of God into human life and time.[19] I suspect, however, that he would have welcomed the emphasis on "the actual life of Christ" which one finds in historical Jesus research. Yet it's also clear that he would have rejected the skeptical tenor (agnostic and even atheist) of at least some positions in that research. He would, in other words, have agreed with New Testament scholar Luke Timothy Johnson's critique of some historical Jesus research—that it fails to use its efforts to deepen faith, but instead replaces Gospel proclamation with typically modern skepticism.[20] I suspect as well that Lynch would have been interested in the strong emphasis on the humanity of Jesus in various Christologies "from below," yet would *finally*, for reasons evident throughout this book, have wanted to incorporate the insights of such Christologies within the more traditional image or framework of a Christology "from above."[21]

History and The Holy Spirit

As the final step in this presentation of the theological foundations of Lynch's thought, I want to return to his discussion of "the irony of Christ" in *Images of Faith*.[22] First, though, two preliminary notes: one about the title of this final section, and a second relating *Images of Faith* (1973) back to *Christ and Apollo* (1960).

My rhetoric may be seduced by a Trinitarian temptation when, following sections on "God and Creation" and "The Actual Life of Christ," I name this final section "History and the Holy Spirit." Lynch rarely uses the language of spirit, and never to my knowledge provides even a briefly developed discussion of the Holy Spirit. My guess is that he generally avoided

---

with Christ's divinity or "from above" and then understood the humanity of Jesus in terms of the "descent" or "incarnation" of the divine Logos. For an immensely helpful introduction to these terms and to the impact of contemporary biblical scholarship on recent Catholic Christology, see Elizabeth Johnson's *Consider Jesus*.

19. So central is the image of descent in Lynch's thinking that, lest we miss his point, he even provides, at two places in the first chapter of *Christ and Apollo* (pages 12 and 17), linear diagrams of arrows moving from above "down" into the finite and time before returning "upward" to meaning or God.

20. See Luke Johnson's *The Real Jesus*.

21. Lynch might, for instance, have appreciated novelist Anne Rice's effort to reimagine "the actual life of Christ" because it remains framed within a fairly subtle "Christology from above." As of this writing, two volumes of Rice's *Christ the Lord* series have appeared.

22. See pp. 156-58 above.

talk about "spirit" since, given the tendencies of this "new theological age," it could too easily have led away from the incarnational perspective which we have again been emphasizing. I also suspect that during the period when he wrote the Holy Spirit remained, at least for Catholic theology, what has since been referred to as the "forgotten person" of the Holy Trinity. Finally, when speaking of "the irony of Christ" in *Images of Faith*, Lynch clearly wanted to emphasize, as he puts it in that book's final words, that "the irony of Christ is Christ himself" (IF, 175). And by "Christ himself" he clearly meant the foundational Christian irony that God really became human and actually lived through human time, even unto death. Whether Lynch *also* meant the "Spirit of Christ" coursing through human history, and whether, then, my title for this section has some justification, I will leave to the reader's judgment about what follows here.

It is at least clear that, in the final, brief and "provisional" (CA, xii) chapter of *Christ and Apollo*, Lynch speaks quite directly of Christ as the real and specifying form of a "new creation"—the new ordering which Christ brought to all Creation:[23]

> *Is it true or not that the natural order of things has been subverted and that there has been a new creation, within which the one, single, narrow form of Christ of Nazareth is in process of giving its shape to everything? To think and imagine according to this form is to think and imagine according to a Christic dimension.* (CA,187, italics in original)

> Yet there has been a second and a new creation. And now the form which shapes it is no longer [simply] an [act of] existence which becomes different in everything it touches . . .[24] Now the action is Christ, rigidly one person, born in that place, at that time, with all those specificities, with this body . . . How can this Nazarene be imagined as the form of a new creation. (CA, 189–90)

---

23. This chapter, called "The Christian Imagination" (CA, 187–97), raises "one final possibility and hypothesis" (187) that Lynch wants to explore as part of his study of "the dimensions of the literary imagination" (the subtitle of *Christ and Apollo*). I take him to mean that the idea of a specifically "Christic" dimension of the *literary* imagination is a hypothesis, not that Christ as the specifying form of a new Creation is hypothetical. It is, rather, a matter of Christian belief even if its meaning always needs further exploration. See, for instance, Christopher Pramuk's book, *Sophia*, as a recent and important example of such exploration.

24. Lynch is here referring back to the discussion of analogy in his book's sixth chapter, "The Analogical." See especially CA, 148–52.

For Christ, we have said, is not another item of the first creation
. . . The real point is ever so much more crucial. For he has sub-
verted the whole order of the old imagination. Nor is this said
in the sense that he replaces or cancels the old; rather, he illumi-
nates it, and is a new level, identical in structure with but higher
in energy than, every form or possibility of the old. (CA, 192)

He shall have his narrow personal march from Bethlehem to
Calvary, but he is already having his great march, by dramatic
generative analogies, through history . . . Thus . . . we already
have two Christs, one taking on the dimensions and the concreteness of an actual life, the other the dimensions and concreteness of human history. (CA, 192–93)

In giving the title "History and the Holy Spirit" to this section, I
am clearly understanding Lynch's talk of "two Christs" and of the second
"already having his great march through history" by means of "dramatic
generative analogies" that bring "a new level . . . higher in energy" to "illuminate . . . every structure of the old creation" as a reference to the Paraclete,
the Spirit of Christ sent into the world to empower the drama of this new
creation.

How, then, does the Spirit of Christ "march through history" and work
in the body of this world? By inspiring courage, enabling patience, enflam-
ing love, and in many other ways.[25] Yet in his final book Lynch, as we have
seen, had chosen to emphasis "the irony of Christ" as central to the form, to
the dramatic generative analogies, and the higher level of energy and illumination which the Spirit of Christ brings to the new ordering of the world
and its history. Thus my suggestion in this final section on the theological
foundations of Lynch's thought shall be that the Holy Spirit works by developing an appropriately ironic sensibility both in us as individuals and in the
body of faith that is our city.

If describing the work of the Holy Spirit as "developing an appropriately ironic sensibility" seems strange, that is undoubtedly both because
of the impoverished understanding of irony in our culture and because of
the pervasiveness of "ironies of contempt" among us.[26] I suspect that most
Christians would readily describe the work of the Holy Spirit as "developing
a loving sensibility within us" or a "faithful sensibility" or a "courageous

25. The Christian tradition speaks of "seven gifts of the Holy Spirit" (wisdom, understanding, counsel, knowledge, fortitude, piety and fear of the Lord) as well as "twelve
fruits of the Holy Spirit (charity, joy, peace, patience, kindness, goodness, generosity,
gentleness, faithfulness, modesty, self-control, and chastity).

26. See pp. 149–56 above for the contrast between ironies of faith and ironies of
contempt.

sensibility." Hopefully the present book's discussion (in chapters 5 and 6 above) of Lynch's contribution in *Images of Faith* will make it equally appropriate to speak of the work of the Holy Spirit in terms of the development of "an ironic sensibility." For, to put the matter in traditional terms, the irony of Christ developed in us through the action of the Holy Spirit is an essential element or mode of the supernatural virtues of faith, hope, and love. There is, to repeat, no essential distinction between Lynch's ideas about sensibility and traditional understandings of virtue and vice. There are among us ironic sensibilities filled with such contempt that they are clearly held captive by vice. And, in Lynch's way of putting things, the Spirit of Christ works against such ironies by deepening and bringing "a new level . . . higher in energy" to the more constructive forms of virtue and irony which have grown in us as we move through the stages of human development.[27] Such a developed ironic sensibility is, then, a way of "putting on the mind of Christ" by embodying "the irony of Christ." It is the virtue or sensibility that empowers us to embrace time and live through its many challenges, to resist its absolutizing temptations to contempt and violence, to endure suffering and real evil. It is a sensibility for living through, with, and in the Spirit of Christ as we proceed through "the valley of the human."

This discussion of faith as irony and of Christ as ultimate model and source of faith's ironic sensibility is taken up, in typically complex fashion, throughout *Images of Faith*. Yet for present purposes the best way explore that book's theological ideas may be to start with the "problem of evil." Lynch most clearly addresses this problem (it is really more an agonizing mystery) in his book's final section, "The Images of Faith in Human Time" (IF, 109–75). There he looks at various forms of suffering as challenges faced by irony in each of the stages of faith's development. And there we find a reflection on evil and on the life of irony that is both intense and extensive.[28]

In focusing on evil in its many forms—including both moral (and perhaps even metaphysical) evils such as the Holocaust and physical evils (which Lynch describes as "the effects of the curse" brought by the sin of our first parents[29]) such as the poverties of limitation, ignorance, suffering, and

---

27. This is, again, the theme of Chapter 5 above.

28 Early in this final section, for instance, there is important discussion about the Holocaust (107–9, 136–37, 143–44), followed almost immediately by an extended discussion (147–54) of Dostoevsky's classic presentation of "the problem of evil" in *The Brothers Karamazov*, and then by three concluding and interwoven sections: first on "The Passage through the Curse" (156–64, referring to "the curse" of suffering and death resulting from the sin of Adam and Eve), then on "The Tragic" (164–68), and finally on "Death and Nothingness" (168–75).

29. See IF, 156 -64, and Gen. 3:16–19.

death—Lynch takes us into the theological center of God's relationship to the world. He also takes us to its emotional and imaginative center, to the place and to the set of issues which raise, for all of us I suspect, some of the most difficult challenges about both God and the world. For how can we imagine a loving God given the pervasive evils of the real world? How can we proclaim the goodness of creation and attain a good taste of both self and world in view of such evils? With such challenges, Lynch also takes us to the center of his discussion of irony. For one key way to understand the ironic structure of faith, and especially "the irony of Christ" (and thus the work of the Spirit of Christ "already having his great march through history"), is simply to reiterate that such irony is the strong force that enables us to encounter, to live with, and move through the evils of the world—not by keeping some ever-so-tenuous tie to transcendent realities, but by actually bringing those realities into a dramatic and transformative relationship with evil and suffering.

I will not here repeat what was said previously, especially in chapters 5 and 6, about Lynch's understanding of irony, though the reader may wish to review those pages.[30] Here I will focus directly on Lynch's claim in *Images of Faith* that "we cannot imagine a greater irony than the Christian" (130). He makes this claim because of the magnitude of "the gap created by the good news itself, between things as we see them and the incredible promise" (IF, 130) and because "the irony of Christ" does not somehow (paradoxically or miraculously) simply manage to hold together "things as we see them" and "the incredible promise," but works *through* things as we see them— "through death and weakness," through "age, sickness, and death," through "precisely what we are" as finite and fallible and sinful—to realize "the good news" and its "incredible promise." Let me again turn to Lynch's words:

> Some of the central contrarieties of the interior life of Christian faith are immediately evident. There are the promises of Christ and the death of Christ. There are the great thoughts, the great visions, the great promises, the great things that are here and are to come. Eye hath not seen, nor ear heard. Then there are the common human thoughts, the extremely common human feelings, the common human tasks and needs . . . There is the part that thinks divine thoughts, almost without limit; there is the other part that is weakness itself and that shall die. (IF, 88)

> [Yet for] Christianity there is more than [this] fascinating coexistence of the low and the high. The lowliness is the very

30. See especially pp. 149–56 and pp. 170–74 above.

instrument to be passed through to reach the high. It is also right to say that it *is* the high. (IF, 89)

The irony of Christ is unique . . . [I]t works through death and weakness . . . and establishes the movement through the human condition . . . as the way. Weakness becomes one of the great forms of power. (IF, 101)

Not only was the good news to be preached especially to the poor, but poverty and death, the very final qualities of all human nature, were declared to be the permanent ironic modes leading to their opposites of salvation and well-being. (IF, 131–32)

[W]hat happens here in Christian faith is . . . the building of an image of nothingness based on the most final of ironies: death becomes the final nothing, the final weakness . . . but it becomes enormously productive in the hands of God. (IF, 172)

If it is the role of all the ironies we need to integrate the great contrarieties of human life—and not, as in all ironies of contempt, to curse the one and flee to the other—then there can indeed be "no greater irony than the Christian." Christ himself, the incarnation of God into poverty and marginality and death as a political criminal, is "the final model" (IF, 95) for such irony and the source and cause of its spread into our lives by His Spirit.

True enough, one might say. This is the Christian claim and belief, though perhaps not usually described as "ironic" and "the greatest irony." For Christians do indeed believe that the Holy Spirit works in and through weakness and evil and even death to bring the promised "fullness of life." Thus it is possible for us to begin to imagine the operation of this great irony so that we might at least begin to grasp how death, "the final nothing, the final weakness" and "all its parallel points," has become "the supremely productive area in man" (IF, 169, 172).

One thing is very clear. For Lynch's theological imagining, as for Ignatius, the irony of Christ does not work by magical leaps out of real time. Yes, there are miracles; yet even miracles (I do not refer to the eschatological or end-time "events" of Christ's resurrection and seconding coming) are but one part of the animating work of the Spirit *in real human time*. Rather, the best image we have of the irony of Christ is, again, the actual life of Christ: His full entrance into the human condition and His movement into its limitations, weaknesses, and evils, even unto death on a cross, as God's way of bringing strength from weakness, life from death, good from evil. Thus the ironic (and saving) sensibility into which we are formed by Christ's Spirit follows this same temporal pattern and human rhythms. It works through the human and through time, especially through weakness and the experience of evil and death.

Yet in so working, the Holy Spirit does not render us passive. Rather, as I have suggested repeatedly in speaking about Christ working *within* the dynamic passions of Apollo, Dionysus, and Prometheus, God's grace operates within our energy and activity and, as Lynch sees it, especially within our imaginations and sensibilities—within the many forms of *imaginative action* that transform and build our lives and our city. "Faith therefore makes the imagination take on an extremely active and not a passive role" (IF, 111). In response to many real evils, the Spirit of Christ works to build in us that kind of sensibility which does not simply endure, Stoic fashion, but responds and transforms the understanding and thus the reality of weakness and suffering. *This* sensibility enables us to live ironically, that is, faithfully: to live with the active faith and hope and love of Christ as we move through the valley of the human towards the great promises of faith.

Let me give two of Lynch's examples, from the final part of *Images of Faith*, of such Spirit-led imaginative action, and ask the reader to identify related examples—to remember, for instance, evil and suffering they have experienced or witnessed and to try to discern the inner transformations of imagination and life to which they, in response, may have been led by the Spirit and irony of Christ, even if they never thought of it in those terms.

The first example involves Lynch's discussion of the powerful cry raised, in *The Brothers Karamazov*, by the middle brother, Ivan the intellectual.[31] This passage in *Images of Faith* (IF, 147–54) is as close as Lynch gets to a direct and traditional discussion of the problem of evil. Ivan tells us that, given just one instance of the terrible reality of evil—he has just told the story of a Russian nobleman who'd had his dogs rip a little peasant boy apart, with his mother as witness, because of a small accident—he wants to "return his ticket." He says it's not God, but God's world that his "Euclidean mind" cannot accept, and argues that promises of eternal harmony mean nothing since the terrible evil of that act still remains. Lynch agrees with Ivan "that these images of symphony and harmony are not images of faith" (IF, 149). Rather he argues (and suggests that Dostoevsky may have been arguing) that "the Euclidean mind" or the human hunger for intellectual clarity, with *its* images of eventual cosmic harmony and of God as Lord over all, is the real source of our problem. Without suggesting that there is any easy solution to the problem of evil, Lynch clearly says, in other words, that it is not the kind of problem the rationalist mind can even begin to deal with. Rather we must struggle in life through such realities, open to God's Spirit

31. See Bk. 5, 4 ("Rebellion") in *The Brothers Karamazov*.

and in the light of "the actual life of Christ," if we are gradually to come to the kind of transformation of images and of sensibility that will embody real faith—faith that is faithful *both* to the hard facts of the world and to the reality of God. In this instance, Lynch's suggestions about a transformation of images concern primarily our image of God and of the world. Here again are a few of his words:

> But in many senses everything finally does *not* work out. The sheer evil that will have been so multiply done will remain done and evil. Of course there is also incredible order and harmony in the universe. But there is also incredible disorder, and the point I am and will be making is that God perhaps emerges incredibly greater for "going ahead anyway with it all" on these and not other terms. (IF, 149)

> We must also explore the question whether or not the traditional and sacrosanct idea of God that has been given to us by a long line of Christian philosophers working within the vocabulary of Aristotle is not itself part of the problem of overly rational images of faith. If God is only immutable (and not also mutable), if we are indeed related to God but not he really to us, if the action of God in history produces no history in God, if all the sorrow of this world does not produce an affection within an all-perfect God, if nothing we do can add to the fullness of Being, then we are dealing with a God who satisfies the needs of a very distinctive rationality, but cannot be said to satisfy the needs of biblical reality or human feeling. (IF, 150)

> Surely there is an intensely important way in which a God in the middle of history, reacting to everything in history, remains the same. He is corrupted by nothing and surrenders his identity or his thoughts to nothing. His thoughts remain not our thoughts. The light he throws on everything comes from the center of himself. It is as though he were the universal image for the good man who living in the world does not lose his soul. (IF, 152)

In saying these things, Lynch in no way wants to suggest any clear resolution to the problem of evil.[32] Rather he gives us an example of struggling with that problem in a way that, moved by the ironic life and Spirit of Christ, ironizes the pretensions of our intellectual images of both God and world and thus stays closer to both facts and faith. Such a Spirit-shaped

---

32. Agreeing with Ivan to reject rationalist "images of symphony and harmony," Lynch then asks "But why did this happen to the child?" And answers: "I don't know. And that is a better image of faith" (IF, 149).

and ironizing sensibility would better enable us to become (or at least approach becoming) "the good man who living in the world does not lose his soul." More, it might enable us to reflect Christ's transformative light onto the darkness about us.[33]

My second example from Lynch involves a far longer discussion (the entire final three sections of *Images of Faith*, 156–75); yet at this point I must and can be briefer. Lynch says that we must distinguish between "a curse upon the human race and upon the earth" because of the sin of our first parents (Gen 3:16–19), a curse that "exists no more because the Son of God took [it] upon himself," and "all the consequences and children of the curse" which nonetheless remain in our lives (156). Among those consequences Lynch mentions: "death . . . sorrow, suffering of body and mind, all the ills that flesh is heir to, separation, misunderstanding, ill repute, grief and mourning, poverty, weakness, mental illness, war perhaps without end" (156–57). (He gives slightly different lists in other places since his point is to be suggestive, not exhaustive.) These things, he insists, "are not a curse. In fact many of the things that were once a curse are now numbered among the beatitudes, the things that are blessed (by the irony of faith the curse is a blessing)" (157). Yet experiencing them we still typically feel them as a form of curse. Thus the problem for faith and for imagination is to find ways, to find ironies that might enable us to better understand and live with these effects of the curse, above all to understand and experience them with the mind of Christ and so to live into the "incredible promise" through these experiences.

"Nothing is more difficult for the imagination," Lynch says, "than to make a successful composition [or imaginative integration] of all the elements of curse and consequences . . . but nothing is more crucial" (IF, 158). As a nation, he suggests, we typically "hide or deny or romanticize the consequences of the curse" (though they remain hard and inescapable) or, moving in the opposite direction, "we are nationally obsessed with a sense of the curse and its accompanying guilt, an obsession that has its own kind of joy" IF, (159). Yet what is demanded of "each imagination" is that it "must make the passage, as Christ did, from darkness into the light of a new image," but never a new image that denies the facts of real suffering and death (IF, 159). Rather it is through the action of the Spirit—by "co-passage through the life of Christ and through [our own] human form" with its sorrow, pain, and death—that we are formed into an ironic sensibility that can find wealth in

---

33. Two excellent recent films, one about an Irish priest (*Calvary*, 2014), the second about a Polish novice (*Ida*, 2013), provide important dramatic images of the good person who does not lose their soul, but sheds light onto the surrounding darkness.

our own poverty and life through our suffering and death, and thereby bring light and life and the pearls of great price into this world.

Easy to say, but very hard to do without the help of friends, without *a body of faith's sensibility* (operative in our families, our stories, our churches and schools, and our city), without the regular practice of some form of spirituality (Ignatian or other), and without the ironic action of the Holy Spirit moving within the deep passions that move through all these human things.

Such, then, are the theological foundations of Lynch's writing—of everything he had ever written. These beliefs clearly developed and deepened over time, yet they were with him from the beginning and from the beginning nourished and guided his thinking about our human city. For we in that city must remain in the valley of the human, as images of the God who created, as disciples of "the actual life of Christ," as led through history by His Spirit.

Afterword

I t was the goal of all of Lynch's writing to inform us about the need for "a new heart and a new spirit" (CA, xv) and thus the need for an Ignatian kind of spirituality. Were such a spirit and sensibility more alive today, in us and in our city, our faith could "in the best sense . . . become completely 'political'" (IF, 161).

It has been the goal of this book to provide an introduction to those writings and to Lynch's call for the new heart and spirit and sensibility needed "to build a human city" (IH, 26).

Yet even more, or so I believe, his writings can actually serve, by the crisscrossing, circling, and challenging style of their thinking and imagining, to lead us gradually into that sensibility. They are themselves, in other words, a form of exercise or training in the spirituality and sensibility they call for.

I have tried in a modest way to imitate that style in this book's overview of Lynch's ideas. I have reviewed the content of his major writings, yet I have tried not to reduce them by a neatly conceptual and sequential summary. Finally, though, this book remains at best a weak imitation of the scope and depth, the form and sensibility of Lynch's works.

Thus it is my repeated hope that my writing might not only introduce readers to Lynch's thought, but lead them to read and wrestle with some of his books, two still in print and the others available in good libraries, through second-hand book distributors, and perhaps someday electronically. For, as I have tried to show, his writings have much of importance that could assist our ongoing efforts to build a more human city.

Glossary

William Lynch cautioned against quick and simply conceptual definitions, urging us to come gradually to fuller understandings. Yet his own use of terms can initially be difficult for the reader. Hopefully the explanations below may provide a first step towards understanding his meaning.

Absolutizing instinct—the deep human tendency to escalate ideas and causes, fears and hopes, into absolute positions and thus into either-or polarizations.

Analogy, analogous—a traditional way of understanding how all realities are so interwoven or connected that each thing is both really different, its own particular existence, and simultaneously the same, as existing and sharing essential characteristics. Thus realities are neither "univocal," or entirely the same despite the appearance of differences, nor "equivocal," or totally unique and different from everything else.

Apollo—Greek god of the arts of music and poetry and drama.

Artists and writers—the intellectual and literary elites, commentators and critics, and occasional university and religious professionals, who are influential in shaping our culture's body of faith or unfaith. Our contemporary "culture wars" arise from growing distrust and contempt between such elites and the broad "middle class" composed both of managerial, civic, and religious leaders, and of "the people," the blue and white collar workforce and their families.

City—the entire and interwoven social, cultural, economic, and political dimensions of human community, whether in a large city or a small town or village. Lynch imagines "the city" as an embodiment of faith or unfaith (see "faith" below).

Contraries, contrariety—the fact that human existence always involves tensions or polarities between opposed dimensions such as self and world, freedom and limitation, past and future. The lived integration of such polarities is dynamic and fruitful rather than polarized and conflictual.

Definite, finite—the nature of all actual or created realities as limited, particular, temporal, and thus changing.

Dionysus—Greek god of the life-force or desire, of biological dynamism and fruitfulness, of excitement and ecstasy.

Drama—the reality that all human action takes place in time and involves a rhythm of action and response or reaction, and ideally involves learning from such experience. Also the forms of art such as theater and cinema, fiction and narrative poetry, which depict the rhythms of human stories.

Faith—initially the inner dynamism of Dionysian desire reaching out to the world in hope and fundamental trust. Yet such primal faith is educated and developed by the already-existing "body of faith" or trust found in family and culture. Thus it is typically also shaped by forms of religious faith. Yet faith can also become a body of unfaith, of contempt and distrust, because of experience and "miseducation" by the fears and rigidities found in family and culture.

Gnostic, Gnosticism—an ancient yet still pervasive worldview or sensibility which sees this world as dark, sinful, fear-filled and untrustworthy, and encourages retreat to an inner spark or soul which both reflects and leads to transcendent or otherworldly light and goodness.

Ignatian—the incarnational or this-worldly spirituality and sensibility deriving from the *Spiritual Exercises* composed by St. Ignatius Loyola, founder of the Jesuits.

Image—a complex and largely inherited or cultural perspective through which we perceive and move into the actual, concrete world. An image of something is not a snapshot but a larger framework for perception and experience.

Imagination—not a single "creative" faculty, but all the resources of thought, perception, feeling, and understanding by which we receive from culture and develop through experience the images whereby we perceive and experience reality.

Incarnation—the inescapable fact that humans are embodied creatures living within real limitations and acting in time (see "contraries," "drama" and "definite" above, and "time" below). Also the Christian doctrine that God really and fully entered this world and lived through time in the human life of Jesus of Nazareth.

Irony—the dramatic contrasting, both in literature or theater and in life, of opposed realities, typically of something "high," exalted or supposedly special, with something "low" or ordinary and even supposedly degraded, so that the contrast upends or overturns their expected relationship. Ironies of contempt typically mock the pretensions of the "high," as when the emperor has no clothes. Deeper ironies help us see that the "low" is the way to the "high," as when Socrates' ignorance leads to real truth.

Prometheus—the Greek demi-god who rebelled against the father-god Zeus by stealing fire and then other gifts, such as the alphabet, and gave them to humans so that humanity might be liberated from darkness and ignorance.

Secular—the human world, especially the modern or post-Enlightenment world of political and economic freedom, scientific discovery and technical invention, which has developed outside of, and often in opposition to, religious control and direction.

Taste of self and world—the reality that we always live with some deeply sensed feel for the good or bad of our own life and of the world around us, and of the fundamental connection between these feelings. So crucial for fruitful living is feeling the basic goodness of ourselves and of the world that Lynch equates such feeling with the Gospel parable's "pearls without price" (Matthew 13:45–46).

Time—the inescapable form of finitude or limitation within which human life and action occur since we always live between past and future. Lynch is always concerned with human time, not clock or calendar time, and thus often speaks of "the stages and phases of human life" (see also "drama" above).

Complete Bibliography of Writings by William F. Lynch, SJ

This bibliography updates the first published listing of William Lynch's writings in Gerald J. Bednar's *Faith as Imagination* (New York: Sheed & Ward, 1996) 180–85.

Books (in chronological order; the first listed is the edition cited in this book)

An Approach to the Metaphysics of Plato Through the Parmenides. Washington, DC: Georgetown University Press, 1959. Reprinted by Greenwood, 1969.

The Image Industries. New York: Sheed & Ward, 1959. (National Catholic Book Award for Most Distinguished Catholic Book of the Year and the Thomas More Award for Creative Publishing.)

Christ and Apollo: The Dimensions of the Literary Imagination. Notre Dame, IN: University of Notre Dame Press, 1975. (Original edition: Sheed & Ward, 1960; first paperback edition: New American Library, 1963; most recent edition: ISI Books, 2004.)

The Integrating Mind: An Exploration Into Western Thought. New York: Sheed & Ward, 1962.

Images of Hope: Imagination as Healer of the Hopeless. Baltimore: Helicon, 1965. (New American Library edition, 1966; University of Notre Dame Press edition, 1974.)

Christ and Prometheus: A New Image of the Secular. Notre Dame, IN: University of Notre Dame Press, 1970. (National Catholic Book Award, 1971; Conference on Christianity and Literature Book Award, 1971.)

Images of Faith: An Exploration of the Ironic Imagination. Notre Dame, IN: University of Notre Dame Press, 1973.

A Book of Admiration. See archival material below.

Essays and Reviews (in chronological order)

"Plato and the Absolute State." *The Modern Schoolman* 16.1 (1938) 14–17.

"Art & the Objective Mind." *Jesuit Education Quarterly* 2.2 (1939) 78–82.

"Of Rhythm and its End." *Spirit: A Magazine of Poetry* 6.5 (1939) 148–51. Reprinted in *Return to Poetry: Critical Essays from Spirit*. New York: The Declan X. McMillan, 1947, 85–88.

"Value of the Arts as Inspirer of Poet and Saint." *America* 62 (Dec. 30, 1939) 327–28.

"The Meaning of Mud." *Spirit: A Magazine of Poetry* 6.6 (1940) 178–85.

"Bringing the Furies to Fordham." *America* 67 (Apr. 18, 1942) 45–46.

"Can the Church Revive the Drama?" *America* 67 (Aug. 29, 1942) 577–78.

"Liturgy and the Theater." *Liturgical Arts* 12 (Nov. 1943) 3–4, 9–10.

"On the Catholic Word." *America* 70 (Nov. 6, 1943) 129–130.

"A Play." *Messenger of the Sacred Heart* 83 (Mar. 1948) 52–53.

"The Sacrament of Our Times." *Messenger of the Sacred Heart* 83 (Mar. 1948) 56–61.

"We Must Make Reparation." *Messenger of the Sacred Heart* 83 (May 1948) 66–70.

"Your Family and the Sacred Heart." *Messenger of the Sacred Heart* 83 (June 1948) 52–55, 90–92.

"A Message for the Alcoholic." *Messenger of the Sacred Heart* 83 (July 1948) 39–41, 94–97.

"A Return to Real Christianity." *Messenger of the Sacred Heart* 83 (Aug. 1948) 11–15.

"The Sacred Heart and Catholic Action." *Messenger of the Sacred Heart* 83 (Sept. 1948) 48–51, 83–85.

"The Fight Against Atheism." *Messenger of the Sacred Heart* 84 (Feb. 1949) 11–13, 92.

"All Roads Lead to Rome." *Messenger of the Sacred Heart* 84 (Mar. 1949) 30–35.

"*Ingredere in Civitatem.*" *Thought* 25 (1950) 5–7

"Culture and Belief." *Thought* 25 (1950) 441–463. Reprinted as chapter 5 of *The Integrating Mind*.

"The Partisan Review Symposium." *Thought* 25 (1950) 681–91.

"Plato: Symposium (The Banquet)." In *The Great Books: A Christian Appraisal*. Vol. 3. Devin-Adair Co., 1951, 16–20.

"Adventure in Order." *Thought* 26 (1951) 33–49.

"Confusion in our Theater." *Thought* 26 (1951) 342–60.

"Blanshardian Democracy." *Thought* 26 (1951) 581–85.

"Mirror of the Magazines." *Thought* 26 (1951) 598–605.

"Theology and the Imagination." *Thought* 29 (1954) 61–86.

"Nationalism and Internationalism." *The Catholic Mind* 52 (Mar. 1954) 149–58.

"For a Redeemed Actuality." *Spirit: A Magazine of Poetry* 21 (July 1954) 83–86.

"Theology and the Imagination II: The Evocative Symbol." *Thought* 29 (1954) 529–54.

"Theology and Imagination III: The Problem of Comedy." *Thought* 30 (1955) 18–36.

"Saint Ignatius and the New Theological Age." *Thought* 31 (1956) 187–215. Excerpted as "Ignatius and the New Age." *Commonweal* 64 (Aug. 1956) 442–43.

Review of *Martin Buber* by Arthur A. Cohen. *America* 98 (Mar. 22, 1958) 728–29.

"The Imagination and the Finite." *Thought* 33 (1958) 205–28.

"Art and Sensibility." *Commonweal* 70 (Apr. 10, 1959) 47–50.

"The Catholic Idea." In *The Idea of Catholicism: An Introduction to the Thought and Worship of the Church*, edited by Walter J. Burghardt and William F. Lynch. New York: Meridian Books, 1960, 57–64.

"Ritual and Drama." *Commonweal* 71 (Feb. 26, 1960) 586–88.

"The Problem of Freedom." *Cross Currents* 10 (1960) 97–114. Reprinted as chapter 4 of *The Integrating Mind*. Also reprinted in digest form in *Theology Digest* 9 (1961) 182–86.

"Theology and Human Sensibility." *The Critic* 18 (April–May 1960) 15–16, 84–86. Reprinted as chapter 7 of *The Integrating Mind*.

"Metaphysics and the Literary Imagination." *Spirit: A Magazine of Poetry* 27 (November 1960) 137–44.

"Let's Have Film Festivals." *America* 104 (Mar. 11, 1961) 753–56.

"Reality and Realism: A Distinction with a Difference." *The Critic* 20 (April-May 1962) 43–47.

"Christianity and the Passive Imagination." *The Catholic Messenger* 80 (Aug. 30, 1962).

"The Freedom to Be Human." In *Freedom and Man*, edited by John Courtney Murray. New York: Kennedy, 1965, 70–86.

"Toward a Theology of the Secular." *Thought* 41 (1966) 349–65. Reprinted in digest form in *Theology Digest* 15 (1967) 175–78.

"Can Ministers and Psychiatrists Work Together?" *Redbook Magazine* 128 (Dec. 1966) 52–3, 123–26.

"Ugliness." *New Catholic Encyclopedia*, 14:368. New York: McGraw-Hill, 1967.

"A Re-Appraisal of Christian Symbol." *North American Liturgical Weekly* 28 (1967) 66–76.

"Death as Nothingness." *Continuum* 5 (1967) 459–69.

"Counterrevolution in the Movies." *Commonweal* 87 (Oct. 20, 1967) 77–86.

"Psychological Man." *America* 117 (Nov. 25, 1967) 635–37.

"Commentary on Ritual and Liturgy." In *The Religious Situation*, edited by Donald R. Cutler, 749–57. Boston: Beacon, 1968.

"The Crisis of Hope." *Sister Formation Bulletin* 14 (Summer 1968) 6–10.

"Images of Faith." *Continuum* 7 (1969) 187–94.

"Images of Faith II: The Task of Irony." *Continuum* 7 (1969) 478–92.

"Madness as an Existential Solution to an Existential Situation." Review of *The Divided Self* and *Self and Others* by R.D. Laing. *Commonweal* 92 (Sept. 25, 1970) 484–85.

"Faith, Experience & Imagination." *New Catholic World* 215 (July–August 1972) 170–73.

"In Admiration of Teilhard." *America* 132 (April 12, 1975) 274–76.

"Euripides' 'Bacchae': The Mind in Prison." *Cross Currents* 25 (1975) 163–74.

"Advent From Head to Toe." *America* 133 (November 29, 1975) 382–83.

"What's Wrong with 'Equus'? Ask Euripides." *America* 133 (Dec. 13, 1975) 419–22.

"The Imagination of the Drama." *Review of Existential Psychology and Psychiatry* 14.1 (1975–1976) 1–10.

"The Task of Enlargement." *Thought* 51 (1976) 341–55.

"The Psychologically Disabled." In *Human Life: Problems of Birth, of Living, and of Dying*, edited by William C. Bier. Pastoral Psychology Series 9. New York: Fordham University Press, 1977.

Review of *Body as Spirit* by Charles Davis. *Commonweal* 105 (Mar. 31, 1978) 219–21.

"A Dramatic Making of the Human." *Humanitas* 14 (1978) 161–71.

"Foundation Stones for Collaboration between Religion and the Literary Imagination." *Journal of the American Academy of Religion* 42 (1979) Supplement H, 329–344.

"The Life of Faith and Imagination." *The Month* (Jan. 1979) 5–9.

"The Drama of the Mind: An Ontology of the Imagination." *Notre Dame English Journal* 13 (1980) 17–28.

"The Life of Faith and Imagination: Theological Reflection in Art and Literature." *Thought* 57 (1982) 7–16. An expanded version of the article which appeared in *The Month* (Jan. 1979).

"Archetypal Theory and Spirituality." *Studies in Formative Spirituality* 4 (1983) 83–93.

"Me and the East River." *New York Images* 1 (1984) 3–5.

"The *Spiritual Exercises* of St. Ignatius and Their Images." *New York Images* 1 (1984) 12–13.

"Easy Dramatic Lessons on How to Miss Reality...How to Hit It." *New York Images* 1 (1984) 14–19.

"Imagining Past, Present, Future in One Piece." *Studies in Formative Spirituality* 6 (1985) 65–72.

"Architecture and Theater in Greece: The World as Actor." *New York Images* 2 (1985) 12–15.

"Final Image: Sancho Panza and Imagination." *New York Images* 2 (1985) 28–30.

"Introduction: On the Transformation of Our Images." *New York Images* 3 (1986), 2–3.

"The Bacchae of Euripides: An American Parallel." *New York Images* 3 (1986) 20–23.

"Three Stories About . . . A Cat, A Dog, The Dreamy Mediterranean." *New York Images* 3 (1986) 28–30.

Dissertations

"Plato and the Tri-Partite Soul." MA (Philosophy), Fordham University, 1939

The Central Problem in Aeschylus' "*Eumenides.*" PhD (Classics), Fordham University, 1943.

Edited Works

Burghardt, Walter J., SJ, and William F. Lynch, SJ, eds. *The Idea of Catholicism: An Introduction to the Thought and Worship of the Church.* New York: Meridian, 1960.

During his career, Lynch was editor of three journals. In 1948 and through the spring of 1949 he edited *The Messenger of the Sacred Heart*, a popular Jesuit monthly. For more than six years, from 1950 through early 1956, he edited *Thought*, Fordham University's scholarly quarterly of humanities and politics. Finally, toward the end of his life, he founded and edited *New York Images*, a journal devoted to the interdisciplinary study of imagination and society; three issues appeared, in 1984, 1985, and 1986.

Although not explicitly listed as editor, Lynch was instrumental in the publication of a special issue of *Thought* (March 1982) on "Faith and Imagination" and in the earlier publication of a series of articles on the same topic which appeared in the British Jesuit journal *The Month* throughout 1979.

Archival Material

There are several boxes of Lynch material at the Fordham University Archives in the Walsh Library. Included are drafts for various published works, some scripts, some unpublished papers and lectures, correspondence (mainly letters to Lynch), and drafts for two book projects.

Of particular significance are the following:

The Drama of the Mind. Diverse texts for a 1970s book project on the "cognitive and ontological" significance of theater, both classical and modern. Most of the content was either from earlier published articles or from newly written material which appeared as articles in the 1970s and early 1980s (see p. 90 n. 1 above).

A Book of Admiration. Text for a 1970s book project on the great human importance of admiration, with examples of things Lynch especially admired.

Images of Hope. Scripts for a four-part television series for The Catholic Hour on NBC-TV (May 9, 16, 23, and 30, 1965). There are scripts for three of the four programs: 1, "The City of Man"; 3, "The Gift of Depending"; 4, "Help As an Image of Hope."

"What is an Image?" Carlton College Convocation (November 26, 1965).

"The Imagination in the City of Man." A slightly expanded version of the Carlton College Convocation lecture.

"Toward A Popular Culture." An undated article seemingly written sometime in the mid-1960s.

Bibliography of Works Cited

(Does not include citations from books
referenced with in-text abbreviations.)

Allen, Steve. "How Will It Work?" *America* 104 (Mar. 11, 1961) 756.

Arbery, Glen. "The Act Called Existence." In William F. Lynch, *Christ and Apollo*, vii–xl. Wilmington, DE: ISI, 2003.

Auerbach, Eric. *Mimesis: The Representation of Reality in Western Literature.* Princeton: Princeton University Press, 1953.

Bednar, Gerald. *Faith as Imagination: The Contribution of William Lynch, S.J.* New York: Sheed & Ward, 1996.

Bellah, Robert. "Can We Be Citizens of a World Empire?" (lecture Jan. 28, 2003). http://www.robertbellah.com/lectures_8.htm. An abbreviated version entitled "Righteous Empire" was published in *Christian Century* (Mar. 8, 2003) 20–25.

Bellah, Robert, et al. *Habits of the Heart: Individualism and Commitment in American Life.* Berkeley: University of California Press, 1985.

Bellow, Saul. *The Dean's December.* New York: Harper & Row, 1982.

Berger, Peter L. *The Sacred Canopy: Elements of a Sociological Theory of Religion.* Garden City, NY: Doubleday, 1969.

Berrigan, Daniel. "Father William Lynch Dies, Jesuit in the Grand Manner." *National Catholic Reporter* (Jan. 23, 1987) 4.

Black, C.E. *The Dynamics of Modernization.* New York: Harper & Row, 1966.

Borgmann, Albert. *Crossing the Postmodern Divide.* Chicago: The University of Chicago Press, 1992.

Boyle, Nicholas. *Who Are We Now? Christian Humanism and the Global Market from Hegel to Heaney.* Notre Dame, IN: University of Notre Dame Press, 1998.

Burghardt, Walter J., and William F. Lynch. *The Idea of Catholicism: An Introduction to the Thought and Worship of the Church.* New York: Meridian, 1960.

Burke, Kevin F., and Eileen Burke-Sullivan. *The Ignatian Tradition.* Collegeville, MN: Liturgical, 2009.

Cohn, Norman. *The Pursuit of the Millennium: Revolutionary Millenarians and Mystical Anarchists in the Middle Ages.* New York: Oxford University Press, 1970.

Dodds, E. R. *The Greeks and the Irrational.* Berkeley: University of California Press, 1951.

Donoghue, Denis. *Adam's Curse: Reflections on Religion and Literature*. Notre Dame, IN: University of Notre Dame Press, 2001.

"Downward to the Infinite." *Time* 75.21 (1960) 81–82.

Eagleton, Terry. *Reason, Faith, and Revolution: Reflections on the God Debate*. New Haven: Yale University Press, 2009.

Ellis, John Tracy. "American Catholics and the Intellectual Life." *Thought* 30 (1955) 351–88.

Ellul, Jacques. *The Technological Society*. Translated by John Wilkinson. New York: Knopf, 1964.

Farnell, Louis Richard. *The Cults of the Greek States*. Vol. 5. Oxford: Clarendon, 1909.

Fennell, William O. "The Theology of True Secularity." In *New Theology 2*, edited by Martin Marty and Dean Peerman. New York: Macmillan, 1965.

Fergusson, Francis. *The Idea of a Theater*. Princeton: Princeton University Press, 1949.

Fleming, Thomas. "Metaphysics and the Human Imagination." Senior Thesis, Georgetown University, 1978. Fordham University Archives, Box 2, Folder 17.

Finnegan, John D. "William Lynch and the Poetics of Analogy." PhD diss., Ohio University, 1970 (University Microfilms, Inc., 71–4790).

Fowler, James W. *Stages of Faith*. New York: Harper and Row, 1981.

———. "The Vocation of Faith Development Theory." In *Stages of Faith and Religious Development*, edited by James Fowler et al. New York: Crossroad, 1991.

"Friends Who Will Be Missed." *Christianity and Crisis* 47 (Mar. 16, 1987) 85.

Fussell, Paul. *The Great War and Modern Memory*. New York: Oxford University Press, 1975.

Fustel de Coulanges, Numa Denis. *The Ancient City: A Study of the Religion, Laws and Institutions of Greece and Rome*. Garden City, NY: Doubleday, 1956.

Gilligan, Bernard. "Images of Hope." *Catholic Book Club Newsletter* 57.8 (1965).

Grant, George. "Faith and the Multiversity." In *Collected Works of George Grant*, Vol. 4, *1970–1988*, edited by Arthur Davis and Henry Roper, 607–39. Toronto: University of Toronto Press, 2009.

———. "The University Curriculum." In *Collected Works of George Grant*, Vol. 3, *1960–1969*, edited by Arthur Davis and Henry Roper, 558–76. Toronto: University of Toronto Press, 2005.

Harrington, Michael. *The Vast Majority: A Journey to the World's Poor*. New York: Simon & Schuster, 1977.

Hart, David Bentley. "Infinite Lit: On William Lynch's *Christ and Apollo*." In *In the Aftermath: Provocations and Laments*, 170–75. Grand Rapids, MI: Eerdman's, 2008.

Hart, Ray. *Unfinished Man and the Imagination*. New York: Herder and Herder, 1968.

Heller, Erich. *The Artist's Journey into the Interior and Other Essays*. New York: Random House, 1965.

Hopkins, Gerard Manley. *Poems and Prose of Gerard Manley Hopkins*. Baltimore: Penguin, 1963.

Huntington, Samuel P. "The Clash of Civilizations?" *Foreign Affairs* 72 (Summer 1993) 22–49.

"An Image of Hope." *Commonweal* 114 (Jan. 30, 1987) 37.

Jaspers, Karl. *The Origin and Goal of History*. New Haven: Yale University Press, 1968.

Jenkins, Philip. *God's Continent: Christianity, Islam, and Europe's Religious Crisis*. New York: Oxford University Press, 2007.

Johnson, Elizabeth A. *Consider Jesus: Waves of Renewal in Christology.* New York: Crossroad, 1992.

———. *Truly Our Sister: A Theology of Mary in the Communion of Saints.* New York: Continuum, 2003.

Johnson, Luke T. *The Real Jesus: The Misguided Quest for the Historical Jesus and the Truth of the Traditional Gospels.* New York: HarperCollins, 1996.

Kane, John F. "William F. Lynch, S.J., Catholic Intellectual Pioneer." *Conversations on Jesuit Higher Education* 36 (2009) 23–26. epublications.marquette.edu/conversations/vol36/iss1/13.

Kennedy, Eugene. *Tomorrow's Catholics/Yesterday's Church.* New York: Harper & Row, 1988.

———. *The Unhealed Wound.* New York: St. Martin's, 2001.

Kenny, Herbert A. "Faith and the Ironic Imagination." *Boston Sunday Globe* (Jan. 27, 1974) A94.

Keppel, Jules. *The Revenge of God.* University Park: Pennsylvania State University Press, 1994.

Knox, Ronald A. *Enthusiasm: A Chapter in the History of Religion, With Special Reference to the XVII and XVIII Centuries.* New York: Oxford University Press, 1950.

Koyré, Alexander. *From the Closed World to the Infinite Universe.* Baltimore: Johns Hopkins Press, 1957.

Lakeland, Paul. *The Liberation of the Laity.* New York: Continuum, 2003.

Lynch, William. "Adventure in Order." *Thought* 26 (1951) 33–49.

———. "Architecture and Theater in Greece: The World as Actor." *New York Images* 2 (1985) 12–15.

———. "Art and the Objective Mind." *Jesuit Educational Quarterly* 2.2 (1939) 77–78.

———. "The Bacchae of Euripides: An American Parallel." *New York Images* 3 (1986) 20–23.

———. "Bringing the Furies to Fordham." *America* 67 (Apr. 18, 1942) 45–46.

———. "The Catholic Idea." In *The Idea of Catholicism: An Introduction to the Thought and Worship of the Church,* edited by Walter J. Burghardt and William F. Lynch, 57–64. New York: Meridian, 1960.

———. "Confusion in Our Theater." *Thought* 26 (1951) 342–60.

———. "Counterrevolution in the Movies: Words, Ideas and the Artist as Thinker." *Commonweal* 87 (Oct. 20, 1967) 77–86.

———. "Culture and Belief." *Thought* 25 (1950) 44–63. Reprinted in *The Integrating Mind,* 97–120.

———. "Death as Nothingness." *Continuum* 5 (1967) 459–69.

———. "The Drama of the Mind: An Ontology of the Imagination." *Notre Dame English Journal* 13 (1980) 17–28.

———. "A Dramatic Making of the Human." *Humanitas* 14.2 (1978) 161–71.

———. "Easy Dramatic Lessons on How to Miss Reality . . . How to Hit It." *New York Images* 1 (1984) 14–19.

———. "Euripides' 'Bacchae': The Mind in Prison." *Cross Currents* 25 (1975) 163–74.

———. "Final Image: Sancho Panza and the Imagination." *New York Images* 2 (1985) 28–30.

———. "For a Redeemed Actuality." *Spirit: A Magazine of Poetry* 21.1 (1954) 83–86.

————. "Foundation Stones for Collaboration Between Religion and the Literary Imagination." *Journal of the American Academy of Religion* 47.2 (1979) Supplement H, 329–44.

————. "The Imagination and the Finite." *Thought* 33 (1958) 205–228.

————. "The Imagination of the Drama." *Review of Existential Psychology and Psychiatry* 14.1 (1975/1976) 1–10.

————. "*Ingredere in Civitatem.*" *Thought* 25 (1950) 5–7.

————. "Introduction: On the Transformation of Our Images." *New York Images* 3 (1986) 2–3.

————. "Let's Have Film Festivals." *America* 104 (Mar. 11, 1961) 753–56.

————. "The Life of Faith and Imagination." *The Month* (Jan. 1979) 5–9.

————. "The Life of Faith and Imagination: Theological Reflection in Art and Literature." *Thought* 57 (1982) 7–16.

————. "Me and the East River." *New York Images* 1 (1984) 3–5.

————. "The Meaning of Mud." *Spirit: A Magazine of Poetry* 6.6 (1940) 178–85.

————. "Plato and the Absolute State." *The Modern Schoolman* 16.1 (1938) 14–17.

————. "Plato: Symposium (The Banquet)." In *The Great Books: A Christian Appraisal*, Vol. 3, edited by Harold Charles Gardiner, 16–20. New York: Devin-Adair, 1951.

————. "The Problem of Freedom." *Cross Currents* 10 (1960) 97–114.

————. "Reality and Realism: A Distinction with a Difference." *The Critic* 20 (April–May 1962) 43–47.

————. "The *Spiritual Exercises* of St. Ignatius and Their Images." *New York Images* 1 (1984) 12–13.

————. "St. Ignatius and 'The New Theological Age.'" *Thought* 31 (1956) 187–215.

————. "The Task of Enlargement." *Thought* 51 (1976) 345–55.

————. "Theology and the Imagination." *Thought* 29 (1954) 61–86

————. "Theology and the Imagination II: The Evocative Symbol." *Thought* 29 (1954) 529–54

————. "Theology and the Imagination III: The Problem of Comedy." *Thought* 30 (1955) 18–36.

————. "Theology and Human Sensibility." *The Critic* 18 (April/May 1960) 15–16, 84–86.

————. "Value of the Arts as Inspirer of Poet and Saint." *America* 62 (Dec. 30, 1939) 327–28.

————. "What's Wrong with 'Equus'? Ask Euripides." *America* 133 (Dec. 13, 1975) 419–22.

Marsden, George. *The Soul of the American University: From Protestant Establishment to Established Nonbelief.* New York: Oxford University Press, 1994.

McBrien, Richard. *Do We Need the Church?* New York: Harper & Row, 1969.

Modras, Ronald. *Ignatian Humanism.* Chicago: Loyola, 2004.

————. "The Spirituality and Humanism of the Jesuits." *America* (Feb. 4, 1995) 10–16, 29–32.

Murphy, Francesca. *Christ the Form of Beauty.* Edinburgh: T & T Clark, 1995.

Neary, John. *Like and Unlike God: Religious Imaginations in Modern and Contemporary Fiction.* Atlanta: Scholars, 1999.

Niebuhr, H. Richard. *Christ and Culture.* New York: Harper, 1956.

O'Connor, Flannery. *The Habit of Being: The Collected Letters of Flannery O'Connor*, edited by Sally Fitzgerald. New York: Farrar, Strauss & Giroux 1979.

Pascal, Blaise. *Pensees*. Translated by A J. Krailsheimer. Harmondsworth, UK: Penguin, 1966.

Peters, F. E. *Ours: The Making and Unmaking of a Jesuit*. New York: Marek, 1981.

Pope Francis. "Speech to Congress" (Sept. 24, 2015). http://papalvisit.americamedia. org/2015/09/24/full-text-of-pope-francis-speech-to-congress/.

———. *Laudato Si': On Care for Our Common Home* (2015). http://w2.vatican. va/content/francesco/en/encyclicals/documents/papa-francesco_20150524_ enciclica-laudato-si.html.

Pope John Paul II. *Ex Corde Ecclesiae: On Catholic Universities*. (1990). http://w2.vatican.va/content/john-paul-ii/en/apost_constitutions/documents/ hf_jp-ii_apc_15081990_ex-corde-ecclesiae.html.

Pramuk, Christopher. *Hope Sings So Beautiful: Graced Encounters across the Color Line*. Collegeville, MN: Liturgical, 2013.

———. *Sophia: The Hidden Christ of Thomas Merton*. Collegeville, MN: Liturgical, 2009.

Purdy, Jedediah. *For Common Things: Irony, Trust, and Commitment in America Today*. New York: Knopf, 1999.

Rice, Ann. *Christ the Lord: Out of Egypt* New York: Knopf, 2005.

———. *Christ the Lord: The Road to Cana*. New York: Knopf, 2008.

Roth, Philip. *The Human Stain*. Boston: Houghton Mifflin, 2000.

Ruthven, Malise. *Fundamentalism: The Search for Meaning*. New York: Oxford University Press, 2004.

Scott, Nathan. "Religion and the Imagination: Some Reflections on the Legacy of William F. Lynch, S.J." *Thought* 66 (1991) 150–60.

Scruton, Roger. *The West and the Rest: Globalization and the Terrorist Threat*. Wilmington, DE: ISI, 2002.

Shils, Edward. *The Intellectuals and the Powers and Other Essays*. Chicago: University of Chicago Press, 1972.

Spohn, William. *Go and Do Likewise: Jesus and Ethics*. New York: Continuum, 1999.

Stravinski, Igor. *Poetics of Music in the Form of Six Lessons*. New York: Vintage, 1956.

Toolan, David. *At Home in the Cosmos*. Maryknoll, NY: Orbis, 2001.

———. "Some Biographical Reflections on William F. Lynch's Thought." In *American Catholic Traditions: Resources for Renewal*, edited by Sandra Yocum Mize and William L. Portier, 133–35. College Theology Society Annual Volume 42, 1996. Maryknoll, NY: Orbis, 1997.

Volf, Miroslav, and William Katerberg. "Introduction: Retrieving Hope." In *The Future of Hope*, edited by Miroslav Volf and William Katerberg. Grand Rapids: Eerdman's, 2004.

Weiss, Peter. *The Persecution and Assassination of Jean-Paul Marat as Performed by the Inmates of the Asylum of Charenton under the Direction of the Marquis de Sade*. New York: Caedmon, 1966.

"William F. Lynch, Author of Nine Books." *The New York Times*, Jan. 12, 1987.

Wittgenstein, Ludwig. *Philosophical Investigations*. Translated by G. E. M. Anscombe. Oxford: Blackwell, 1963.

Index

Lynch Books and Book Projects

Names and Topics